WOMEN WHO HURT
THEMSELVES

WOMEN
WHO HURT
THEMSELVES

A Book

of Hope

and

Understanding

DUSTY MILLER

BasicBooks
A Division of HarperCollins Publishers

To Judith V. Jordan
With love and gratitude

Copyright © 1994 by Dusty Miller. Published by BasicBooks, A Division of HarperCollins Publishers, Inc.

Designed by Ellen Levine

Library of Congress Cataloging-in-Publication Data
  Miller, Dusty, 1944—
    Women who hurt themselves: a book of hope and understand-
  ing / by Dusty Miller
      p.   cm.
    Includes bibliographical references and index.
    ISBN 0-465-09220-9
    1. Self-destructive behavior. 2. Women—mental health. 3. Post-
  traumatic stress syndrome. I. Title.
  RC569.5.S45M54   1994
  616.89'0082—dc20   93-47203
                                                          CIP

94 95 96 97 ❖/RRD 9 8 7 6 5 4 3 2 1

CONTENTS

ACKNOWLEDGMENTS

I have had the good fortune to have several wonderful mentors. The first was my mother, Anne Small Miller, whose inspiration as a gifted teacher has guided me throughout my life. Another important teacher, Adeline ("Paties") Potter, has been watching over me since one hour after my birth.

I owe my start in the field of psychology to Evan Imber-Black. Evan has supported me intellectually and emotionally throughout my career, showing me again and again that failure is impossible. Other mentors who have influenced my thinking and excited my faith in the power of the written word include Judith Lewis Herman, Bessel van der Kolk, Rachel Hare-Mustin, Claudia Bepko, Jo Ann Krestan, Joan Laird, and Ann Hartman. Each of these writers has shaped my ideas about psychotherapy, women, and trauma. Collectively, they are leaders in a community of scholars who have pioneered the way in sharing knowledge, both within and beyond the professional community.

Many professional colleagues have provided inspiration and support over the years. I gratefully acknowledge the many years of collaboration with Mardie Ratheau, Judy Davidson, Bill Lax, and Dario Lussardi, all treasured colleagues. I also thank Ellen Keniston, Amelia Stevens, and Judith V. Jordan, who have provided essential personal support to me over many years.

My colleagues and students in the Clinical Psychology Department at Antioch New England Graduate School have been patient with me when my attention was too often absorbed by this book. I wish especially to thank Provost James Craiglow for his belief in the importance of this project, and my faculty colleagues, who have been loyal and generous friends over the long haul. My clients and students have given me precious gifts of their questions, their ideas, and their trust. I wish I could name them all individually and thank each for her contributions.

There are several women who have played central roles in the creation and production of this book. I wish to express my gratitude to Michelle Loris for the generous insights and support she has provided over the entire course of the project. I am grateful to her for her many contributions to the development of "The Inner Circle." Lindy Norlander has given me superb editorial assistance in times of crisis. I owe so much to Marsha Passoja, my administrative assistant, who has provided valuable editorial comments and tireless technical support over the past two years. Marsha and Sharon Milkey also helped me greatly in their thoughtful responses to early drafts of the book. Jo Ann Miller, my editor at Basic Books, conceptualized this book before I knew I had the capacity for such an undertaking. She convinced me to begin and then guided me skillfully and brilliantly through the entire process. Nina Gunzenhauser provided consistently trustworthy maps for how to make my ideas coherent, slogging through many hours of challenging collaboration with unflagging equanimity. Jill Harkaway and I originally began evolving ideas for this book in 1986, and I thank her, Mardie Ratheau, and Judy Davidson for collaboration and significant contributions, especially in regard to the description of family dynamics and their replication in individual dynamics and the therapy relationship.

Finally, I want to thank my "family of friends": Patricia Ouellette, Katie Tolles, their daughters, Krystal Ouellette-Tolles and Erika Ouellette-Tolles, Carol Peed, Leslie Dubinsky, Michelle Loris, and Carol Morgan. Most of all, I am tremendously grateful to Judith Jordan, who has helped me develop a Protective Presence to carry me through this project, and to my colleague and partner, Pat Wieland, for her gift of transformation through love and humor.

PART I

TRAUMAS REENACTED

1

Women at War with Themselves

Imagine a long, black marble wall, inscribed with names, reaching far into the distance. Imagine a quilt, covered with names and images of loved ones who have died, stretching over acres of land. But instead of war casualties and AIDS victims, the names on this wall and this quilt are those of women who died by their own hand. They died from alcoholism, drug addiction, anorexia, bulimia, excessive dieting, self-inflicted burns and slashing, and a hundred other ways of harming one's own body.

These are women who killed themselves, yet they could be considered murder victims. In childhood they suffered sexual abuse, physical abuse, neglect, or psychological terrorism. Their names would stretch for hundreds of miles if inscribed on a memorial wall or stitched on a memorial quilt. These women are not remembered as brave victims of a war or an epidemic illness, but they should be. Instead, they are often blamed for their deaths because the fatal wounds were inflicted by their own hand. These wounds, however, were a direct consequence of earlier injuries inflicted by parents, grandparents, and other primary caretakers, injuries that never healed and proved deadly.

Like the women I am writing about in this book, I have my own story. There are many reasons, both personal and professional, why I care so much about the lives of women who hurt themselves. A dear friend, a woman I'll call Fiora, first made me aware of the crucial connection between early trauma and self-inflicted pain. Fiora was my closest friend when we were young women and she was the first person I ever talked to about the central and buried shame of a common history: our shared experiences of childhood abuse.

Fiora remembered being sexually and physically abused by her father from an early age (probably three or four) until she was first hospitalized as a teenager. She was a musical prodigy and traveled with her family in Europe, from concert hall to concert hall, throughout her childhood. Fiora's father managed his daughter's career, demanding total obedience and endless labor. When Fiora showed signs of exhaustion and mental confusion, her father began procuring amphetamines for her from doctors with whom he had black-market connections. Thus Fiora became drug-addicted by the time she was twelve years old. Soon she also began a secret habit of cutting her body, a ritual that persisted for years.

Like most abused children, Fiora had no language to describe what was happening to her. She lived most of her life deep within herself in a split-off world of partial awareness, with no friends to support her. Fiora was in and out of psychiatric hospitals during her teen years. She would be detoxed from amphetamines during each hospital stay, only to become addicted again when she was released to her parents. The hospital system never treated the addiction, virtually ignored the cutting, and failed to detect the abuse. They did not investigate the possibility that her "illness" was engendered and maintained by her relationship with her father.

The mental health system's failure to understand Fiora was not at all unusual. Until the mid-1980s, the dissociation and terror-related symptoms of Post-Traumatic Stress Disorder were often misdiagnosed as caused by drug abuse or biologically based mental illness. Women like Fiora ended up in state hospitals or cycling in and out of halfway houses or private mental hospitals, condemned to be treated as mental patients for the rest of their lives.

In her mid-twenties, Fiora took a lethal dose of drugs and died, finally successful in her efforts to kill herself.

Fiora could see no way out of her despair and pain. Although I too was an abuse survivor with many scars and desperate moments, I was luckier. I had a network of friends, allies, and professionals who helped me find ways to heal. I had the support of a partner who loved me, work that I liked, and a therapist who had helped me stay alive when I wouldn't have been able to do it on my own. Fiora had been too badly hurt to allow the kind of attachments I was able to use in my recovery. Ultimately, she was a victim of both her father's sadistic exploitation and the professional helping system.

Ever since I began to understand that Fiora was reenacting the pain that had been inflicted on her in childhood, I have looked for answers that might have changed her destiny. I became a psychologist, driven by my determination to create new ways to understand and help women like Fiora. It is painful for me, even now, to tell Fiora's story, but, paradoxically, whenever I have felt discouraged in my work, it strengthens me to think about her life and untimely death—and to realize how much I learned from her about adult self-injury and early trauma. It is for Fiora, and for the thousands like her, that I have sought ways to provide better treatment for all those women who are trapped in a world of pain and secrets.

Childhood trauma takes many forms. It can be experienced through physical or sexual abuse or through invasive caretaking. The trauma can come through chronic physical or psychological neglect as a result of parental illness, addiction, dysfunction, or premature death. Whatever the cause, such trauma results in a sickening of the child's whole being and the loss of a sense of safety. Worst of all, the psychological wounds inflicted whenever a child is violated may never heal. From childhood into adulthood, the victim may psychologically bleed from these internal wounds without anyone noticing.

Traumatized children grow up to be many types of adults. A fortunate few experience only the ordinary problems of daily life. Most, however, are afflicted with psychological scars that cripple them in myriad ways; some feel anxiety or depression but lead relatively quiet lives, while others manifest the wounds suffered in childhood in troubled relationships, life-threatening symptoms, and dangerous behavior patterns.

Men and women who experienced childhood trauma feel similar types of pain, but they often express it in different ways. There are many ways to explain why women hurt themselves more often than men do. Men who have been traumatized in childhood are likely to inflict on others what was done to them; they are socialized to act aggressively and to fight back rather than to allow someone to harm or humiliate them. Women are socialized not to fight back; allowing themselves to be hurt or humiliated is far more socially acceptable than being aggressive or violent toward others. Although some women become abusers themselves, it is much more likely that female victims of childhood trauma will inflict pain on themselves. Men act out. Women act out by acting in.

Many studies of trauma survivors confirm the high incidence of self-harming activities, especially self-mutilation. The writers Ellen Bass and Laura Davis, in their popular book for incest survivors, *The Courage to Heal* (1988), explain this pattern by pointing out how natural it is for adult survivors to replicate the childhood violence, not knowing how else to act. One of the most powerful and overwhelming emotions that abuse engenders is anger. This rage, bubbling and seething within the victim like lava in a volcano, is one of the explosive fuels that feed self-injurious behavior. Bass and Davis quote the poet Adrienne Rich: "Most women have not even been able to touch this anger except to drive it inward like a rusted nail" (p. 123).

Various experts have noted correlations between certain types of self-harmful behavior and a history of sexual abuse, physical abuse, or neglect. The psychiatrist Judith Herman, in her overview of trauma theory and treatment, *Trauma and Recovery* (1992), notes that self-mutilation, purging and vomiting, suicidal behavior, and compulsive exposure to danger are common sequelae. The psychologist Kathleen Bollerud (1992), in a well-named chapter on alcoholic women, "Long Night's Journey into Day," makes the connection between early trauma and the tendency toward dissociative disorders and substance abuse.

The psychiatrists Bessel van der Kolk, Christopher Perry, and Judith Herman (1991), who also found a high correlation between severe childhood abuse or neglect and adult self-destructive behavior, link the adult behavior patterns to a lack of secure attachments in childhood and to the tendency of the severely traumatized individual to dissociate. A number of studies (reviewed in Landecker, 1992) view self-injurious behavior as an attempt to escape feelings of emptiness, depersonalization, and unreality; to ease tension; to express emotional pain; and to punish the body as a way of expressing responsibility for the abuse. Other clinical experts (van der Kolk, 1987; Herman, 1992; Shapiro and Kaminlak, 1992) see the self-destructive behavior that is characteristic of many trauma survivors as attempts to alleviate inner rage when feelings cannot be expressed verbally, to provide a sense of control over the body, to express shame, and to provide biochemical relief.

I agree with these theories, but I also believe there are additional reasons for self-harmful behavior. Although self-injury may express rage, shame, and other feelings common to trauma survivors, and while it may ease tension or help the individual to escape feelings of emptiness or unreality, these functions are only part of the motivation for such behavior; this book addresses the physical and psychological reenactments of childhood trauma expressed in self-harmful behavior. The women described in these pages harm their bodies in a wide variety of ways: through eating disorders, substance abuse, self-mutilation, prescription drug abuse, frequent and often unnecessary cosmetic surgeries, and excessive dieting. In each case the woman is reenacting her experience of childhood trauma.

Over the years, I have heard the stories of many women in pain. I have used these women's voices to illustrate their lives as children, their experience before and during treatment, and their lives now.* Although most of these stories were revealed to me in a clinical context, here they are told as if the women were speaking directly to the multitude of other women who share similar stories.

I describe a treatment approach that I have found effective in helping these women work with therapists, peers, family members, partners, and a variety of professionals. While it is painful to hear their stories of anguish and shame, it is inspiring to hear how they were eventually able to triumph in their war against themselves and to join in the empowering force of women united in health and strength.

Hidden Pain, Visible Hurting

Karen is bulimic. June, alcoholic. Lee cuts herself and is addicted to pain medication. Nancy diets incessantly, takes numerous prescription drugs, and has frequent cosmetic surgery. What do these women have in common? If you met them in the supermarket, you might think them very different from one another. Karen is an attractive young woman, age twenty-three, who radiates pleasure when she talks about her job as a nurse in a big city hospital. June is forty-one, aged by years of drinking, coping with the hardships of poverty, and raising three children

---

*To protect the identity of my clients, I have used fictitious names and altered identifying material. The voices of the women are not actual transcriptions, but rather representations of the many voices I have listened to and learned from.

without a dependable partner. Lee, childless at thirty-six, is a shy but successful businesswoman whose husband, David, is her only close friend. Nancy is a wealthy, fifty-year-old suburban woman who travels with her executive husband, plays tennis, and attends doctor's appointments religiously.

Their childhood histories are also different. Karen was the eldest child and only daughter of a successful lawyer father and an alcoholic mother; she was sexually abused by her father from age four until puberty. Nancy was raised primarily by her grandmother because her wealthy parents were busy with other activities and unavailable for the demands of daily parenting. Nancy's grandmother doted on her and intruded on her body through a pattern of excessive caretaking. June had an alcoholic father who was periodically absent; her mother was fanatically religious and verbally abusive, alternating between being overly strict and completely neglectful. Lee's father was a high school teacher. Her mother managed a nursing home. Lee used to believe that her family was "normal" until she began to remember fragments of terrifying psychological and sexual abuse.

Perhaps these women's self-abusive patterns are similar. Karen and Nancy both have problems with body image and eating disorders. However, it is unlikely that Lee, a reclusive businesswoman who cuts herself, would be viewed as similar to Karen, an outwardly cheerful young nurse who is bulimic. Although most bulimics are ashamed of their symptoms, it is likely that Karen could disclose her bulimia and not be rejected, while Lee could not reveal her cutting without fear of being thought crazy or in need of institutionalization; women who hurt themselves through acts of self-mutilation are more stigmatized and pathologized than women who hurt themselves through eating disorders. Finally, June's alcoholism could easily separate her from the other women if alcohol abuse is seen solely as a chemical/behavioral addiction problem, genetically determined and treatable only in a program such as Alcoholics Anonymous (AA).

My view is that despite their differences, Karen, June, Lee, and Nancy share a common syndrome. They are all women who hurt their bodies as a result of childhood histories of interpersonal or family trauma; they reenact the harm done to them as children and reinforce their belief that they are incapable of protecting themselves because they were not protected as children. These women suffer from what I call "Trauma Reenactment Syndrome" (TRS), the central characteristic of which is a pattern of intentionally inflicting harm on one's own body.

The key to recognizing TRS is the connection between an adult woman's symptomatic behavior and her own unique story of childhood trauma; TRS women do to their bodies something that represents what was done to them in childhood. Karen almost literally reenacts the childhood sexual abuse by forcing food (representing her father's penis) down her throat and then vomiting (gagging) it back out of her body. June reflects her mother's neglect-and verbal abuse by neglecting and abusing her body through drinking. Nancy's diets and weight-loss pills replicate her grandmother's invasive enemas and excessive fussing over her body, repeating the pattern of constantly struggling to fix, clean, and improve the body. Lee's cutting symbolically reenacts childhood terrors and pain, as well as possibly physically reenacting the sadistic abuse she experienced.

The pattern of symptoms tells a story of how the child learned to be in relationships and learned to be with herself. The symptom is her survival skill, no matter how dangerous and hurtful it is. The self-injurious behavior serves many functions: in a strange way, it serves both to keep others at a distance and to keep her from feeling alone. She experiences the behavior itself as a relationship. It may help her feel alive when she is overwhelmed by feelings of numbness. Paradoxically, it can serve as well to keep her from feeling unbearable tension, rage, or grief. Her behavior is also a cry for help, a request for the protection she did not receive as a child.

TRS takes a variety of forms. It can involve alcoholism, drug addiction, and eating disorders. It can also include self-injuring behaviors such as cutting, burning, punching, slapping, or pinching one's own body, pulling out hair, and swallowing toxic substances or inserting them into the vagina or anus. TRS behaviors can also show up in a medical guise as excessive dieting, endless cosmetic surgeries, doctor-shopping, or prescription drug abuse. Some women who warrant inclusion in the TRS population engage in only one of the behaviors. Others engage either sequentially or simultaneously in a cluster of them.

It is important to remember that for these women their self-abuse connects them to their trauma, even though they, their partners, or their helpers may find it difficult to see or understand the connection. While some of the behaviors, such as bulimia, may closely mimic the type of trauma inflicted, other behaviors, such as substance abuse, may not have as clear a relationship.

Many writers specializing in the effects of trauma on women (Courtois, 1988; Herman, 1992) have linked eating disorders to childhood violation. Self-starvation (anorexia) can be seen as a reaction to traumatic degrees of invasive caretaking and explicit sexual abuse. The emaciated body resulting from anorexia and the obese body associated with compulsive overeating can be understood as forms of self-protection against being viewed as sexual and thus as a logical response to sexual abuse. Experts on bulimia also describe how bingeing and purging are related to the anxiety and body shame associated with childhood trauma.

To date, however, little has been written linking trauma histories with other types of self-destructive behavior. Obsessive dieting, compulsive cosmetic surgeries, alcoholism, drug abuse, and even smoking may be directly related to a history of abuse or neglect, but the connection has not been addressed by those studying these areas. This book begins to fill that gap by exploring the connection through the stories of women who hurt themselves as a way to articulate their trauma histories.

Whatever the particular symptom, for all TRS women the self-inflicted harm resonates with the pain that was inflicted upon them as children. Their self-destructive behavior tells the secret story of their childhood experience over and over again.

KAREN'S STORY

My name is Karen. It's hard for me to say this because parts of my life have been secret for what seems like forever. My voice sounds shaky and I feel like I'm going to be sick. I'm really scared to talk about this.

I look good on the outside, but inside I am fighting a life-or-death battle. I am my own worst enemy, or perhaps I should say my body is my worst enemy. If you saw me during an ordinary day at work, you would see an ordinary woman, maybe even a woman you could say is attractive. I am small, I have dark Mediterranean eyes, and my patients sometimes say I have a beautiful smile.

I am a hospital nurse, and I am still new enough at my work to tell myself that I love what I do. The patients, the doctors, and even most of the other nurses are all fooled by me. They think I'm kind, cheerful, and steady as a rock. "Karen," someone is always saying to me, "how can you manage to stay so calm? How come you're never angry?"

I am not calm. I am not steady or cheerful. I am not kind. I am angry, very angry.

Most of the time, no matter how much I seem to be enjoying my work, I am thinking about how much I hate my body. I am thinking murderous thoughts about my body. I am planning how I can eat lunch and then vomit in the staff bathroom without someone hearing me. I am thinking about how soon I can go home and begin drinking my nightly bottle of wine, and how long it will take to drink the whole bottle.

At night, when I am alone, I feel such rage that I am afraid sometimes that I'll do something terrible to someone. I fantasize about what kinds of torture I'd like to inflict on the most obnoxious, mean, conceited doctor at the hospital. But the victim of my torture is really me.

I am at war with myself, and I think that there is no exit, no possible cease-fire. I feel like those Moslem men you see on TV who beat themselves on the head until they bleed and who seem thrilled to die for their beliefs. I have to fight to the death, and yet I have no wish to die. I don't even know what I believe, so I'm not like those men.

If anyone knew what I do to my body, they would think I was completely nuts. This one girl at work, a nurse I like to work with because she's really funny and also takes no crap from anyone— she's an AA person—she would say that I'm alcoholic or that I'm bulimic. But I'm more than that. I'm not just an alcoholic or a food addict. These labels don't explain me. I don't know what I am or who I am. The women on the talk shows and the women in all of the self-help and recovery books . . . those women sound like parts of me. But no one seems to be as complicated or as hopeless as I feel about myself. No one has all the different parts of themselves that I seem to have. Am I depressed? Am I a multiple personality? I don't think so, but I do feel like there is more than one me.

By the way, you may be surprised to learn that I actually have boyfriends. At least I have had boyfriends. Lately I just can't make myself go out. My last boyfriend and I broke up about six months ago, and although I feel lonely sometimes, I don't actually miss him. My best friend, Ellen, says I like the idea of being in a relationship better than I like the actual guys I get involved with.

Ellen gets so impatient with me about this. She's married. The last time she and her husband, Dennis, fixed me up with a friend of theirs, she got so angry with me for screwing things up that I thought she was going to quit on me, too. I couldn't stand to lose Ellen. She and Dennis are my closest, long-time friends.

But here's the really weird thing: even though Ellen is my closest friend, she has no idea about the things I do to myself. She tells me I drink too much, but she has no idea what I do when I'm alone. After I saw a talk-show program on eating disorders, I tried to talk to her about it, but I lost my courage after she made a really mean remark about people who make themselves throw up. I knew then that I could never tell her about what I do. I'm not sure what other people would think about me. I don't think anyone would think that I'm a multiple personality, but they probably would think it's more than just being depressed. *I* know it's more than that.

The TV programs and the talk shows wouldn't know what to do with me, I guess. I'm an incest victim, by the way. But these days, who isn't? They say that incest victims can be depressed or they can sometimes be sort of crazy or they can be alcoholics or prostitutes or women who hate sex. They don't say that there are women like me who look normal but are doing all these horrible things to themselves. They don't really talk about how there's a war going on between different parts of my mind, the part that feels murderous, the part that wants to do the right thing, the part that keeps telling me to drink or to vomit my lunch. The only people I know personally who do stuff like that are usually in detox or on psych wards in hospitals. We're not supposed to be the nurses in the hospitals, just the patients.

I would lose my job as a nurse, I would lose my best friend, Ellen, and I would certainly lose any guy if they ever knew what kind of living hell my life has become.

Probably if I went to a therapist they would tell me I had to go to AA or a group for eating disorders. Or I'd get committed to a hospital. I'm so desperate and so lonely and so tired of living like this. Sometimes I can't figure any way out of this except suicide, but I don't want to die.

I think that's the strangest thing of all, that I don't want to die. But this is not a life.

Karen came to see me because her health insurance allowed twenty sessions at the psychotherapy clinic and she wanted help with "relationship problems." She was fashionably attractive, although her skin seemed unusually pale and her carefully made-up eyes looked chronically exhausted. In our second session, she disclosed to me that since age thirteen she had been binge-eating and purging by vomiting and using laxatives. No one knew Karen's secret until she decided to tell me. She later revealed her drinking habits and eventually told me that she engaged in occasional bouts of pulling her hair and bruising and scratching her body.

Like many women who hurt themselves, Karen read every self-help book she could find. She had a few close, supportive friends, including Ellen, some other nurses, and an old school friend. Even with all these resources, Karen felt desperately alone and hopeless. She considered joining a support group and telling her friend at work about her eating disorder, but she was terrified at the thought. She finally sought individual counseling with me because of her reluctance to engage in intimate relationships.

Dating episodically, Karen would find herself in a predictable cycle. After a short period of excitement about the new relationship, she would begin to feel close to her boyfriend but would soon break it off, becoming obsessively critical of even his smallest habit or mannerism. With some embarrassment she told me that she disliked sex. She avoided most kinds of physical contact with boyfriends, family members, and even her closest female friends.

Karen was holding another secret, which she disclosed to me after several therapy sessions; she revealed that she had been sexually abused by her father from the age of four until she entered puberty. Her father, a prominent lawyer, had divorced Karen's alcoholic mother when Karen was eighteen and had married a woman fifteen years his junior, with whom he now had a four-year-old son and two stepdaughters, ages twelve and nine. Karen's mother was living with Karen's youngest brother, age twenty, and both mother and son were active alcoholics.

Like many children of alcoholic parents, Karen spent much of her time worrying. Karen told me tearfully that she worried about her parents, about her youngest brother, and more recently about the safety of her two young stepsisters. She wondered if she should share her concerns with her mother, but avoided doing so because it would mean talking to her mother about the sexual abuse. She alternated between thinking that her mother already knew and blamed her for it, and worrying that her mother would refuse to believe her. Karen had always thought that she was her father's favorite child and that her mother and the other children envied her.

Karen was trapped in an intricate web of secrets. She was keeping the secret of the incest, the secret of her mother's and brother's alcoholism, and, most dangerous of all, the secret of her self-harmful behaviors. Her symptoms were potentially as toxic as if she were cutting her wrists or drinking a quart of Scotch nightly. The difference was that her forms of self-harm were well hidden from sight. As a nurse, Karen knew all about the damage the bulimia was doing to her body. Already her teeth were discolored and becoming loose. Her skin was sallow and often blotchy. Her esophagus and intestinal tract were chronically irritated. And once she had a major scare when she showed signs of cardiac irregularity.

Knowing that her bulimia was connected to her history of sexual abuse was helpful to Karen. She and I were able to make the link between this particular choice of symptom and the way she had been traumatized. Just as her father had forced her to have oral sex, Karen forced uncomfortable, sickening amounts of food down her throat and then vomited. Unfortunately, although she could recognize that what she was doing to herself was what her father had done to her, the insight alone did not alleviate her self-injuring patterns:

I am starting to build up those feelings of rage again. I want to stuff the rage back down my throat. I want to stop the terrible feeling of anxiety that sweeps over me at times like this.

When I feel like that, I have to have a drink. The wine soothes me, it keeps me from killing someone, it helps me not be really present at work.

Today a doctor humiliated a patient. I wanted to grab his head and pound it against the bed rail until he bled. I wanted to rip him to shreds.

I wanted to go down to the cafeteria and get something to eat so I could get away from him. I got some of that cake I was looking at when I went through the lunch line.

The cake made me feel full, awful. I was filled with its awfulness. I hate chocolate cake. What made me eat it? I had to throw up.

I felt so alone, so empty. When I got home I drank some wine and just skipped dinner.

The wine was just what I needed. I felt okay. I felt peaceful. I thought about calling Ellen and her husband, Dennis, to see if I could go over there for a visit. But then I thought, what if they're not home? I hate being alone when I feel like this. Maybe I'll have more wine.

Oh God, I thought, I'm ridiculous. Even Ellen can't do anything to help me. I'm hopeless, I'm disgusting. Ugly, ugly. Bad.

Pulling out each hair on my arm is interesting. All of the little points of pain, like points of light. Lies. Men and lies. Kill them. Kill him.

Why am I doing this?

Women who engage in self-harmful medical cosmetic activities also often suffer from TRS, although the relationship to childhood trauma is usually less clear than with other forms of the syndrome. In addition, it is less likely that people will recognize that these women are hurting themselves. TRS women in this category go from doctor to doctor, gathering a drugstore of often contraindicated prescriptions. Some of these women engage diet specialists who collude with them in dangerous or at least seriously unhealthy weight-loss programs. There are also women who undergo numerous elective surgeries. Their bodies become like clay—shaped, distorted, and worn out by surgeons for whom they are medical objects and sources of revenue. These women take a seemingly more passive role in their self-abuse in that they often invite others to harm their bodies, but the abuse is no less destructive—and no less a cry for the protection that they cannot provide for themselves.

NANCY'S STORY

My name is Nancy. My husband, Chip, is a lawyer and my children go to an expensive prep school. Besides our beautiful home, we have a cottage in the mountains and we just bought a little place at the beach. My life is enviable, I know. But I feel like there's this big hole inside of me.

I know some of you won't understand my despair. I'm not sure that I understand. You talk about trying to pay the rent, or how your family mistreats you. You hate yourselves for your drinking or your eating problems or for the scars you leave on your body. I have everything that you want. How can you relate to my story?

I've always thought I had a happy childhood. My brother and I were given so much. We knew that we were rich and I liked that, and I liked seeing my parents dressed in gorgeous clothes going off to parties. My father was a vice president in a very prestigious national company and Mother was always working with her charities or playing bridge. My parents were always busy, jetting off here and there. Sometimes they went to Europe, sometimes they went out to the West Coast. Sometimes they went together, but more often they were apart. I didn't go with them because they were always so busy on their trips. I didn't see my brother very often because he was away at boarding school or camp most of the time. I remember that we did all go down to St. Thomas a few times, so my parents didn't always leave me totally alone.

Whenever my parents were gone, my grandmother took care of me. Gram was my father's mother, but she was really unlike Daddy. She'd kiss and hold me all the time. Daddy would barely notice if I walked into the room. Gram followed me everywhere.

Even into the bathroom! She slept with me too. She said that she needed to be close to me so that she could take care of me if I had a nightmare or got sick. She was always touching me or putting a thermometer in my mouth to make sure that I didn't have a fever. Sometimes I would get terrible tummy aches, so she used to give me enemas to help prevent them. She always wanted me to tell her how I felt, and I had to tell her everything. She took really good care of me. She was always changing my clothes and fixing my hair so that I would look pretty for my daddy.

And I was pretty. I always had dates and I had a wonderful group of friends. I met Chip when we were both in college. We got married during his second year in law school.

I am very happily married and proud of my children. I even have a nice job working with my closest friend, Babs, at a little travel agency that we own. It's a great business, because sometimes I can talk Chip into going to new, exotic places on our vacations so I can check them out for the agency.

Chip probably drinks too much for a man in his late forties, but aside from that he's a responsible husband and father. He's a lot like my own father, actually. He's kind of aloof, not really very involved in family life, but that's because he has so many pressures at work. I know he loves us.

Ever since I had my first baby, I've been worried about keeping myself trim. Having a baby does terrible things to your figure. I really don't like looking at myself in the mirror, and now that I've passed that dreaded fortieth birthday, I can't help but notice my face sagging too. I approach these problems from every direction. I work out every afternoon at the health club and play tennis seven days a week. I diet constantly. I've spent hundreds of dollars on cosmetics each month for the past twenty years. But I have to do more and more. Fortunately, I've found some fabulous doctors over the years, true geniuses at restoring youth through surgery and medication.

The trouble is that with all this work I do to keep myself attractive, I always seem to be sick or in pain. Chip says that we can't have socialized medicine in this country, or at least in the

Northeast, because he's got all the doctors in New York and Connecticut fully employed just taking care of me. I have a lot of stomach problems, just like when I was young, and skin problems and terrible headaches. I've tried every kind of medical expert, from neurologists to chiropractors to homeopathic healers.

My friends complain of similar problems, but they all seem so much healthier to me. I'm the only woman I know who spends so much of her life trying to win all these battles against her body, and yet I keep losing.

I don't know how I'll ever get through twenty or thirty more years in this body.

Maybe I won't.

Nancy's form of self-abuse could be seen simply as a reaction to society's dictates that women must avoid aging, wrinkles, and weight gain, but Nancy also suffers a form of Trauma Reenactment Syndrome. She is a victim not only of societal pressure to be eternally young and beautiful, and of doctors who exploit her fears by giving her unnecessary drugs and surgeries, but also of her busy and uninterested parents' neglect and her grandmother's invasive and overbearing caretaking. Finally, and most painfully, she is a victim of her own self-injurious choices.

Because Nancy is unable to identify clearly the harm done by her parents and grandmother, she has a hard time recognizing that she lacked protection in childhood. She does not consider her family to have been abusive and believes that she actually did receive care—in the form of presents from her parents and attention from her grandmother. Nancy has internalized her grandmother's intrusive and violating behavior and her constant emphasis that Nancy needed to be pretty to make her father proud. Now she allows and even seeks out medically intrusive procedures in her attempts to remain attractive. She has also recreated her parents' "benign" neglect in her relationship with her husband, who jokes about her excessive medical involvement but does nothing to stop it. The despair Nancy feels keeps her desperately alone, trapped in a body that she views as an enemy, with no one to help her make sense of her battle or to offer protection.

JUNE'S STORY

My name is June. I've got my problems, but we all do, don't we? Just let go and let God and live one day at a time. I guess you can figure out I'm an alcoholic, but I'm "in recovery," as they say. Or at least some of the time I am. Been going to meetings for five years and two months, ever since Jack got his third drunk-driving ticket and lost his license. There but for the grace of God could have gone me.

Jack was my second husband. I divorced him about two years ago. I was married to Roy for a while, but he got on my nerves and was always fighting with my son Tony Jr. So I let him go.

My life is never boring, I'll have to say that. I've got my three teenagers still at home with me, God help me. Tony Jr. is eighteen, Richard is sixteen, and Dawn, fifteen. They all give me a hard time, one way or another. Tony is the best one—no drugs, a steady girlfriend, but also no sense. If there's trouble, he finds it, and the boy always gets caught. Richard is my handsome son and my biggest worry: drugs, booze, fights. He'll end up dead like his father if something doesn't happen to straighten him out. But I've turned it over to my Higher Power. Can't change anyone but yourself. Especially can't change your kids. But my Richard breaks my heart, even though I could kill him. When I forget to let go and let God, I think I can save him.

And Dawn? I want everything for her. I want everything for her I never had. But I'll be honest with you, I get madder with Dawn than with anyone else in the world. She shuts me out, she won't eat—a skinny little thing, fifteen years old and no figure, no period as far as I can tell—and sometimes she seems to hate me. I put good food on the table but she won't eat. But I keep trying with her.

I'm not like my mother. She didn't care about us. Her whole life was church and cleaning. When Ma was cleaning, like scrubbing the toilet with scouring pads, she'd hum to herself, and she'd be really happy. She was as religious about her cleaning as she was about church. Went to Mass three times a week. But she could be really mean, too. My dad would get drunk and he'd take

off, and then Ma would turn around and be so mean to me and
my younger sisters. Those were the only times that she ever really
paid attention to us. Those times, and when we were dirty or
messed up her precious house. Then she'd scream at us. Hell, she
even resented feeding us, 'cause it meant that we'd dirty the
dishes. We used to eat cereal out of the box to keep her happy.
Ma used to say that cleanliness was next to godliness, and by
God, she was going to have a clean house.

She used to say things like "children should be seen and not
heard" and "thou shalt respect thy parents," which meant that we
had to be really quiet. If we gave her any lip, then she'd scream or
not give us any dinner. We also got sent to our rooms. I think that I
spent most of my childhood in my room, staring at this huge crack
that ran down the wall or playing with my doll, Eliza. I gave Eliza
so many hugs that her arm fell off. Then Ma threw her away
because she said that she was disgusting. Sometimes I miss that doll.

Yeah, it wasn't easy in that house. But you can't change the
past, can you? Can you?

June, forty-one years old and currently single, is an intelligent, highly
verbal woman. When she became pregnant during her senior year of
high school, she dropped out. She has worked as an aide in various
hospitals, nursing homes, and daycare centers, and has also periodically
tried home sales of products such as Tupperware.

Episodic involvement in AA and AlAnon has partially helped June
with her addictions to alcohol, amphetamines, and tranquilizers. She
has entered several detox programs and even stayed for three months in
a specialized substance-abuse facility. June knows how to "talk the
talk" of the AA twelve-step recovery program, yet she continues to fall
back into drinking-based relationships and then return to alcohol abuse
for several weeks at a time.

I was the supervisor for June's therapist, Lynn. When I met with her
for a supervision session, Lynn, a normally calm and compassionate
woman, spoke of June in a tone that suggested she was quickly losing
her patience because of June's frequent relapses. What she was telling
me, however, was the story of June as blameless victim. I listened carefully for the unexplored clues, the underbelly of the case.

In therapy, June readily talked about her childhood history of severe neglect. Lynn told me that June's father was an alcoholic who periodically abandoned June's mother and the family. The mother was in turn verbally abusive to June and her younger siblings. "June doesn't remember her mother ever giving her any physical affection," said Lynn. "Her father would occasionally hug her, but more often than not he was either not home or drunk and passed out on the couch. June remembers that she and her sister spent most of their time in their room, sometimes locked in, while their mother cleaned or read religious tracts. She also remembers being hungry often."

June did not hide her addictions either. Although she was trying hard to stick with the AA program, she felt hopeless about any kind of lasting recovery. What concerned June the most, however, was her children.

"What kind of parenting has June been able to give her own kids?" I asked, knowing the answer I would probably hear.

Lynn sighed and shook her head. I knew we were thinking the same thing: How many times have we heard this tragic story? How can we expect parents who were abused and neglected as children to miraculously discover how to be a good parent?

"June's own children have also had difficult lives," she replied. "One of her teenage boys is heavily involved in drug and alcohol use, and her daughter is periodically anorexic. This is really upsetting to June and also confusing for her, because she clearly remembers that she often went hungry."

June was sometimes protective toward her daughter, wanting to save her from a life like her own, and at other times angry, verbally abusing her daughter for being "a patronizing, holier-than-thou little bitch" who could, as June put it, "starve herself to death if that's what she wants to do."

"What about current friends?" I asked.

"It's a little hard to know how to answer that question," Lynn responded. "June has a whole gang of pals, both AA friends and old friends from her drinking days. She seems attached to her younger sisters, too. I'd have to say, though, that she really doesn't let anyone get very close. She's been seeing me for two years now and I still feel like she barely notices my support or even, at times, my physical presence."

"What do you mean?" I asked.

"Well, at times during our sessions, I feel almost invisible. I could be anyone, I could be a tape recorder. Then at other times June is effusive in her gratitude. The worst times—and there are a few of these I'll never forget—are when she gets cold and nasty and devalues my efforts to help her. I'm a little reluctant to say this," concluded my colleague, "but lately I often find myself wishing that she would just quit therapy, as she occasionally threatens to do."

The way Lynn feels about June is probably similar to how many others in June's life feel. In all of June's relationships there is a shifting pattern of closeness and distance, overvaluing and devaluing, engaging and disengaging, self-reliance and a desire to be dependent. Because of her parents' scolding and lack of affection, June learned early to remain hypervigilant and not to allow anyone to get too close. Because of their neglect, she learned that no one would care for her. At the same time, she yearns to be close, to feel accepted and loved, but because she cannot allow herself to be so vulnerable, she cuts herself off from what she really wants. Consequently, she is enraged at those who tempt her to let down her guard and then "disappoint" her when she subsequently pushes them away.

Not all TRS women engage in continuous self-harmful behavior, as do June, Karen, and Nancy. Sometimes there is a relatively stable period in adult life, characterized by ongoing depression or anxiety but not involving self-harmful activities, which appear later (or reappear, having occurred in the teenage years). Some women seem to have at least superficially successful lives that are suddenly disrupted by an unexpected outbreak of self-destructive behavior—to the surprise and shock of their partners, families, and friends. Such events are often triggered by the awakening of memories of previously forgotten abuse.

Because of the recent change in social awareness of child abuse and neglect, many adult survivors are beginning to uncover buried memories of childhood trauma. Indeed, the number of women experiencing such awakenings is so large that there is growing controversy in professional circles about "induced" or "false" memory versus "real" memory of childhood trauma.

Some mental health professionals believe that trauma memories can be falsely induced in patients who think they may have been abused but have no clear memories. The false memory controversy has stirred up considerable pain, anger, and confusion on both sides of the debate and has become a legal issue as well as a clinical one. In my own work, I find that women who have developed entrenched patterns of seriously self-harmful behavior are unlikely to do such things to themselves without an underlying history of abuse or neglect. I have yet to encounter a woman with a severe eating disorder, unremitting substance-abuse problems, or a history of self-mutilation who did not experience some childhood trauma, whether it was sexual abuse, physical abuse, severe neglect, or, in a few cases, chronic and incapacitating childhood illness. I listen to the stories of childhood very carefully, noticing other indications that something clearly was not right. If a woman suddenly remembers childhood trauma but has no self-harmful symptoms or serious problems in relationships, I might be suspicious about the possibility of induced memories. But I believe that women who are in chronic psychic pain and engage in self-harmful behavior were usually traumatized in childhood.

While the recovery of buried memories is generally a progressive and necessary activity, a survivor may go through a period of terrible distress as she begins to remember and to give voice to early trauma. Consequently, she may enter a period of reenactment of childhood abuse manifested through self-destructive behavior, even if such behavior has not previously been typical. The following story is about this kind of woman.

LEE'S STORY

My name is Lee. I never would have believed I would be telling you about myself. I still try to pretend I'm not a woman who hurts herself, and I'm also a very private person. I've been married to David for fourteen years and there is still a lot about me even he doesn't know.

Two years ago, soon after my thirty-third birthday, I began to cut myself again. I did it for a while as a teenager, but teenagers sometimes do weird things. I thought that I was beyond such bizarre behavior. It's true, of course, that I used to smoke a lot of pot at one time in my life, but I really never saw that as a problem. Certainly it's not what I would call bizarre. My therapist knows about my cutting myself, and some other things like that. So does David. I can't tell anyone else.

The other thing that I guess puts me in the category of "women who hurt themselves" is how many different kinds of painkillers I take. I have terrible headaches, so bad that I have to leave my business and go home when I feel one coming on. The headaches have been part of my life for a very long time, but in the past several years they have definitely gotten worse.

Between my therapist and David, I've been sent to at least six doctors to see if anyone can help with the headaches. No one can, but they all prescribe pills for me, so it's worth it to keep trying, I guess.

My therapist and I have been together for more than ten years. Her name is Martha and she's like a mother to me. Two or three years ago, Martha started really urging me to remember more abuse stuff from my childhood. That's how the cutting began again. Martha and I have pieced together what seems to happen when I get into the cutting episodes. This is what it's like. Something will set me off so that I start thinking about all the bits and pieces of how scared and alone and sad I was as a child. I can actually notice myself feeling as small as if I was, literally, a child again. Then, at a certain point, I know that the pain is going to start; I'm headed for one of my headaches and I have to do something. I start to agonize over how I'm going to fail to outrun the pain. Sometimes I take my pills and kind of psychically buckle my seatbelt and just head into the pain. Other times I get myself so totally terrified and sad that I just can't do anything. I'm kind of frozen like that, and then I'm likely to head for the bathroom and get a razor and start cutting.

While this is going on, I know I should stop myself from doing it. But I can't. Both my therapist and David have made me promise I'll call one of them or go to one of them when this cycle starts up, but I just can't.

I hear myself say, "No, I can't do this to myself," and then this harsh, terrible voice tells me I have to do it or the headache pain will get me and kill me. Then there's a voice that just seems tired and weak and says, "I can't help it. I can't stop myself from doing it." So it's as if there are at least three parts of me: the little scared kid me, the horrible cutting me, and the worn-out me who says I can't stop it.

You would think that ever since Martha and I got that scenario figured out I'd know how to change it. But I can't.

When I'm at work or when I'm just having a nice time with David or with friends, you'd never think I had these kinds of problems.

I often wonder if people make up memories of being sexually abused to explain something about themselves that feels really crazy. Everything about my life tells me I'm not crazy. Look at how successful my business is, and look at what a good marriage I have. But some of what I seem to remember makes me feel crazy. Nothing comes too clearly at all.

I just keep stumbling through my life inside my mind. I've got horrendous pictures, flashes, images, then nothing. Or I've got pain.

Martha wonders if my mother abused me. I wonder how *many* people abused me. I wonder if I'm making it all up. I wonder if the pain in my head will ever stop.

For years Lee had severe headaches and was chronically depressed, but was able to cope with daily life. In therapy, memories of abuse arose as Martha gradually helped her to remember specific details of her childhood. When Lee began to remember fragments of being sexually abused, she began cutting herself.

Lee is a successful businessperson; she owns a small chain of video rental stores in the city where she lives with her husband, David. They have been married for fourteen years. She is thirty-five and he is thirty-six. They have no children. David always wanted them, but Lee was strongly reluctant without really knowing why. Lee began individual psychotherapy ten years ago when the conflict about having children became an increasingly urgent problem. The marriage remained stable despite the tension, but David became increasingly frightened and angry with the onset of Lee's cutting episodes.

The family that Lee began remembering seemed almost impossible to match with the family seen by the outside world. Lee's father and mother were both well liked and respected in their jobs and in the community. There was no alcoholism in the family and very little overt conflict. Lee grew up believing that her family was normal, but during her ten years of therapy she began learning to question surface appearances.

The one cloud hanging over Lee's family was the suicide of her maternal grandfather when her mother was only fifteen years old. Lee's mother, an only child, seems to have been extremely attached to her father and had clearly resented being left to take care of her widowed mother, with whom she had a noticeably tense relationship. Lee grew up hearing how much she was like her grandmother in both looks and temperament.

The years of individual psychotherapy created a deep bond between Lee and her therapist, Martha. Over the past few years, however, Martha expressed worries that they were reaching an impasse because of Lee's self-harmful behavior. When Martha suggested that Lee might need a different kind of treatment, Lee became so distraught that Martha backed off until the next round of self-injury occurred. Lee, her husband, David, and her therapist were all increasingly frustrated and frightened.

What eluded Martha, Lee, and David was the pattern of abuse that began in childhood: what was initially external became internalized. Without naming this pattern of abuse reenactment, the therapist and the client deal with only a piece of the problem, which is often not enough to stop the self-harming behavior. Looking at Lee's behavior as a manifestation of TRS, we have a useful way of understanding it. This is the first step in beginning the healing process.

Central Characteristics of Trauma Reenactment Syndrome

TRS women, whose rage, pain, and shame lead them to hurt themselves, reenact the trauma inflicted upon them in childhood through a pattern of behaviors, a set of distinct personality styles, and a number of predictable and distressing problems in living. There are four central characteristics that distinguish women who suffer from Trauma Reenactment Syndrome from other women with self-abusive habits or a history of trauma: (1) the sense of being at war with one's own body; (2) excessive secrecy as a central organizing principle of life; (3) inability to self-protect, often evident in a specific kind of fragmentation of the self; and (4) relationships in which the struggle for control overshadows all else.

My Body, My Enemy

TRS women are in a constant battle with their bodies. Their harming of their own bodies is confusing, to both professional helpers and the TRS victims themselves. The behavior seems to reflect a condition of being out of control, yet for many women it creates the illusion of being in control of their bodies. Whether the TRS woman is cutting herself, drinking, taking diet pills, or purging, she is making a choice to do so. This sense of being in control is important to her, because as an abused, neglected, or invaded child, she lacked control; someone else often had power over her body.

Self-destructive behavior often provides a sense of relief. It can provide escape from feelings of rage or grief. It can relieve the self-injurer from the sensation of numbness. It can reduce feelings of anxiety.

Some forms of self-harmful behavior are widely perceived as providing relief. Almost anyone who enjoys an alcoholic beverage can relate to the idea of having a drink to "unwind" from tension and anxiety, or even to take the edge off anger or sadness. Similarly, most people can relate to the use of alcohol to allow for disinhibition in social situations such as parties, dancing, or sex. So when a TRS woman uses alcohol or one of the more socially acceptable drugs such as marijuana or cocaine, and explains that it helps her experience some form of relief, most people can identify with her.

Using diet pills, dieting excessively, having numerous cosmetic surgeries, and going frequently to doctors for help with "cosmetic" problems may also be relatively understandable to the average American woman, who is induced by the culture at large to worry about her weight, her breasts, her buttocks, her skin, her height, her age, her hair, and so on. When a woman such as Nancy talks about her efforts to keep herself looking young, trim, and attractive, few women would ask whether she has a serious mental health problem.

Eating disorders are now also relatively easy for most people in our culture to understand. Many men and women overeat, even though obesity is stigmatized, especially for women. "How can she let herself go like that?" people often ask about obese women; their comments indicate that while worrying about overeating is a cultural norm, the judgments made about obese people deny any empathy for those whose eating habits result in being severely overweight.

Anorexia is paradoxically both stigmatized and encouraged in our culture. If an anorexic woman is a beautiful model, she is admired, envied, and rewarded. If she is an ordinary girl or woman who is not labeled as "beautiful," she upsets everyone around her. "Why can't she just make herself eat?" her family, friends, and even strangers ask in exasperation.

Bulimia is generally the least understandable or tolerated behavior among the eating disorders. People are astonished at the thought that anyone would choose to vomit or induce diarrhea. The bulimic woman is therefore especially secretive about her self-harmful activities and often has normal body weight.

TRS women who self-mutilate are the most stigmatized and isolated group. They are viewed as mentally ill and often diagnosed as suffering from Borderline Personality Disorder. Whether they cut themselves, burn themselves, pull out their body hair, or put toxic substances into their mouths or vaginas, they engender fear and disgust in others. A person who is not a self-mutilator cannot easily empathize with these women, who are aware of others' reactions. They are the most secretive among TRS women and are often viewed by these other women and even by themselves as having no kinship with other types of TRS victims.

Chapter 2 describes the various ways in which TRS women engage in the war with their bodies. Whether it is June going on another drinking binge, or Karen vomiting her lunch at work, or Lee being overpowered by her compulsion to cut herself, or Nancy frantically trying to outrun the aging process, these women are all waging an all-consuming war against their own bodies. Sadly, it is not a popular or "just" war, so there is little recognition of their terrible suffering or their many efforts to help themselves and put an end to the war.

Secrets

TRS women are enslaved by secrecy for several reasons. The most obvious impetus for secrecy is that self-abusive behavior is usually unacceptable to everyone else in the woman's life, from loved ones to professional helpers. Even alcoholism and drug abuse are more likely to be kept secret by women than men, who are often more open about such problems. Experts on female alcoholism, including Claudia Bepko and Jo Ann Krestan (1985), describe how female alcohol abuse is stigmatized and therefore kept underground. Other forms of self-harm, with the possible exception of excessive dieting, are even more likely to be kept hidden. Even women who, like Nancy, have had numerous cosmetic surgeries (face lifts, tummy tucks, buttocks tucks, or liposuction) often try to hide the fact from others.

Another reason for secrecy is that it is often a habit carried over from childhood. Abused children are usually threatened with dire consequences if they do not keep silent about the abuse, and neglected or invaded children often keep their treatment secret because they are ashamed of it. Because TRS behaviors are reenactments of childhood traumas, it is logical that secrecy remains a central characteristic, even when the abuser has become the woman herself.

Loyalty to and protection of the abuser encourage secrecy among traumatized children. In the adult TRS victim, loyalty to and protection of the symptomatic behavior create the mandate for secrecy. Not only does the symptom become a sort of relationship or "friend" for the TRS woman, but the secret-keeping too takes on a life of its own, so that the secret becomes another such hidden friend.

As I will describe further in chapter 3, these functions of secrecy are complicated and deeply entrenched. In addition, because secrecy keeps people at a distance from the TRS woman, it makes treating her an especially difficult challenge. The role of secrecy in treatment will be taken up in part II.

The power of the secret is well illustrated by Karen's situation. Karen desperately wanted to get better but felt overwhelmed and trapped by her shameful secrets. A significant part of the work that Karen and I had to accomplish together was to break through her defensive patterns of secrecy, which had become a way of life. For Karen, giving up excessive secrecy was like giving up a vital part of herself.

Secrecy had been forced on Karen in childhood, and it had come to serve a protective function in her adult life. By keeping her secrets, she could keep a polite but impenetrable boundary between herself and everyone else. By finding fault with her various boyfriends and then leaving the relationships, she could keep the shame of her incest, her bulimia, and her drinking a secret from them and, to some extent, from herself. By valuing her secrets more than her relationships, Karen could keep her distance and avoid getting hurt. The process of slowly uncovering the secrets was critical. Just as important for Karen was understanding how secrecy functioned to both harm and protect her. Once she trusted someone enough to begin to change her habits, she could stop protecting her father at her own expense and could take better care of herself and eventually her young, at-risk stepsisters.

No Protection

The TRS pattern of self-harm is rooted in an inability to self-protect and a fragmented sense of self. Despite the TRS woman's longing to stop the abusive cycle, she does not have the capacity to protect herself. In childhood, there was no one who kept her from harm, and therefore no way that she could learn to keep herself safe. She has no internalized "Protective Presence." Because of this inadequate protection from serious harm and violation in childhood, she never developed a sense that might give her advance warning signals and help her avoid the various cycles of trauma reenactment. She also cannot soothe herself when she is hurt.

While each TRS woman hurts her body in a different way and each has suffered a different childhood trauma, all these women dissociate: the mind fragments into several different parts as a result of the trauma. Dissociation is what happens when the mind cannot tolerate a traumatic event and responds by splitting off the experience, separating it from the conscious mind. The physical experience of dissociation may be a feeling of numbness, floating, and disconnection of mind and body. Memory becomes fragmented and thinking is confused. The child or adult who dissociates may feel as if she is outside herself, seeming to watch herself from a distance.

Dissociation is something we have all experienced at some time to some degree. When we get very angry or very frightened, we often have a sense of temporarily being a different person from who we are most of the time. When I am really furious, for example, my face and voice change, and I say things I would never say under other circumstances. For the TRS woman, this is a frequent experience, central to her self-harmful activities.

The process of dissociation will be explained more thoroughly in chapter 4. In this chapter, I will look briefly at just one aspect of dissociation: the experience of the fragmented self. In the dissociative process, the mind can seem to split into separate parts. In Karen's case, when her father sexually abused her, the trauma was too unbearable for her four-year-old psyche to endure. What she did was to split off the "bad" part of her father and take it inside her mind as a separate part of herself. This became the internalized Abuser. Equally unbearable was the absence of protection Karen experienced from her alcoholic mother. Karen split off the Nonprotecting Bystander part of her mother and took it inside to become another part of herself. Karen began to adjust to these fragments of self. While she is not a multiple personality, she does have the dissociative problem of fragmentation.

The sense of the fragmented self is central for women who reenact their trauma. The TRS woman experiences the feeling that she is more than one person. Although some of these women suffer from severe dissociative problems in which the different parts of the self seem to be completely separate (requiring long-term, specialized treatment) most self-harming women can relatively easily integrate these discrepant parts. Their problem is that the various "selves" are not in harmony with each other and actively collude in the patterns of self-harm.

This sense of fragmentation causes TRS women to say "I felt like I wasn't myself when I said that" or "I don't know what got into me that made me act like that." Sometimes when the TRS woman is "beside herself" with rage, she can be frightening and, to the target of her anger, may not even resemble herself.

In listening to the stories of TRS women and how they speak of themselves, I realized that their conception of self incorporated more than the duality of "good" and "bad" self. Over and over again I saw the configuration that I call the "Triadic Self." This self reflects the relational patterns that these women experienced during their abusive childhoods. The three aspects of the Triadic Self are the Victim (the "wounded child within"), the Abuser (an internalized representation of the abusive adult), and the Nonprotecting Bystander (usually a representation of the adult figure who was often unable or unwilling to protect the child victim).

The experience of the Triadic Self is repeatedly enacted when the TRS woman engages in self-harmful behavior, including symptoms and self-destructive relationship patterns. When an episode of self-abusive behavior begins, the Abuser is the dominant voice, commanding the harmful activity. Then there is a small, timid response from the Victim, trying to stop the inevitably injurious behavior. Next is the entrance of the Nonprotecting Bystander, who says, in effect, "I'm sorry, but I can't stop this from happening, I can't help it, I can't protect you."

Karen is enacting the dynamics of the Triadic Self when she binges and purges. An episode may begin when she is struggling with herself about her obsession with a boyfriend. Fearing dependency and acute vulnerability, she switches instead to obsessing about her craving to binge. As she begins to binge, she is saying both "I have to eat this whole cake" (the voice of the internalized Abuser, her father) and "No, I don't want to do this to myself" (the voice of the internalized child Victim). When she says to herself, "But I can't help it, I have to do this, I just can't stop myself," she is also evoking the voice of the internalized Nonprotecting Bystander (her mother).

Every time a woman such as Karen, June, Lee, or Nancy engages in self-harmful behavior, she is fragmenting herself into the Triadic Self configuration: the Abuser harms the Victim and cannot be stopped because the Nonprotecting Bystander is incapable of intervening. What has to happen in the recovery process is for the adult woman to gain control of this pattern of dissociation. She needs support in identifying it and in consciously learning to replace the Nonprotecting Bystander with a Protective Presence. The development of an internalized Protective Presence, which can be seen as the healthy transformation of the Nonprotecting Bystander, is both the most difficult part of recovery for the TRS woman and the most important.

Relationships

Relationship dynamics can exacerbate the problems of the TRS woman. Just as self-abusive behavior affects the relationship, the relationship affects the behavior. Most self-harming women will agree that they are characteristically very reactive in relationships of significance. They tend to be very sensitive and extremely watchful. The themes that seem to pervade the relationships of these women are fear of abandonment, a belief that there is or has been deception, humiliation and shame, obsessional thoughts, and a simultaneous fear of and longing for compensatory love and protection.

Women who hurt themselves experience a variety of relationship challenges. While not exclusively the province of TRS women, feeling close to others is especially troubling for this population. Some women who hurt themselves are very good at disguising their problems, appearing to be easily connected to those with whom they are involved. Some of these women are, in fact, very charming, even charismatic. Some of them have achieved genuine connection and closeness in most kinds of relationships but cannot manage intimate involvements. All of these women feel a painful sense of aloneness and they know that an important part of themselves remains unseen and untouched.

There is no single way that TRS women interact in relationships. Moreover, the individual woman is usually different in one type of relationship than she is in another. Each of these women was in a primary childhood relationship with the perpetrator of the trauma and also with one or more people who allowed the trauma to occur. She was also forced to relate to other hurtful or disappointing members of her childhood environment. Her understanding and learning of relationships arose within a troubled system. In the same way that these women reenact their trauma, they also reenact the relationships of their childhood. The exact nature of their current relationships depends on the specifics of their interactions as a child, the situation in which they find themselves, and the response evoked in them by the person with whom they are involved; however, there are some general patterns I have seen again and again in working with TRS women.

Four types of relationships are particularly problematic for TRS women. Intimate relationships and friendships are frequently fragile and complicated, alternating between extremes of intense engagement and distancing. Family of origin relationships are another area of stress and challenge, especially relationships that carry the memory of abuse, failed protection, or neglectful parenting. Current family relationships with children, adult siblings, grandparents, and in-laws can also be complicated and unusually stressful. Finally, relationships with professionals and other helpers are loaded with challenges and disappointments, especially around issues of authority and trust.

Depending on the woman, the needs of the self or the needs of others often predominate. Some self-harming women have little capacity to perceive or respond to the needs of other people, while others have little awareness of their own needs and behave like the classic "codependent" who needs to be needed. Personal boundaries may be blurred, so that there is inappropriate sharing of confidential or personal information and intrusions into another person's private space or business. The other side of the same coin is when a woman neglects her own needs and tolerates such intrusions from others.

The TRS woman may avoid close relationships by vacillating between an intense longing for connection and an equally intense mistrust of closeness. Her relationship avoidance is a result of the invalidation or devaluation of self in relation to others. Devaluing herself may include minimizing her own ideas, thoughts, wishes, and accomplishments in relation to those of others. The rage that so many TRS women feel creates chronic difficulty with interpersonal conflict, which may appear in the form of rage attacks, constant bickering to avoid direct, serious confrontation, or extreme repression of anger.

Many of these patterns are especially visible in the TRS woman's sexual relations. She may be preoccupied with sexual conquest, sexual comforting, sexual masochism, or sexual control, or she may avoid sexual closeness almost entirely. Intimacy issues are often most clearly revealed in the sexual patterns of these women, yet this may be an especially difficult area of exploration and discussion in therapy.

Many self-harming women engage in highly dramatic behavior that can serve to distance others or test their commitment. Many TRS women suffer intense depressions and exaggerated physical complaints, and they may express their distress in an operatic style or else freeze others out through sullen withdrawal.

All of the relationship behaviors become understandable with full comprehension of the factors that cause and maintain the patterns of TRS. Once a woman begins to develop this understanding, she can begin to create more functional and fulfilling relationships. Only in safe relationships is the TRS woman able finally to experience protection, and it is within the fertile soil of an accepting and caring relationship that the seed of the Protective Presence begins to grow and flourish.

A New Approach to Recovery

Each of the four women introduced in this chapter has a different story about her attempts to get help for her self-destructive behavior. None of them, however, were able to achieve a healthy, normal life; with these four women, as with millions of others, the complexity of the TRS patterns was not fully understood or addressed in treatment.

Karen had tried several approaches to her eating problems. She read numerous magazine articles and several books about such disorders. From her reading, she became aware that eating problems are not simple in either their origins or their cure. She felt relieved to discover that her failure to solve them was not a failure of will power. Most experts she read seemed to agree that women with eating disorders could not reasonably be expected to "just say no" to their desire for too much food or to regurgitate their food, or even to the desire to starve themselves. They considered eating disorders to be caused by poor self-image, by the wish to avoid being perceived as a sexual being, and by a history of dysfunction in the victim's family. They recommended various approaches to treatment, but there seemed to be a consensus that, to achieve successful recovery, the eating-disordered woman needs group support as well as support from friends and loved ones.

The literature Karen read described the various types of eating disorders: bulimia (bingeing and purging), anorexia (starving), and compulsive eating (both as part of the bulimic cycle and as a problem of obese women and men). Although many diets were recommended as part of the recovery process, Karen was most attracted to the idea that many women with eating disorders suffer from the problem of addiction. She felt hopeful that she could approach her problems with food—and drinking—by focusing on her patterns of addiction. Bolstered by the idea that she was both a food addict and possibly an alcoholic, Karen went to Overeaters Anonymous (OA) and Alcoholics Anonymous (AA) meetings several times a week. Eventually she began attending both groups on a daily basis. Both OA and AA are so-called twelve-step programs. The steps refer to a series of designated stages in becoming involved in the program and letting go of the addictive behaviors, or "being in recovery." In the twelve-step program approach, the recovery process includes not only stopping the addictive behavior of choice, but also working on related patterns of interpersonal behavior that tend to be part of the addict's profile. An important part of the process is working with a sponsor, someone with a history of successful involvement in the program, who can be called for support and guidance between meetings. Karen was able to begin speaking in meetings early in her attendance and found a sponsor within the first two months of "recovery."

Despite Karen's best efforts, she was increasingly discouraged by her continued mental distress. No amount of meeting attendance seemed to help her inner turmoil, nor did contact with her sponsor or supplications to her Higher Power (the twelve-step approach's term for God or the spiritual presence invoked to help a person experience serenity in the difficult process of recovery). Karen continued to feel tortured by feelings of rage, self-hatred, fear, emptiness, and a terrible loneliness and isolation. She never felt safe enough to disclose her childhood experience of sexual trauma at the meetings. The less she depended on her bulimic and drinking behaviors to escape from these terrible memories and feelings, the more desperate she felt.

June also used the twelve-step program to help recover from alcoholism. While she felt less alone than Karen in her AA program, she too felt discouraged, helpless in ending her occasional binge-drinking episodes. She knew all the reasons offered by the program to explain her "slips," but she was unable to make the program's teachings work for her when she was headed toward a relapse. June, like many other TRS women, would scold and blame herself for not being able to "work the program right." She was sure the problem lay within her, not within the program's limitations. She was unable to make connections between her mother's harsh neglect and her pattern of self-abusive drinking. Instead, she was taught to explain her alcoholism in terms of her alcoholic father's influence. She thought of herself as someone who grew up in an alcoholic family and thus was constitutionally predisposed to become alcoholic.

June had in fact made some progress in beginning to move toward the development of a Protective Presence by getting into the twelve-step recovery program. What she also needed was a more personal relationship, most likely with a therapist or a therapy group, in which she could begin to explore the painful childhood feelings she had buried for so long. By developing a tolerance for these disturbing experiences of shame, rage, sadness, and fear in a safe but intense therapy relationship, she could begin to allow herself to feel real love and vulnerability. For the TRS woman, her therapist or group often becomes the model for caring that she never had.

Lee chose a different route to try to get her life under control. Her individual psychotherapy was the lifeline she hoped would help her escape her profound experience of isolation. Later, she also expected the therapy to help her understand and stop her cutting. Unlike Karen and June, Lee was given ample opportunity to explore her childhood history of trauma. Unfortunately, just as with Karen and June, the internal distress as well as the self-abusive symptoms did not seem to diminish. In fact, the more Lee tried to remember and talk about her childhood victimization, the more she felt compelled to harm herself, and as with Karen, the more her relationships suffered. Karen withdrew from friends, Lee withdrew from her husband, David.

Nancy was not in any kind of treatment. Because she did not see her extreme dieting, overexercising, and excessive medication as symptoms or addictions, she did not actively try to change her behavior. Like Karen and Lee, Nancy felt terribly alone and out of control. She too was searching unsuccessfully for a way to escape the tyranny of her body as enemy. Her attempts to get help from doctors were very much like Karen's and June's attempts in twelve-step programs and Lee's attempts in psychotherapy, doomed to fail because only part of the picture was seen and treated; Nancy did not make the connection that her grandmother's invasive caretaking and her parents' neglect could be related to her battles with her body or her sense of personal failure in life.

These examples of treatment failures are not intended as a criticism of any one treatment approach. Twelve-step recovery programs work extremely well for many people who suffer from addictions of various sorts. Psychotherapy is often extremely effective as well, including for many victims of childhood trauma. Diets, cosmetic surgeries, and other medical procedures are also not without their usefulness for those people whose troubles stem primarily from certain physical problems. For the TRS woman, however, it is frustrating and depressing when none of these approaches helps her escape the tyranny of self-destructive behavior. As I note in chapter 6, treatment for the TRS woman has historically been poor because the complexity of the TRS cycle and its origins has not been fully understood. I cannot emphasize strongly enough that any single diagnosis and treatment designed exclusively for alcoholics or for eating disorders or for self-mutilators cannot adequately meet the needs of TRS victims. Successfully treating these women requires a thorough understanding of the complexity of TRS.

It is vital to establish a more comprehensive way of describing, understanding, and treating the myriad behaviors that characterize Trauma Reenactment Syndrome. My approach to treatment and recovery challenges some fundamental beliefs about treatment of substance

abuse, eating disorders, and self-mutilation; alcoholics are not separated from self-mutilators, nor are eating disorders treated solely as
problems of addiction or "bad eating habits." Many self-abusive
women can be viewed as suffering from Post-Traumatic Stress Disorder
(PTSD), but such a diagnosis is not broad enough. The TRS woman
needs to be understood from a more holistic perspective. She is an intricate amalgam, and to treat only one aspect of her denies the importance of the varied components of the syndrome. Any treatment
approach must recognize that letting go of the symptom should happen
in a careful, supportive series of steps. Both the history of the behavior
and the various functions it serves must be addressed. Because of the
destructive nature of the TRS woman's memories and rage, the therapist must traverse the landscape of the woman's wounded psyche very
carefully.

Four major assumptions underlie my proposed approach to Trauma
Reenactment Syndrome treatment and recovery. The first assumption is
that the contexts of the symptom are central to understanding and
treating the TRS victim. By *contexts* I mean the situations in which the
person lives, interacts, thinks, and experiences herself in relation to the
world. There are multiple contexts that create and continue to support
the logic of the symptom.

The second assumption is that the symptom must be viewed from a
historical perspective. The behavior must be seen as an adaptation, an
attempt to cope, and an indirect communication about the anger and
pain from past trauma and about the disparate parts of the self that
were internalized from abusive and nonprotective childhood relationships.

Third, the symptom has several important functions. The self-
abusive behavior may have developed to serve various purposes: to dis-
tract from unbearable pain, rage, or shame; to punish the hateful self;
or to communicate abuse. Even when it is no longer "necessary," it
may still serve the function of being a familiar companion of sorts, less
frightening than relationships or new experiences in the real world. As
paradoxical as it may seem, the relationship with the symptom may feel
more real and dependable to the TRS victim than relationships with
people.

The final assumption is that the TRS woman needs a healthy, caring
relationship before she is able to revisit her traumatic childhood. If she
does not have the security of a safe and supportive relationship, she will

not be able to confront successfully her memories or the pain and anger that fuel her destructive behavior. While it is possible that she may be able to find such a relationship outside the therapeutic setting, it is most likely that a therapist or therapy group will be best equipped to accompany her on the difficult journey to health.

I am convinced that it is necessary to use several different theoretical perspectives and several different levels of treatment when designing a recovery program for women who hurt themselves. This book illustrates how various treatment approaches currently being used can be integrated to create a more effective recovery model. Through understanding both the history that initiates self-abusive behavior and the context that perpetuates it, TRS women can help themselves to get the best combination of treatments and thus achieve lasting recovery.

2

The Body as Battleground

Trauma Reenactment Syndrome can manifest itself in a variety of self-destructive behaviors. Some of these, such as alcoholism, drug abuse, and eating disorders, are widely practiced in our society. Others are not only common in our culture, but socially acceptable as well, so that they are not likely to be considered symptoms; such fashion-focused behaviors as cosmetic surgeries and extreme diet regimes may not be recognized as self-destructive. I also include chain-smoking among the self-harmful behaviors associated with TRS. This is controversial, since, in many circles, smoking remains a socially acceptable type of self-harm; however, because it is as lethal as the other forms of behavior, I believe its inclusion is justified. At the other end of the spectrum of self-destructive behaviors are various forms of self-mutilation. The TRS woman may cut, burn, or punch her body, bang her head, or pull out her hair. She may insert toxic substances into her vagina, rectum, or mouth.

Given this wide range of symptoms, how can we know when an activity indicates TRS? For example, how can we distinguish the TRS woman who chronically abuses alcohol as a way to reenact her trauma from a woman who is drinking too much for another reason? My criteria for deciding whether a behavior, including such socially acceptable behaviors as smoking, drinking, and poor eating habits, constitutes TRS are the following: (1) there is a history of childhood trauma—physical or psychological abuse, neglect, or invasive caretaking; (2) the behavior is chronic and deeply troubling to the client; and (3) it is clearly injurious to her health. When these factors are present, I can begin to look for ways in which the behavior may be serving as a reenactment of the childhood trauma.

The Difficulty of Identifying the TRS Woman

Karen, the young nurse described in chapter 1, is one of many women who find their way to a therapist's office, a recovery group, or even a hospital bed. These women want to change their lives, but they can't find the right door or the key to open it. They feel fragmented within themselves. They feel desperately alone. They feel misunderstood and they blame themselves for it. No single label fits them or seems to describe their suffering.

If Karen had come into my office ten or fifteen years ago, I would have diagnosed her as alcoholic. If instead I had first met her around eight years ago, I might have been more likely to explore the eating disorder as well and then to generalize, giving her a broader diagnosis of Addictive Personality Disorder. My primary objective would have been to get her to go to twelve-step meetings, where the goal would be sobriety and recovery from bulimic patterns.

Had Karen come into my office for her first visit only six or seven years ago, I might still have been concerned about the alcoholic drinking and bulimia, but I probably would have concentrated more on her history as an incest survivor and diagnosed her as suffering from Post-Traumatic Stress Disorder, which would have meant a major shift in treatment. Instead of confronting her addictive behaviors, I would have wanted her to uncover rather than bury her story. I would have helped her gain access to her emotional memory of the abuse. I would have focused on the past and invited the painful stories, rather than admonishing her to concentrate exclusively on the daily goal of abstinence from alcohol and binge-eating.

Perhaps, however, instead of concentrating on her addictions or her trauma history, I might have responded most actively to Karen's problems in relationships. As a family therapist, I often used to focus on the dysfunctional relationship patterns—or ideas about relationships—in my work with someone like Karen. I would certainly have urged her to find a way to use either a twelve-step program or some other means to gain control of her drinking and eating disorder, possibly suggesting a women's support group. I would not have ignored her history as an incest victim, but I might have thought that since she was not present-ing her trauma history as a primary issue in her current life, it was not useful to push her to work on those memories. I probably would have invited Karen to bring people with whom she had significant relation-ships to her therapy sessions: the goal would have been to enable these various relationships to function more effectively.

Other therapists might have seen Karen's self-harmful behavior pat-terns, her rage at work, and her failure to stay in an intimate relation-ship as red flags, clear signals of Borderline Personality Disorder—a diagnosis that often includes bodily self-harm and unstable relation-ships. Had a colleague suggested this diagnosis, however, I would have argued that Karen did not seem to fit it, at least not in its more extreme presentation. Borderline clients are characterized as categorizing people as all bad or all good. Karen did not do that, except perhaps at work, where she viewed the "bad" doctors as abusing power in relation to "good" patients and nurses. She frequently evidenced rage, but it seemed most often to be directed toward herself.

If another clinician had diagnosed and treated Karen as the "classic borderline," her therapy would have been different from my approach. She would have been confronted about present reality, with the insis-tence that she not distort what was happening in her relationships. Therapy would not have encouraged or rewarded her painful memories or her longings to be gratified through a more supportive and empathic therapy. She probably would not have been encouraged to allow herself to feel like a child when her fear or rage took over.

Another clinician might have diagnosed Karen as suffering from Multiple Personality Disorder (MPD). Was it one of her other "selves," or "alters," who drank? Another who vomited? Another who was friends with Ellen? Another who was so steady and cheerful at work? Could she be a "multiple" and seem so "normal" on the outside?

In fact, the fragmentation of self that Karen seemed to be expressing in her cycles of bulimic activity and binge-drinking was not unlike the fragmentation experience of many trauma survivors diagnosed with Multiple Personality Disorder. Karen was in a state of dissociative frag-mentation when she hurt herself. The self-abusive parts were distinctly separate from the person who cheerfully accomplished her work at the hospital or was a good friend to Ellen and Dennis. Multiple Personality Disorder would probably be a misleading diagnosis for Karen, however. Those parts of her activated in the Triadic Self were not complete entities, or alters. Even without therapy, she was aware of various parts of herself simultaneously existing within her, unlike the more severely dissociated MPD patient, who is not conscious of how her various alters are different parts of her mind and cannot integrate them.

Karen could fit each of the diagnoses I have just reviewed. She probably could have responded to each of the treatments. The problem with these diagnoses is not that any one of them is wrong or that the related treatment is useless. Each diagnosis, however, addresses only one of the complex problems associated with TRS and does not penetrate to the sources of the problems and the factors that keep these problems so deeply entrenched.

The frustrating tenacity of self-harmful behaviors has been challenging to me as I have worked over many years with women who hurt themselves. As a psychotherapist and teacher, I have frequently encountered the problems of interpersonal trauma: incest, child abuse and neglect, rape, battering, and psychological terrorism. In my work as a professional and in my personal awareness as an abuse survivor, I have realized that no single approach is adequate to the understanding and treatment of interpersonal trauma. Because of Karen and many other clients like her, I have learned that working exclusively from one perspective is a serious, life-threatening mistake. To approach Karen's healing process by focusing only on her addictions, or her relationship system, or her trauma history, or her dissociative problems is not enough.

Karen herself felt that no single label or treatment seemed to fit. Together we needed to find a bigger, more complex framework to make sense of all she was and all she knew and felt. In listening to Karen's stories and those of other women like her, I began to hear similar themes and ways that these women conceptualize themselves.

The Logic of Self-Abusive Behaviors

It is a challenge to explore the logic of any of the behaviors associated with TRS, whether it is Karen's bulimia, June's drinking, Nancy's com-

pulsive surgeries, or Lee's self-mutilation. Those who have not wit-
nessed Trauma Reenactment Syndrome firsthand will have to depend
on a less immediate process of recognition and empathy. A TRS
woman who has engaged in one kind of self-injuring behavior may
even feel baffled or disgusted by another form of TRS.

Despite the many differences among TRS symptoms, there are as
many commonalities. Once a woman who is reenacting a trauma
through self-destructive behavior realizes this, she is more likely to
address the underlying meaning of her symptoms, rather than being
distracted by how much "better" or "worse" her self-harmful habits
are than someone else's. It is often hard, however, for the professionals
and peer support groups that have always made strong distinctions
between various self-harmful activities to accept the similarities.
Twelve-step program members are probably the most likely to recognize the common ground, because their philosophy of addiction encompasses a broad spectrum of behaviors and relationships. Unfortunately,
the twelve-step philosophy may recognize the connecting pattern but
may oversimplify the roots of the problem and the comprehensive
treatment needed.

All forms of Trauma Reenactment Syndrome are manifested in a
common cycle of thoughts, feelings, and behavior. We could begin to
describe this cycle at any point in its sequence. We could say that the
cycle begins when the TRS woman feels unbearable rage or shame or
fear that causes her to act self-abusively. We could say that the cycle is
self-generating: when she hurts herself, she feels disgust at what she has
done and so punishes herself further through another round of self-
harm. We could also say that it is likely to occur when she finds herself
too close to a loved one and panics, creating distance through hurting
herself. We could include her partner in the description and say that the
TRS cycle is perpetuated when the partner becomes outraged at the
repetition of the self-inflicted suffering.

Wherever we begin, the cycle follows a somewhat predictable pattern. There is a strongly held belief, usually expressed by the woman
herself, that she is "bad," "incompetent," "unlovable," "disgusting."
This belief activates feelings of rage, fear, grief, or anxiety. These distressing feelings then trigger the self-abusive behavior.

Perceiving the pattern of the cycle is important. It is equally important to understand the various functions that the act of self-abuse can

serve. It can feel like relief because it anesthetizes against the pain of despair, rage, fear, or shame. It can serve as a distraction from unbearable feelings and thoughts. It can be a form of self-punishment, appropriate to feelings of being bad, undeserving, disgusting, and selfish. In addition to these functions, the behavior can serve as a communication about the woman's childhood experiences, which are replicated not only in the behavior but also in the beliefs and feelings that trigger it. It can communicate the story of what was done to her, symbolically or sometimes literally. It can be a communication about the longing for protection she did not receive in childhood: as she hurts herself, she communicates both how she was not protected then and how she longs for help and protection now. And it can serve as a statement that the woman has control of her own body. She can starve her body, or cut it, or fill it with toxic drugs: no one else can control her body when she demonstrates such strange ownership.

Self-harmful behaviors also play a part in relationships. The most obvious role is to draw others closer in a helping and rescuing capacity. Even though the helper is generally thwarted, the addiction, cutting, or surgery does act to rally aid to the woman in emotional and physical pain. The other side of this coin is that, paradoxically, the very same behavior serves to distance the TRS woman from others. The secrecy attached to the activity and its disturbing elements (extreme weight gain or loss, or unpleasant drug-induced behavior, for example) keep a manageable distance between the woman and other people. No matter how many ways she asks others for contact, she is always ambivalent and is simultaneously finding ways to distance herself from the very people she cries out to. Finally, the TRS symptoms themselves come to be experienced as a relationship; many women describe their involvement with their self-harmful behavior as similar to a relationship with a friend or lover. As I explore each of the functions of self-abusive behavior in greater detail, it will become evident how this peculiar companionship comes to be created.

The following excerpt of Karen's incest memory contains all the elements from which the common cycle of thoughts, feelings, and behavior is formed. It is difficult reading, likely to arouse nausea, fear, sorrow, and anger. But the painful experience of reading it can help in beginning to understand how the TRS woman is able to harm her own body.

A TEDDY BEAR NAMED I LOVE YOU

I am six years old. I have a very pretty dress, don't I? My daddy says I am the prettiest little girl in the world, but Mommy says he's just teasing me.

When Mommy is sleeping off her cocktails before dinner, she sits in the big chair in the living room and her mouth is open and she snores! Daddy and I try to keep from laughing out loud.

I get very hungry when they drink their cocktails. Daddy gives me some nuts. I like the nuts, but then I'm still hungry. So sometimes if I'm a very good girl and do what Daddy likes, he makes me something to eat. Sometimes I just have to wait until Mommy wakes up from her cocktail nap before I get something to eat.

Daddy likes me to play with his lollipop. I like to touch it and make it stand up, but I don't like to lick it. Sometimes he hurts me with it. But if I'm good and do what he wants, then he says I'm his beautiful princess and he gives me macaroni or spaghetti for dinner.

Sometimes when Daddy snuggles with me, it feels good. Sometimes he puts his fingers between my legs and it's all warm and nice and kind of tickles. But then sometimes it feels scary and it hurts.

One time Daddy really hurt me. I was choking and I couldn't breathe and he was pushing my face against him and I was crying. I thought I was going to die. Then he slapped me for crying. He slapped me really hard. He told me I was asking for it.

He says those words in different voices. When he's nice and he's playing with me and wants to play Daddy's lollipop game with me, he says, "My pretty little princess, you're just asking for it, you know that?" Then we snuggle up and we laugh and play find Daddy's lollipop and I make it stick up. But when he's mad at me afterwards, if I cry, he says it very mean. He says, "You little slut, you were asking for it."

I asked Mommy if I am a slut and all she did was laugh. She told me little girls can't be sluts.

Daddy told me never to tell Mommy about the lollipop game or they would come and take me away and I would never see Daddy or Mommy again.

I wish I had a brother or sister. I wish I could play with someone after school. But I am afraid they will find out I'm bad and
then they won't play with me. Daddy says I'm bad because I make
his lollipop get hard. Sometimes he pretends to spank my bum
while I kiss his lollipop, but sometimes he spanks me too hard
and makes me cry. I try not to cry because it just makes him
spank me harder.

The bad me hates Daddy sometimes, but I know that I'm really
his little princess and I love him even more than my kitty cat.

Daddy says I'm very special. He will love me forever.

I have a teddy bear named I Love You.

When she is bulimic, Karen illustrates the many functions of self-
destructive behavior. She thinks about herself and her secrets, including
her bulimia, the incest with her father, and her fear that she is not doing
anything now to protect her father's stepchildren from him. She thinks
she is disgusting, cowardly, and selfish. These thoughts fill her with
anger, fear, and shame. Most of all, she feels agonizingly depressed and
hopeless. To try to escape these unbearable feelings, she eats a gallon of
ice cream, a package of cookies, and half a loaf of stale bread when she
runs out of desserts. Then she becomes desperate to get rid of what
she has stuffed down her throat and into her painfully full stomach. She
vomits and feels exhausted but strangely peaceful. Unfortunately, the
peaceful feeling is brief. Soon she is again filled with disgust and self-
loathing, this time because of her binge–purge episode. Eventually the
horrible feelings overwhelm her and she is driven to begin the cycle
again, seeking elusive relief from her sense of failure and shame.

In addition to the cycle of "bad" thoughts, "bad" feelings, and
"bad" behavior (symptoms), Karen's choice of self-abuse tells a graphic
story about how she was abused in childhood. She stuffs unwanted
objects into her mouth, down her throat, and into her stomach. In a
sense, this is against her will. It replicates the childhood violation of her
mouth, throat, and abdominal/vaginal area. After bingeing, she frantically vomits, replicating actual gagging during the childhood experience
of oral penetration and also, symbolically, the wish to expel the object,
the fluid, and the shame of it. Like the childhood violations, the
bulimia must be kept secret, and Karen feels once again that she is the
bad one and that she is to blame. In being unable to stop herself, she

reenacts how alone and unprotected from harm she felt during the abuse.

Because Karen felt deeply attached to her father in childhood, the good feelings of being close to him became confusingly intertwined with the horrific experience of being orally raped by him. The ingesting of comforting, sweet-tasting foods as well as stale bread replicates how good and bad became all mixed up together. Similarly, the relationship with her bulimia feels comforting and essential to survival, even though Karen understands it is destroying her health, just as the relationship with her father felt frightening but also provided an intense feeling of connectedness.

This is a critically important part of understanding the TRS cycle. However illogical it may seem, abused children often are intensely attached to the abusive parent and will protect that person. In a similar way, women who hurt themselves become very attached to and protective of their symptoms. They do not give up the self-abusive behavior easily, because it provides the familiar reassurance of relationship, no matter how much it harms them.

Like all children, Karen sought connection with and approval from both her parents. Unfortunately, because of her mother's alcoholic neglect, her father seemed more likely, from her perspective as a child, to provide these basic needs. It is also important to recognize that some of the fondling and snuggling involved in the abuse may have been pleasurable for Karen. Every child likes to be held, and children are sexually responsive to genital stimulation just as adults are. Experiencing some parts of the abuse as pleasurable makes it very confusing for the child to cope with the frightening, painful, and sickening aspects of the abuse. Karen did not enjoy being abused, but the connection with her father was her emotional lifeline. Even the pain and fear associated with the trauma became transformed into part of her feeling of connectedness. Thus, when she is stuffing herself with food and then disgorging it, she feels a peculiar form of being connected to something, a symbol of relationship. Her bulimia becomes a form of company for her.

Any desire Karen felt to disclose the abuse was overridden by the fear that if she told, she would be taken away from her parents and would lose her father's love and attention. Karen's tenacity in secretively holding on to her adult patterns of self-abuse makes perfect sense in the context of this childhood history.

Relief and Arousal

Self-harmful behavior functions to regulate and relieve intense feelings. Many women who drink, do drugs, binge, or cut themselves describe how their self-injuring activities help them cope with unbearable feelings. Some choices of behavior may seem more obviously suited than others to function as relief mechanisms. Alcohol and drug abuse, for example, would seem to provide relief from painful feelings more directly than an activity such as cutting, which for most of us causes rather than relieves pain. But for the woman whose symptom of choice is self-mutilation, cutting creates a powerful release from her psychic suffering. This kind of relief may feel like welcome numbness, whereas for non-TRS people, this form of self-harm would stimulate quite the opposite feeling, that is, excruciating pain.

Self-harmful behavior also regulates feelings in the opposite direction. Trauma in many ways creates a higher level of arousal in the victim. When the trauma is chronic, the pattern of persistent arousal can actually change the person's biochemistry. Many adults who suffer from Post-Traumatic Stress Disorder have developed a craving or need for frequent experiences of excitement. The TRS symptoms, even while they may be serving a numbing function, can also increase sensations of excitement. I will describe this process in more detail later in this section; first, I will look more closely at the various ways in which TRS symptoms function to bring relief.

Unbearable Feelings

Drinking and using drugs are similar to the dissociative techniques used by the trauma victim to shut off the pain, fear, and rage experienced during the abuse. The abused child learns to evoke the numbing and disconnectedness necessary to endure the violations. The adult survivor, wishing to recreate this experience of escape, searches for other avenues to this state of oblivion. In a strangely paradoxical way, chemical abuse provides pleasurable sensations of excitement and at the same time induces numbness and a sense of being outside one's own mind and body.

Women who drink or abuse drugs are most likely to describe their activity as a form of self-medication, an anesthetic against pain, rage, fear, disgust, intimacy, or any other feeling they wish to escape. June describes her drinking as if it were a lover who soothes and comforts her, distracting her from pain, loneliness, and disappointment.

JUNE'S STAIRWAY TO PARADISE

I get myself sober and for a while it's okay. But I never stop missing the anticipation, imagining I'm going to have a drink in another minute or an hour or whenever it's going to happen. I'll be feeling pretty much like I can get through the day sober, you know, but there's still the feeling of being disappointed, kind of empty. I end up missing the feeling of anticipation almost more than I miss the relief I feel when I start to drink. It's silly, but it kind of reminds me of when I was a kid and I just started going out with guys. I'd enjoy imagining how great it was going to be even more than I would enjoy being with the guy, even when I was having an okay time, you know?

Then the other weird thing about it is there's a point in time when I'm drinking and I'm not really sloshed or anything yet. And at this time I feel like I'm with a best friend or having a great time in bed or kidding around with my family—you know, those times when you just feel so good—but what's weird is that it's just me and the booze and we're just us, just kind of flying or something. It's hard to explain. I mean, I know that I shouldn't be drinking, and I can even be telling myself I'm going to end up really sloshed and getting sick and making a jackass of myself, but at the same time I'm just feeling this great feeling. It's what they mean by a rush, I guess.

In much the same way, Lee conceptualized her cutting behavior as providing a sense of relief and pleasure. When she was abused as a child, she felt a powerful combination of pain, fear, and pleasure. Because she had no one to talk to about this complex experience, she began to experience herself as "bad" through her feelings of shame, but also as "special" and "powerful" because some aspects of the sexual episodes were positive, especially when she was aroused in pleasurable ways. Lee found it difficult to resolve her emotional and physical responses. It was as if she had betrayed herself by experiencing some "good" feelings. Her body became another enemy. Given the complexity of her response, it is not surprising that her self-abuse cycle, too, contains elements of pleasure, arousal, and a sense of power.

Some TRS women describe their self-harmful behavior as a means of either escaping the sensation of numbness or achieving it. The desire to break out of numbness and the opposite desire to attain it seems to be a goal common to many of the types of self-harm included in the TRS pool. Cutting is perhaps the type of self-injury most commonly associated with the sensation of numbness.

Drinking and drug abuse are often used to escape feelings of pain and despair. A young drug addict described her drug use in this way.

Sometimes I'm just hurting so bad, thinking about how things are in my life. I'll be thinking how my girlfriends keep leaving me, how I can't seem to get my shit together, how I don't have money for the right clothes or for the CD player I keep on wanting to buy. Then I'll be thinking next about something someone did to me—you know, a long time ago. I get so sick and disgusted when I think about it that I just get to hurting worse and worse. Can't even concentrate on the tube. Can't call a friend 'cause my phone's been cut off again. All I can think about is how bad I hurt and how bad I want to just chill out and feel nothing. Just nothing. That would be so nice.

So I decide to get a little buzzed. You know, nothing drastic, just a sweet little high. So I go down to this place where somebody's always got some kind of shit. Either I pay one way or I pay another, depending on whether I got money. Then I get this good buzz on, you know. I let myself do a little more shit and then I get to that place where I'm feeling nothing. Beautiful, awesome nothing. Next day I feel disgusted with myself but I know I'll do it again the next time I get those bad, bad feelings.

At first glance, Nancy's medical forms of self-harm would seem to have little connection to any form of relief or release. Listening to her story, however, reveals that the emotional sequence is not so different from June's or Lee's, although the process is substantially more delayed. Nancy talks about her terrible anxiety and fears. Behind the fear is also considerable grief and sorrow for the struggle her life has always been and for the loneliness she can never quite escape.

NANCY IN NEVER-NEVER LAND

I was having iced tea with Natalie yesterday after tennis, and she was talking about a party she and Jack went to. Anyhow, she said that so many of the women there were obviously second wives and how fabulous they looked and how young. She said to me, "Nancy, you and I are just lucky we have hung on to our husbands, because, dear, we just could not compete with what's out there."

Now Natalie is quite a good-looking woman, a very youthful forty-five. Hearing her talk about both of us that way threw me into a real tizzy. If she thinks we can't compete, then she's seeing my age as clearly as I do. I try to get Chip to tell me what he thinks, of course, but the man is just a dear, sweet liar, because he always tells me I look like a hot butterscotch sundae with a cherry on top, our little code for when he wants sex. Anyhow, I can't trust him to tell me how I really look.

This conversation got me thinking again about the eggplant and oat bran diet I've been on for three weeks now, and I'm positive it's not working. Then I thought again about the new surgeon my friend Ginger found who is supposed to be the best in the field for tummy tucks. I don't think I can do another tummy tuck yet, because I just had one last year. But maybe this man does good buttocks tucking. My ass is just disgusting, no matter how many times I work out each week. Maybe I'll call and see how soon I could get it done. Everyone says that it is really, really painful. But you know what they say—"no pain, no gain."

I wonder if I could get it done at the hospital where I was last year? The nurses there are so sweet. I remember how the last time I really didn't even want to come home, they were so sweet to me. I'd better call and get this all scheduled before the eighteenth, when Chip wants me to go to that party at the new CEO's place.

But then he'll probably go to the party without me, and that could be a little risky. Oh well, I'll just have to go to the damned party and look like shit. But I'll schedule that surgery right after the eighteenth.

The centrality of anger in the TRS woman's emotional system is never to be underestimated. Although anger is a difficult, if not forbidden, emotion for many TRS women to express, some can be impressively bold in their symptom-induced anger. Some women, for example, can get openly angry only if they have been drinking. Others use their self-mutilation to express rage. Women with eating disorders have extremely complicated ways of using their self-harmful behavior to release anger, as well as to suppress it. For example, Karen eats cake she does not even like when she gets angry at work. Then she vomits what she has stuffed down her throat, an indirect expression of her rage. Angela talks about her rage as she describes her compulsive eating.

ANGELA'S SWEET TOOTH

Yes, they like to tease me about my sweet tooth. My older brother still calls me Peaches and asks me for some sugar. Imagine how I feel, a grown woman having my brother call me that and asking me for sugar! Well, he can ask all he wants, but he's not getting any. He took all the sugar I had when I was a young girl.

I was only nine when he started. My brother and his friends sometimes. They gave me money for it. They never really hurt me, but I always felt dirty. I think they told other kids, because I got teased a lot by boys at school, and girls too, kids I didn't even know. So I played with my little brothers most of the time, even when I was too old to be playing with little kids. I was lonely, though, and I could make my younger brothers do whatever I wanted. My parents were divorced and my mother had to work hard to get by. There were four of us, and my father didn't always pay his child support. I was my mother's best friend, so I would never have wanted to upset her about what my brother and his friends made me do.

Now I look back on it and I feel so mad at my brother that sometimes I want to tell his wife exactly what he did just to punish him. I never would do it, really, because Stella would be the one who would suffer, not my brother. It wouldn't be fair. So I guess what I do with my anger is I eat. We talk about that a lot in my women's support group at the church, how we feel overwhelmed with anger sometimes and the things we do to try to make ourselves feel better. I try so hard to ask God to help me let go of my anger. I guess I'm not trying hard enough, though, because He doesn't seem to be able to take this burden from me. When I have prayed and prayed and prayed some more and my anger is still within me, then I finally just say, "Oh, what the heck," and I start my eating routine. I have gone to my pastor many times to ask him to help me understand why I do this and why God doesn't hear my prayers. Pastor Johnson is a very sweet man and he always counsels me to be patient and keep myself busy and not to dwell on the failures. I wonder what he would say if I told him about my brother and the things he did to me. I would be so ashamed.

Last year I had trouble with my legs and a doctor at the clinic told me I had to lose weight or I could end up in a wheelchair or worse. She was a nice woman, very kind. She asked me about what I ate and if I had tried to diet. I told her, Lord, yes, I had tried a hundred times! She sent me to Overeaters Anonymous, OA for short. It's just like AA, except it's for people with food addictions. I tried it, but I just couldn't imagine telling those other people how I felt or what I think about that makes me get so mad that I have to eat. When I went back to see the doctor, she asked how I had liked going to OA. I told her it was just fine, because I didn't want to hurt her feelings. She would never have understood anyhow, because she was so slender and fit and all. The next time I went to the clinic I asked for another doctor, because I didn't want to have to lie to her again about OA. Then I went home and got so mad at myself for my failures that I ate and ate until my stomach hurt all night.

Other women use starvation as a way to express extreme anger. Although much of what is written about anorexia suggests that it is an extreme example of every American woman's body hatred and fear of fat, it is also understood as a powerful tool to release rage. Many of the young women who suffer from anorexia have been subject to childhood trauma, from sexual abuse to extremes of invasive caretaking. The choice to starve themselves is often a way of venting overwhelming rage at those who have taken over their bodies in one way or another. The refusal to eat is an active release of anger and allows the anorexic to feel peaceful and comfortable in her body. Women and girls who are hospitalized because of their anorexia are often helped to begin expressing their rage verbally as the first step to letting go of the anorexia as an outlet for unbearable feelings.

Alcohol and drugs are also vehicles for the release of rage. While high on alcohol or drugs, many women can show anger they otherwise keep well hidden. When one client was using drugs and alcohol, she cursed and fought "like a man," she told me. After she stopped using chemicals to release her rage, she was in agony. The rage was still there, but she knew no way to express it effectively. Her solution was to develop a variety of other, more secretive and bizarre ways to let the rage out; she pounded her head against walls, punched wooden doors, and kicked metal bed frames. Still her rage continued to build up and pour out. Hurting herself was the only way she knew to release the anger.

Grief sits heavy for most women who hurt themselves. Their acts of self-harm can serve to express and release the grief they have stored from the past and the grief they continue to experience in the present. Karen opens herself to her sadness only when she is drinking alone.

"STORMY WEATHER"

I understand all about the blues when I've been drinking my wine at night. I'll start out having a glass of wine just to unwind. Then I'll have another to get mellow. Then the next one makes me feel good, but a little wobbly. Finally it's that fourth or fifth glass that takes me over the edge into my crying time. I'll put on some music, especially blues or soul music, and I'll just cry. I'll talk aloud to myself or to my cat, telling nobody, really, just how bad

I feel. Once in a while I'll call my friend Ellen when I'm like that, but she gets a little pissy with me and tells me to take a shower and go to bed and sleep it off. Then she'll give me a lecture the next time I see her about how I drink too much. So usually I just keep myself company when I'm into the crying thing. Someday I'm afraid I'll kill myself when I'm like that, because I do so much thinking about dying and planning how I'll do it. But I never actually do anything more than just think about it and talk to myself about it.

When I have to get up the next morning and go to work, I have wicked hangovers, and I swear to myself I'll never do it again. But the sadness just creeps up on me and then I have to have those extra glasses of wine and let the tears just rip. I used to cry that way when I was a kid, just cry and cry and rock myself to sleep. Maybe some part of me wants to be the little kid again and just lose myself in the tears. But oh God, is it ever lonely.

The Craving for Arousal

Arousal is another important function of self-harmful behavior. The TRS woman often feels a fascination for various forms of excitement. As a child, she gradually learned that even negative excitement connected her to others, until finally violence became synonymous with relationship. Whether she was being beaten or violated and afterward held and caressed by a remorseful abuser, or constantly touched by a hypersolicitous caretaker, or scolded by a usually neglectful parent, the child may have felt closer and more connected during this time than at others. She may have felt chosen, singled out for this sort of connection.

Another aspect of this pattern develops as a by-product of the repetitive cycle of excitement. When a child or adult is in a state of arousal due to intense fear, rage, or heightened alertness or anxiety, the actual chemistry of the body changes. We all have experienced this phenomenon in situations of danger, when our adrenaline flows and we feel a strong sense of being in an altered state. When the child experiences these changes repeatedly, the biochemistry of the body changes permanently, so that it becomes more difficult for the child, and later the adult, to return to baseline levels biochemically (van der Kolk, 1987). The result in the adult is an addiction to excitement.

When the adult TRS victim is in a cycle of self-harming, often the planning, the anticipation, the secrecy, and the activity itself all create an experience of pain and excitement or arousal that replicates the excitement in childhood abuse cycles. Many TRS women report that when they stop their self-injurious activities, they feel an intolerable emptiness, dullness, flatness, or depression. They experience a terrible loneliness and sense of being disconnected. It is no wonder that so many choose to return to their self-abusive activities when there seems to be no other way to achieve excitement and the illusion of connection.

In all forms of self-abusive behavior, each part of the cycle is part of a reenactment of childhood trauma. This reenactment is both painful and paradoxically pleasurable, as well as being familiar and thus oddly comfortable. June talks about how as a teenager she found that the anticipation of going out with someone was often more exciting and satisfying than the actual event. In the same way, the anticipation of getting high is as important as the actual chemical surge or relaxing effect of the drink or drug itself.

Laura, another client, talked frequently in the early stages of therapy about how her self-abusive activities were charged with a certain thrill, an undercurrent of excitement that reminded her of some of her childhood experiences with her father. She talked about the way their interactions became like the stalking of a hunter and his prey. Although he always "caught" her at the end of this predatory dance, there was a certain element of excitement, a charge of fear, that heightened all her reactions. Her father often gave her lectures on being tough, being able to take care of herself later on in life. When she practiced her various methods of self-harm, she would think about these messages and reexperience the old thrill of fear and excitement.

LAURA'S STORY

I can only allow you to see glimpses of me because I myself am only aware of glimpses and flashes. Looking for myself is like looking at an old photograph for that face in the group you think you recognize. You enlarge the picture, bigger and bigger. You still can't be sure that's the face you are looking for. It's like the home movie some guy named Zapruder took of the Kennedy assassination and the investigators keep going over and over the scenes, the grassy knoll, the number of shots. My life is like the Kennedy assassination. You will never really know what happened or all the parts of who I am. No one can know because I don't know.

My first memory of the abuse is when I'm four or five. My parents have gone out, I think. They go at night and on Sundays.

My father returns home. I don't remember where my mother is. My father and the man take me into my parents' bedroom. My father holds me while the other man opens his pants. He touches me and touches himself. My father holds my legs apart while the man rapes me. I don't remember making any noise, no screams, no crying until they leave. I am terrified of my father. He gets drunk and beats my mother sometimes. My little sister and I have learned not to scream or make any noise when this happens or we'll get it too.

Later I am lying in my bed, blood coming out of my hole between my legs. My mother doesn't know. My father comes back and he takes away the bloody sheets and puts a towel with ice between my legs to stop the bleeding. It hurts so bad. He tells me he'll do what the other man did if I tell anyone. My father hurts me over and over, for years.

I hate my father. But he taught me how to be strong, how to survive. When I used to drink, I'd feel the power in me. I know I could kill my father. I think about it a lot.

I used to do speed and coke. I even got into crack for a few months. I quit after I got raped by a guy at work and some of his friends. I used to shoot up with him and buy from him sometimes too. I ended up in the hospital after I got raped.

It's worse than you could ever begin to imagine now that I'm not using. I can't sleep and I can't stop the pictures in my head. I do other things to try to stop the pictures and to let the rage out, but nothing works the way drugs and booze can. I am so scared

I'll relapse. I don't even know why I'm not getting high or drinking, but I am determined. Determination keeps me from using again.

I can't talk about who I am when I go to the twelve-step meetings. I go because they told me at the hospital that it was the only way I could stay sober. I hate most of the people at those meetings. I don't even look at the men, and I'm uncomfortable if any of the women try to be friendly to me.

They have no idea of how rough someone's life can really be. They talk about being abused, some of them, but they don't sound like I feel inside. I can't tell them that I'll die before I'll ever let anyone touch me again. I have to stay sober to make sure no one can rape me or touch me again. No one is going to hurt me ever again. But what kind of choice is it, to stay in misery, clean and sober, or to get high and get trapped again by some f——rapist. It's no choice, no win, no exit.

Sometimes I purposely go places where I know I might get attacked, and then I see how close I can get to hurting someone. But I get scared and run. So I'm not as tough and brave as I need to be.

Maybe I'm like a soldier and this sobriety is like boot camp.

I've started seeing a therapist at the mental health center. She supposedly specializes in trauma, but I don't think she knows what she's doing. I keep trying to tell her about the abuse that my father did and she keeps telling me to slow down.

The worst thing about going to see her is that sometimes I don't want to leave at the end of the hour. Sometimes I have this fantasy that she'll kind of allow me to live in her office with her. I actually dislike her, so I don't know where this idea is coming from.

I know how to get her, though. I keep telling her about the weird stuff I do. I can see it freaks her out. I tell her about the knife. I even tell her about how I punch myself in the head and punch my legs and stomach. I make little cuts with the knife, jabbing into my legs, my arms. I keep telling myself that I'm tough, I can take it. I punch myself and I tell myself that I can take any pain. I'm as hard as a rock and strong as the wind.

I have to put rubber bands around my wrists really tight when I'm in her office so I can keep the pain focused there instead of crying or screaming. I think she'd like it if I cried or screamed, but I won't give her the satisfaction. If I let myself hurt that way, like the pain could get inside me, I'd be dead. I'd lose. I won't give her that.

Laura told me her story in one of our initial therapy meetings, despite my reluctance to listen. I first saw her when I was doing mostly family therapy, specializing in problems of violence, child abuse, and related addictions. I found Laura's story excruciatingly painful. The stories of her abuse in childhood were chilling. I was horrified by the degree of sadism her father exhibited, and I was sorrowful about the degree of the child's isolation and hopelessness in regard to the need for protection. I was also puzzled and troubled about how to respond to her particular patterns of self-abuse. When she told me about going out of her way to invoke the violence of strangers, I had difficulty understanding why she persisted in doing so. Her cutting and punching herself were also puzzling and scary to me because of the way she told me about these activities: there was a sense of cruel enjoyment in her voice that chilled me but also raised my curiosity.

Because Laura was among the first of my clients to engage in this type of self-harmful activity, and because the acts were severe, I was relatively confused and frightened by her. I had worked with many drug- and alcohol-addicted clients, as well as numerous eating-disordered girls and women. My experience with clients who self-mutilated was limited. I was not sure if I should be exploring the childhood traumas that were at the root of the self-injuring behavior or if I should try to stay in the present and use a more symptom-focused approach. The usual treatment approach for such clients was to confront them about their self-destructive behavior and to get them to concentrate on the present, not the past.

It has been common in the training of most psychotherapists to see clients like Laura as needing "containment." They have been seen as adversaries of the therapist, engaged in a turbulent struggle of demanding help or love and then rejecting it. Their frequent wish to be allowed to regress to a childlike state should not, we were taught, be gratified, as this would only cause them to disintegrate or regress more.

Laura frightened me, but she also touched something in my heart, opening some part of my own memory. I felt intuitively that to interpret her self-abusive behavior as manipulation would be a mistake. Beneath the icy surface hostility, she seemed terrified. Rather than engage in a struggle with her about her self-destructive activities, I felt a strong wish to reassure her, to stay steadily in her gaze as she vigilantly observed me. To gain her trust, I had to make myself accept that there were necessary reasons for her strange, self-hating behavior.

One of the things that I noticed about Laura's choice of self-abusive activities was the degree of excitement she was describing, both when she engaged in these activities and again when she recounted them. I could see the gleam of bravado, the mischievous glint in her eyes; she was relishing trying to shock me with her exploits. Even though her activities seemed to generate cycles of pain, fear, and rage in her, she also seemed to enjoy them. It became clear to me that I had to find a way to understand and remain open to this aspect of her self-abuse.

Most important of all was for me to accept that she needed to keep everyone, including me, at a distance. Her drugs and drinking had kept others from getting close, but now she had given up these distancing mechanisms and she needed new behaviors to maintain the boundaries. If she let anyone get too close, she believed, she would get hurt. The logic of her bizarre activities began to make sense to me.

In chapter 3, I will describe how Laura and I found ways to work together. My intention in beginning her story here is to illustrate how I began my search for more useful ways to work with self-injurious women. My training in addictions, family therapy, and more traditional diagnoses and treatments failed me with Laura. I had to push toward a new way of thinking and responding. My first task, however, was to overcome my fear and my desire to distance myself.

"Body Language"

Few theories about self-harmful activities and addictions include what I consider to be one of the most important functions of such behavior: the reenactment of childhood trauma. The TRS woman's symptom is her way of telling her story. Not all self-destructive behaviors mimic the specifics of the trauma, but the story is always there, waiting to be decoded.

Lee suffered what is perhaps the most potentially damaging of all childhood traumas: sexual abuse involving the active participation of her mother. She was abused at an early age, possibly before she had enough verbal language to create a narrative of her traumatic experience. Because of the severity of the trauma, the age of onset, and the terrible disruption of attachment that maternal abuse creates, Lee's symptoms were indirect, essentially mute, for many years. No one could easily have guessed that her depression, severe headaches, and aversion to children were the result of traumatic abuse. With Karen, June, and Laura, symptoms such as alcoholism, eating disorders, and self-mutilation spoke loudly long before the women could use words to tell their stories. The symptoms were a clue to their histories of abuse and neglect, even though there was a big difference between, for example, Karen's degree of "looking good on the outside" cover-up and Laura's frank drug abuse and antisocial behavior. Even Nancy could be considered a little easier to "read" than Lee in terms of her symptoms. Her extremes of dieting, exercising, diet-pill popping, and undergoing surgeries would suggest both an extreme response to the cultural demands to be young and beautiful forever and a story of internal suffering born of a childhood trauma history.

In contrast, Lee kept her story deeply concealed for many years, even from her own consciousness, because both consciously and unconsciously she felt unsafe. Her symptoms were far too subtle even for her therapist, at least initially. Finally, after seven years of therapy, Lee felt safe enough to begin to face her trauma memories more directly. Then the cutting behavior began, and the occasional bruising, scratching, and burning of her skin. These symptoms seemed completely bizarre at first to her therapist, Martha, to her husband, David, and especially to Lee herself. But they were logical symptoms, telling a childhood story over and over again until Lee became conscious of what they were trying to express.

LEE, AS A CHILD

Hand hurts. Her voice. Loud, angry. Her hand over my mouth. She ties my legs, ties my hands. He hurts me.

No, hurts, hurts.

Someone is screaming. A child is crying. Who's crying?

Her voice. You are a bad girl. Hand over my mouth. She hurts me.

The child stops crying. No more screaming. Bad girl. Don't cry. No one did anything to you.

Wet. Cold. No one comes. Dirty. Bad girl.

Hand hurts Lee. Lee is a bad, bad girl. Be quiet. No crying.

Among the many tragic stories of childhood trauma, Lee's is one of the saddest. When Lee and her therapist, Martha, began to reconstruct these memory fragments, Lee was already thirty-three years old. From the words that Lee used when she spoke of the abuse, she and Martha estimated that the memories were possibly thirty years old. Lee was perhaps only two or three when her sexual torture began.

Lee's fragmented memories seem to place her mother repeatedly not only at the scene of the crime but playing an active role as well. "He" was probably not her father. Lee and Martha began to suspect that the abuse happened away from home and that the mother was involved in something the father knew nothing about. When I first began consulting with them, they were not sure if Lee's mother was really the "she" Lee was remembering. The more we began to piece together the story, however, the more sure Lee became that it was her mother who had participated in the torture.

Because the abuse began when Lee was so young, she had incomplete language to recall it. She had only fragments of sentences and glimpses from memory. Frustrated, horrified, and overwhelmingly depressed by the memories arising in therapy, Lee began to engage in self-destructive behaviors.

LEE'S RITUAL AS NARRATIVE

Everything has to be arranged exactly right. No one must find out. If I cut a line down my thigh just to here, it won't show, even when I wear a skirt. Another one, another, another. The cuts make a pattern. I am creating a beautiful design. The blood makes little red beads, like necklaces of blood on my body. The blood washes me clean.

I cut my breasts to show that I am sorry for my wrongdoings. The pastor would say, "Have mercy upon us, Oh Lord, now and in the darkness of our night."

Lee felt very calm when she was engaged in cutting herself. Later, she looked at what she had done and was deeply repulsed. She told Martha that she could only faintly remember doing it. Sometimes she let her cuts become infected by neglecting to clean the wounds. When David or Martha confronted her about the neglect, she was evasive, but seemed to imply that she deserved to suffer the ongoing pain.

Lee was overwhelmed by her shame at what she was doing to herself and at realizing what had been done to her. She was terrified to ask her family for any confirmation or information related to possible childhood abuse. She and Martha speculated that Lee's mother, too, may have been an abuse survivor. Lee's maternal grandfather's suicide when Lee's mother was fifteen had never been explained, and Lee wondered if her mother had exposed him as an abuser. If so, it may be that Lee's mother carried her own unexplored shame and self-hatred, which could have been expressed in the repetition of the abuse against her own little daughter. This speculation is well founded in current research on incest survivors. The psychologist Denise Gelinas (1983), one of the first writers on the clinical aspects of incest, suggests that sometimes the abuse survivor appears to be unaffected by the abuse until she has a child of her own. Then the trauma resurfaces and she reenacts it in one way or another, including harming herself or, less often, becoming abusive to her own children.

Sometimes, Lee told Martha, she wondered if she was just making up these memories. If she was, then what kind of terrible mental illness was taking over her life and making her do these things to herself, she wondered. Both Lee and Martha needed reassurance that there was a story to be pieced together that could logically connect Lee's cutting behavior to her childhood. This assurance occurs when the cutting is taken seriously and interpreted as a communication about something that had been done to her body in childhood, a critical step in Lee's healing journey.

For another TRS woman, the self-injurious activity might reflect her experience of feeling punished or shamed in childhood. The activity itself might not directly repeat what happened to her in childhood but rather tell a story expressing her feelings of shame or disgust toward her body. Bulimia, for example, does not have to be a communication about something being forced into the child's mouth, as it was for Karen. Some bulimic women who were never sexually or physically abused still experience deep and chronic shaming communications about their bodies. These communications may have been from invasive caretakers or sometimes from hostile or neglectful adults. In the adult woman's repertoire of bingeing-purging activities, she repeats the story of shame and disgust in this disguised narrative.

Nancy, in her repetitive surgeries and diet excesses, tells a story at a deeply unconscious level about her childhood trauma. She internalized her grandmother's anxious fussing over her body, taking in shame, fear, and a desperate longing for affection, which she now communicates through her fashion-focused self-harm. Neither Nancy nor her various professional helpers can easily decipher this story until the degree of the childhood damage is really understood.

It's My Body!

Clients describe their relationship with their self-harmful activities in a variety of ways. Some, like Karen, talk of the pattern of eating and purging as a painful repetition of childhood sexual violation, but also as a comforting ritual and a form of being in control of one's own body. "I am doing what I choose with my body and you can't stop me!" is how some women have stated this relationship.

Margaret, a formerly anorexic woman, explained to me that her rituals of starving herself did not have the same meaning that one would imagine to be attached to the refusal to eat. Starving oneself might seem to be a passive *non*-act: doing nothing, feeling hungry, weak, and empty. To Margaret, however, the rituals surrounding her refusal to eat were active, a series of choices, an energetic experience of controlling her body. She was symbolically fighting off the invasive grandmother who had given her nightly enemas, scrubbed her vaginal area until it was raw, and came into the bathroom without invitation when Margaret was using the toilet or bathing. Margaret experienced her anorexia as her friend, actually visualizing it as an entity: a sturdy, clever little girl who skillfully outmaneuvered the attempts of Margaret's lover, friends, and therapist to help her (which meant trying to make her eat). She told me that when she first stopped her self-starving behavior, she felt weak and helpless without the anorexia to help her stay in control of her body. The anorexia expressed loudly and clearly her message that no one was going to take charge of her body, as had been done in childhood.

My Pain, My Friend

In a book about the world of those with Borderline Personality Disorder, *I Hate You, Don't Leave Me* (1989) by Jerold Kreisman and Hal Straus, the description of the borderline's relationship struggles parallels that of many women who warrant a TRS diagnosis:

> In a sense, the borderline carries only a sketchy map of interpersonal relations; he finds it extremely difficult to gauge the optimal psychic distance from others, particularly significant others. To compensate, he caroms back and forth from clinging dependency to angry manipulation, from outpouring of gratitude to irrational hate. He fears abandonment, so he clings; he fears engulfment, so he pushes away. He craves intimacy and is terrified of it at the same time. He winds up repelling those with whom he most wants to connect [p. 12].

A vital part of the self-abuse cycle is to keep others at a distance. This process is explored in depth in chapter 5, but it is important to highlight here the self-protective function that the behavior provides. Although only an illusion, the TRS woman comes to believe in part of her mind that the drinking or cutting or bingeing actually protects her. Because she is trapped in fear, self-loathing, and shame, she is ambivalent about getting too close to anyone. Whatever her symptom, it serves her well in keeping her from achieving close, dependable, mutually trusting relationships. She is too consumed with the addictive behavior—and also too bound by its necessary secrecy—to make space for anyone either to get close or to stay close; she is so deeply involved in her behavior that she is emotionally and physically unavailable. Also, if known, the activity itself might drive others away because it is upsetting, frightening, annoying, or repulsive.

Unfortunately, the other side of the coin for most TRS women is the fierce longing to be rescued and protected, which may be the most troubling and most entrenched characteristic of TRS women. Many childhood trauma victims share the experience of crying out to "Mama" in the agony of the traumatic moment and discovering that she does not appear to rescue, protect, comfort, or hold and rock the wounded child, as so poignantly stated by the psychiatrist Bessel van der Kolk (1989, personal communication). This terrible disappointment and disillusionment become the central confounding dynamic in efforts to help victims of childhood trauma. The abused little girl grows up to be a woman who has no internalized capacity to protect herself, because in childhood being protected was not a consistent enough experience to become part of her internal structure. Therefore, as an adult she cannot protect herself from her self-destructive behavior and has an equally difficult time allowing her partner, friend, or therapist to function in a protective role.

Mental health professionals and others in the TRS victim's life often make the mistake of believing that she can simply force herself to stop the self-destructive behavior. She makes the same mistake, believing along with everyone else that she is "weak" or "not really trying to quit." Sadly, she simply does not have the capacity to protect herself if she has been repeatedly traumatized during childhood. This impasse deepens the isolation the TRS woman feels, trapped by the very behavior that should function to bring others closer, to get them to protect her. Instead, she is blamed for not being able to protect herself, so her behavior serves a double function to keep others at a painful distance: it separates her from others because of the distancing capabilities inherent in the behavior and because she is blamed for not being able to stop what she is doing to herself.

Given how frequently this sort of isolation occurs in the life of the TRS woman, it is no wonder that her self-harmful activity becomes her most precious companion. Karen, June, and the anorexic woman Margaret refer at times to their self-destructive behavior as if it were a friend. This may seem strange to those who are not themselves chronically self-harmful, but it is easy enough to understand if one amplifies the ordinary experience of, for example, feeling enthusiastic about a pain medication that finally succeeds when other medications have failed to stop a severe headache. Or it may help to think about times when a drink at the end of a long workday eases physical and emotional tensions. For the TRS woman, her self-harmful activity soothes her, reassures her, protects her from dangerous closeness to others, awakens her from numbness, anesthetizes her against anger, grief, and anxiety, tells her powerful and troubling story for her again and again, connects her to those powerful childhood relationships that give her a primary identity, and proves to her that even in violence and pain she is connected to the representation of someone. With all of these functions, the self-injuring behavior clearly qualifies as a "best friend."

Furthermore, the symptom is a best friend who is always available. The TRS woman has control of this activity, much like a pet dog, and therefore "woman's best friend" can be depended on never to desert her. The more others try to separate the woman from her phantom lover (the bottle, the drug, the food, the razor, the surgeon's knife, the cigarette), the more she clings to it in an "us against the world" defiance.

Margaret talks about her anorexia as a protective, sturdy little friend who helps her stay in control of her body. Karen feels soothed by her drinking, discussing her wine as if it were a special friend or therapist cradling her as she cries. June has an exhilarating time with her companion, alcohol, describing her relationship to drinking as if she were out dancing with Fred Astaire. Laura hurts herself as if she is in training with a brutal but revered athletic coach. The young addict's drug use leads her into a sweet release from her tormented brooding, so that the drug becomes her rescuer. Lee's cutting takes her to a place of excitement and peace simultaneously, the cutting taking on the form of a wizard with strange and mysterious magic.

In the trauma-centered environment of childhood, violation and pain come from the same person as food, shelter, and caretaking. It makes sense that the small child will grow up assuming that pain equals connectedness. Self-harm becomes the most familiar and most dependable form of feeling relationally connected that the adult woman knows. Her symptom and her pain protect her and she feels less. Her symptom becomes the relationship in which she feels seen and understood. She can only begin to move away from this relationship with her pain when there is the possibility of being understood by someone outside herself who can fathom the complexity of her self-harmful patterns.

No matter how much every TRS woman wishes for protection and longs to be understood, there is the major obstacle of secrecy and concealment. In the following chapter, I turn to the problem of secrecy, which is central to the intractable nature of TRS and critical in the process that begins the path to recovery.

3

Secrecy:
Silence and Deception

And of course I am afraid, because the transformation of silence into language and action is an act of self-revelation, and that always seems fraught with danger. But my daughter, when I told her of our topic and my difficulty with it, said, "Tell them about how you're never really a whole person if you remain silent, because there's always that one little piece inside you that wants to be spoken out, and if you keep ignoring it, it gets madder and madder and hotter and hotter, and if you don't speak it out one day it will just up and punch you in the mouth from the inside."

—Audre Lorde, *Sister Outsider*

For many women, remaining silent seems safer than transforming "silence into language and action" to reveal the true self. The pivotal challenge for the TRS woman is to find a way to speak out "'that one little piece inside you.'"

In *The Dance of Deception* (1993), the psychologist Harriet Lerner describes the ways that women avoid the polarity of "truth-telling" versus "pretending." It has been costly for women to break out of the traditions encouraging them to say what someone else wants to hear, yet women have sought new ways of telling the truth to each other. As Lerner puts it, "Pretending stems naturally from the false and constricted definitions of self that women often absorb without question ... it is, quite simply, what the culture teaches women to do" (p. 14). At the same time, however, women have created forums for telling their stories, defying the constraints of the social environment.

In her classic book *On Lies, Secrets and Silence* (1979), the feminist writer Adrienne Rich says that "lying is done with words, and also with silence" (p. 186), and states bluntly that women are rewarded for lying. She connects lying with amnesia, defining amnesia as "the silence of the unconscious." She warns us that if we lie regularly, we lose contact with the unconscious and end up lying to ourselves. Lerner, Rich, and the African-American writer Audre Lorde (1984) call on women to reclaim their voices through truth-telling. For those among us who have a history of childhood abuse, breaking our long silence is both liberating and extraordinarily frightening.

Women do not have exclusive ownership of secrets, silences, and deceptions. The family therapist Evan Imber-Black (1993) comments that secrets are kept by individuals, families, even nations, and, she asserts, secrets are endemic to social systems. She focuses on families and secrets, reflecting that "secrets can grow like weeds through the generations, sending unexpected tendrils into every corner of a family's life" (p. 20). In a dysfunctional family, secrecy and concealment are often the strongest family rules. Families in which there are traumatic events and relationships have a much higher ratio of lies to honest communications than do families with more ordinary interactions. The traumas of child abuse and neglect are especially likely to engender deception and silence.

One explanation for the high incidence of this kind of concealment in trauma-afflicted families is the defense mechanism of denial. As adults, we may try to forget or not to hear the cry of the abused child or the battered woman. If we ourselves have been abused, neglected, or violated, we may not even see the trauma right before our eyes because we have learned to blot out what we cannot bear to take in. Alternatively, we keep the silence, in the hope that the violence, the invasions, the neglect will disappear magically. It is another kind of denial, a denial of the power and toxicity of family violence. This is the kind of denial that hums to itself nervously, hoping that someone else will take action or that what we are seeing is really roses, not thorns. Another reason why deception and concealment thrive in dysfunctional families is the rule of fear. A child, a grandparent, even a mother may try to ignore abuse out of fear of the consequences of speaking out.

In recent years, there has been increasing public pressure to take notice of family violence and abuse. Slowly the stories are beginning to emerge. Yet the adult woman's communication of the trauma, if told by an act of violence against herself, is still too often silenced. Part of this silence comes from the silence in the family from which the TRS woman emerges; part is the result of having no language to express the pain and confusion of her story. There is a paradox involved: the identity of this woman is that of both victim and abuser. How can she tell the story of her childhood victimization without revealing the acts of violence committed against herself?

Clients and therapists alike strain for language to express the secrets of the abuse victim, but we are almost mute when it comes to expressing the secrets of those who commit acts of violence, including those who commit violence against themselves. In exploring our attitudes toward women who hurt themselves, it may be useful to consider them as women who are inflicting abuse, akin to those who perpetrate violence against others. We may not easily accept this double description if we are angry, frightened, or judgmental about anyone who inflicts violence on children or women. Most of us do not want to listen to the story of the perpetrator. We prefer to view him or her as sick or criminal, someone whose behavior must be contained through the enforcement of deterrents, be they educational, behavioral, legal, or social. The situation is even more complicated when the perpetrator of abuse is a woman inflicting harm on herself.

The challenge is to hear the full depth and complexity of the abuser's story, whether we are listening to a man or a woman, to our own voice or someone else's. We must learn how to listen to the woman who acts against herself in the role of abuser. Otherwise we once again silence the "wounded child within," just as she was silenced in childhood. It is in this silencing that we replicate old family behaviors and then misinterpret the victim's responses to our silencing as pathologic.

Broken Promises, Shattered Dreams

To understand the silences and deceptions of the TRS woman, we must first understand her history as a traumatized child. Child abuse is a story of misused power, exploitation, and the betrayal of innocence.

The abuser often has no empathic awareness of the victim's experience. He or she may be in a state of rage or sexual arousal that has nothing to do with love for or relationship with the child. Society recognizes child abuse as a breach of faith with the community of humanity. No wonder, then, that child abuse has been "the best kept secret" (Rush, 1980) in the history of humankind.

Evan Imber-Black (1993) says that "those who hold power become entitled to keep secrets that, in turn, feed back and amplify positions of power. Those who have little or no power are intimidated into silence" (p. 22). Because of the power differences between children and adults, the adult is entitled to keep the secret of the abuse while the child is required to do so. The secrecy serves to keep the behavior from being uncovered and terminated. Often the child victim is afraid of telling because she fears reprisals against herself and possibly her mother, siblings, pets, or property. Laura's father, for instance, would abuse her mother and younger siblings unless Laura offered herself as a scapegoat. Talking would also threaten the welfare of the family. The child may be convinced that if she tells the secret, her primary relationship to the seemingly omnipotent and often beloved abuser may be threatened. The child is given complicated messages and injunctions about keeping the secret. Like Karen, she may feel "special," "grown-up," and preferred above all others, or, like Nancy, she may believe that she is privileged to be in her family. A child like Lee may believe that the abuse is somehow her fault and feel ashamed of her participation in the secret.

If the child tries to tell the secret, she may get the message that she is imagining things, overreacting, or lying, or that whatever happened was her fault and she should not continue to talk about it. She may be told that it would be her fault if her parent (or sibling or caretaker) had to go to jail or leave the family. It was this tactic that made June believe it would do no good to tell anyone that her mother was neglecting her and leaving her responsible for her younger siblings.

One of the problems affecting both children and adults when forced into disclosure of abuse and neglect is the threat to the relationship between child and caretaker. Despite the abuse of power, the relationship may mean something positive to both abuser and victim. Karen's father, for example, perceived himself as loving his little girl. For the incest victim, the relationship may be more important than the trauma of the physical violence or violation. The perpetrator is not only a powerful caregiver in the child's world, but, paradoxically, may also be

more present, tender, and loving than anyone else in the child's life.
Many children who are neglected experience sexual attention (and
sometimes the abuser's remorse after sex) as making them feel special
to the adult. Karen felt that when her father abused her he was very
much focused on her and that such attention was desirable in the face
of her otherwise lonely life.

Moreover, as I will describe in the next chapter, children seem to
"take in" the abusive parent as a result of frequent or chronic abuse.
The abuser, who is often both enemy and lover to the child, is internalized and becomes part of the victim's psychic self. Thus, when there is
the possibility of disclosure, the child (and later the adult victim) risks
losing a part of herself.

A child conceptualizes the world in "either/or" terms: there is good
and bad and nothing in between. Abuse and neglect convince the child
that she is bad because bad things happen only to bad people, and if
bad things have happened to her, then she deserved them. Love is given
to those children who deserve loving; if she has not experienced it,
then, in her understanding, she is unlovable. Yet the child, and later the
adult, experiences a powerful longing to be loved, so how can she
admit those things that were done to her, thereby exposing her innate
badness and unlovableness? Shame helps to keep the child and the
adult survivor silent.

In a family where there is pervasive neglect, there are other reasons
why a child keeps secrets. She may never have learned to talk about
shameful events or to express feelings of fear, sadness, or disappointment, or even to communicate her basic needs. She may not have the
language to explain what is wrong with the neglectful parent, especially
if the parent is alcoholic or mentally ill. Some women who hurt themselves come from homes where severe neglect stemmed from the illness
of the mother or primary caretaker. In many families like this, the illness is not talked about in front of the children, and so the children
develop a belief in keeping the silence that they carry with them into
adult life.

One client who was chronically neglected as a child described her
childhood as being organized around her mother's bouts with cancer.
No one called the cancer by its name or explained to the children what
the various outcomes might be. This woman learned as a child never to
talk about her mother's illness either inside or outside the family. The
pervasive neglect, coupled with the family rule of denial, made the ill-

ness seem more like a recurring nightmare than a reality. As an adult, this client chain-smoked and took large doses of over-the-counter diet pills and sleeping pills. Although she was in a long-term relationship, her partner never commented on these self-destructive habits. It was not until my client's sister died of lung cancer that she was able to disclose her smoking and pill-popping addictions and to speak about these problems in her support group and to her friends.

For the child who is subjected to excessive, invasive demands from adult family members to give unconditional access to her thoughts, her space, her activities, and especially her body, secrecy may be a response to this violation of privacy. Refusing to share information becomes an attempt to exert the control that she is not allowed to experience in other ways. Often unable to make the distinction between secrecy and privacy, she keeps much of her life shrouded in mystery. This tendency is frustrating for those who care about her and sense that something is not quite right at home. What may seem like sullen resistance in the violated child is really a desperate attempt to retain some form of control, to establish a semblance of longed-for privacy.

Another way in which childhood becomes the training ground for adult secrets lies in the distortions children experience in many forms of adult communication. Harriet Lerner (1993) uses the example of the widespread practice of mislabeling the female genitalia. Little girls, she says, are routinely taught that they have a vagina, but not that they also have a vulva that includes the labia and the clitoris; the external, easy-to-examine, primary source of sexual pleasure in the girl's body is either given no name or mislabeled. Despite their benign intent, mothers and other adults thus distort and deny an important part of the female experience. In a far more malevolent form of adult miscommunication (Herman, 1992), the perpetrator of child abuse—to escape accountability—manipulates the child's reality by denying that the abuse ever happened, accusing the victim of exaggerating, or claiming that she brought it on herself.

In order for the trauma to be concealed, repression must occur. The manipulation of reality moves from an external source (the perpetrator) and becomes an internal manipulation of reality by the victim herself. Repression is a protective mechanism often associated with traumas such as a car wreck or the death of a loved one: the traumatized person buries some part of the trauma in the unconscious mind because it is too painful or frightening to keep in consciousness. In responding to the trauma of incest, battering, or psychological terrorism, the child represses the events in order to survive psychologically as well as physically. Since the abuse is not talked about, it may remain buried or repressed for years. In this way, the child becomes habituated to repressing painful or otherwise disturbing events, observations, and thoughts.

Lying also becomes part of the child's world. Adults conceal their violations or abandonment of the child using both silence and overt lies. The child's own lies, born of fear, confusion, loyalty, and repression, become indistinguishable from the truth. Finally, the child becomes no more aware than the listener that her communications are lies.

The repetition of distortions and lies in the child's experience of relationship to her parents eventually leads to the creation of what is called the "false self." This concept was originally developed by the British psychiatrist Donald Winnicott (1965). Winnicott, an astute observer of the mother–child relationship, used the idea of the false self in describing normal development, but the idea also has major implications for the development of the child whose sense of self is seriously impaired by chronic abuse or neglect. In less healthy families, the child learns to avoid needing what she cannot get from her parents. She develops a false self that obscures her real needs, desires, and experiences, even from herself. This restricted but adaptive self is what allows the child, and later the adult, to survive disappointments and violations. Because of the false self, the child can continue to function, but her capacity for attachment is seriously compromised. Silences and distortions protect her in lieu of her parents.

Nancy's childhood was fertile ground for the development of a false self. Her parents' neglect was disguised and distorted by her well-meaning grandmother, who tried to protect Nancy by creating lies about how loved she was. Nancy's grandmother did the best she could to create the myth of a loving family in which Nancy was the cherished daughter, the lovely little princess. Unfortunately, the ways in which this anxious grandmother attempted to care for the child were so intrusive that Nancy had to develop a powerful false self to protect herself. Her own wishes and needs were obscured from her by her parents' neglect and her grandmother's violations.

Nancy needed to feel valued and seen as a child, but she was given the message that only a perfect little replica of an adult woman, glamorous and alluring, could get the attention of her busy socialite parents. Her need for personal privacy in relation to her body, her feelings, and her thoughts was denied repeatedly. Gradually Nancy came to accept her grandmother's ideas as her own. She took fewer and fewer risks in asking for what she genuinely wanted and needed, because she could not sustain the frustration of this futile process. Eventually, a well-developed false self emerged, a self that was adaptive in the environment created for Nancy. Her grandmother's efforts to provide what her parents could not demanded that Nancy subscribe to a picture of family love that would satisfy even if it did not nurture.

Nancy and the other TRS women described in this book all had experiences of being silenced and having reality distorted, as well as having to repress their traumatic victimization. All of them developed some version of a false self. This false self, along with the practice of silence and deception, was the wellspring for the secrets of their adult life.

Secrecy in Adult Life

Many TRS women reenact the bond of secrecy required by their childhood abusers. Because child abuse demands secrecy, both during and between episodes, survivors tend to perpetuate the habit of being secretive even when it is not in their best interest. In the adult life of the TRS woman, this pattern of excessive secrecy works to keep her self-harming behavior hidden. Because she developed the habit of secrecy during childhood, she is accustomed to keeping much of her life to herself. She is practiced at concealing problems of any sort, not only from her friends, partner, and family, but also from therapists, doctors, and other concerned professionals. Ironically, the pattern of self-abuse is perpetuated by the very rule she lived with as a child, the "no talk" rule.

There are two major areas of secrecy for the TRS woman. The first is the secret she has carried with her from childhood concerning the abuse, neglect, or violations. Survivors of child sexual abuse are more likely today than in the past to disclose the trauma, but there are still many women (and many more men, proportionately) who do not. In addition to all the victims of sexual abuse, there are many adult survivors of childhood battering, violation, and neglect who remain invisible because their trauma is not so readily identified.

The second area of secrecy for the TRS woman is the concealment of her self-abusive behavior. Although we see thousands of women coming forth with disclosures of eating disorders and chemical dependency in peer support groups, in recovery groups, on talk shows, and in psychotherapy, there are still vast numbers of women with problems of self-abuse who are not revealing them. Women who self-mutilate, for example, are reluctant to disclose their behavior, generally because they are ashamed and because such disclosures are frequently met with revulsion and condemnation. On the other hand, women whose self-harming activities fall more into the "beauty knows no pain" category do not discuss their behavior in public forums because they do not view their diets and surgeries as addictions or self-injury.

There are many reasons why the TRS woman hides her self-injurious behavior. She may fear the practical and social repercussions that disclosure might bring: loss of a job, loss of a partner, even trouble with the law, or simply being considered unattractive, "unladylike," or incompetent. Another set of motivating factors is generated internally. These reasons for secret-keeping include profound feelings of shame.

Shame is a pervasive experience for the TRS woman; she experiences the shameful action or event as part of her identity. The psychotherapists Claudia Bepko and Jo Ann Krestan, in *Too Good for Her Own Good* (1990), describe the "shame trap." Women in this trap feel ashamed of their needs and then ashamed of their self-abusive behavior, which is their response to the initial wave of shame. A "vicious cycle of worthlessness and fear" (p. 51) keeps many women locked in a pattern of shame and abuse, escalating in a self-generated feedback loop to more shame and more abuse.

Karen experiences a complicated mixture of shame reactions attached to her bulimia. When she makes herself so sick that she can barely function at work, she feels shame that she is failing her patients and coworkers. When she thinks about what she is doing in the middle of the night, eating her way through everything in the refrigerator and then vomiting until she cries from the pain in her throat and stomach, she also feels shame. Her feelings become so intertwined that she often cannot tell the difference between "What I did was bad" and "I am bad." She is horrified both by what she is doing and by what she is.

June, identifying herself as an alcoholic mother, has felt like a "bad person" for as long as she can remember. She feels profound shame that she has failed her children. Her shame has been part of her since early childhood, a result of growing up neglected and unloved; she received the message that she was essentially "bad." In her alcoholic drinking, June sometimes finds a temporary escape from her sad and angry feelings, but she can never escape the shame. At other times rage and grief are amplified when she is high on drugs or alcohol, and she is overcome with the self-loathing that her shame engenders.

Like secrecy and lying, shame acts to create a barrier between the TRS woman and other people. Because of their shame, Karen, Laura, and June all feel that no one will really love them, accept them, or stay with them. Each of these women is unable to sustain a lasting relationship because she is dominated by her secret shame. The feeling of "badness" results from the shame that is ever-present in the way TRS women think about themselves. Because they perceive themselves as "bad," they are convinced that others will know or sense the badness if they get too close.

Many women say that they feel like imposters in various parts of their lives, but TRS women feel like imposters most of the time. The more secretive they are about their self-abuse, and the more horrifying or disgusting they believe their symptoms to be, the more they feel like frauds who will inevitably be exposed as perverted, horrible, sick, unfeminine, and most of all, unlovable.

For Lee, the experience of shame is harder to name. Because she cannot clearly recall much of her childhood abuse history, she feels overtaken by shame without having clearly identifiable trigger experiences. Lee and her therapist believe that her headaches and the cutting of her body are related to things she cannot quite remember about her mother and her childhood terrors. These fragmented memories of abuse overwhelm Lee with shame. The more she struggles with the shame of her symptoms and the shame of what she cannot remember, the more she withdraws from friends and family.

Perhaps most painful for TRS victims is the shame of feeling disconnected and isolated from others. Many of us at one time or another have felt discomfort or even slight shame in situations where we felt we were viewed by others—or sometimes just by ourselves—as being alone when we would prefer not to be. Many women feel embarrassed to be seen eating dinner alone in a restaurant or to be alone at a concert, movie, or party. For TRS women, being alone can become so much a part of daily life that they brood about the shame of their solitary condition as much as they suffer their loneliness. The shame of feeling unwanted, unchosen, and unloved is often as acute as the fear of being "found out." To understand why secrecy is the central organizing principle of the TRS woman's adult life, it is important to remember the roots of that secrecy in her abuse history and how the shame of childhood is perpetuated.

Some TRS women feel understandably indignant at being asked by would-be helpers to relinquish the secret of their self-abuse, considering it an invasion of their privacy. There are important distinctions between privacy and secrecy. The ethicist Sissela Bok (quoted in Imber-Black 1993) defines "secrecy" as intentional concealment, while privacy implies appropriate boundaries between self and others (p. 19). Evan Imber-Black (1993) sees the shift from privacy to secrecy as a power-based issue; when we claim the right to *privacy* so that we can conceal something, we are blurring power dynamics, pretending that there is no distinction between these two concepts (Imber-Black 1993). Harriet Lerner (1993) cautions all women that the shield of privacy may isolate them and prevent the sharing of personal experiences. She believes that through sharing, women can find commonalities and confront false myths about the female experience.

Discouragement and weariness keep many women from disclosing their self-harmful activities. Too many TRS women have been told too many times that if they would only follow so-and-so's rules, advice, directives, diets, or guidelines, they could easily stop the problem behavior. These women have been scolded for not following diets, not going to enough support group meetings, not being spiritual enough, not being self-disciplined enough, not going to the root of their problem—in short, not trying hard enough. The accumulation of failures to stop the self-harm often leads to greater shame and concealment. The more the TRS victim goes underground with her self-abuse, the more the isolation and shame will increase the destructive activities, which in turn increases the self-blame. Sadly enough, many helpers remain oblivious or indifferent to the effects of their directives and admonishments. Will power is a concept that should be banished from the vocabulary of all those who wish to help the TRS woman. Entreaties to share are also frequently painful to the ears of the shame-bound TRS woman, who would surely share her pain if only she could.

Despite its negative aspects, secrecy serves several positive functions in the life of the TRS woman. First, it gives her a way of exerting control. When the child victim or the TRS woman experiences chronic powerlessness and views the world as unsafe, there is a constant tension to regain some kind of control. Keeping secrets is a form of control that becomes precious to the child or adult. In the child's narrative, secrecy may be coerced (Laura's story) or cajoled (Karen's story) by the adult abuser, but it is still perceived by the child as something she controls. Even the physical pain and psychological terror of being abused may become a secret the child controls as a way to avoid worse repercussions from the abuser.

In the life of the adult self-abusing woman, keeping the secrets of her self-abuse and her history of childhood trauma is a vital part of feeling in control of her body and her life, forcing others to guess and worry about her and denying them access to a vulnerable part of herself. These stories are a precious commodity, even if they have a toxic effect on her sanity. If therapists or others coerce her to give up control of her story before she is ready, she may feel reabused, in the sense that someone else is taking control of her mind and her memories.

Secret-keeping is also a positive force in giving the TRS woman a way of feeling connected, symbolically, with others. Secrecy takes on a life of its own for the TRS woman because it comes to represent, as it did in childhood, the special, intense quality of being close to another person. Keeping the secret in childhood created feelings of being special, of existing in a relationship, even if that special relationship was terrifying, painful, humiliating, and shameful. Thus, part of the adult's cycle of self-injury is to feel attached to the behavior of secrecy and concealment. Ironically, what keeps the TRS woman separated from others is the very thing that makes her feel reassured that she is in a relationship: she has a relationship with the secret.

The adult perpetrator who persuades the child to resist disclosure often refers to the abusive behavior as "our little secret." "Our little secret" grows up with the child to become a sort of companion in her adult life, much like the symptom. As she works to protect and maintain the secret, she may think of it as a friend, a child, something she owns and keeps hidden away.

One problem with secrecy is that it necessitates not only concealment but also lying. Knowing that information is being concealed may be frustrating or disappointing. Knowing that someone is lying generally leads to anger, deepening mistrust, and eventual disconnection from the relationship. The TRS woman is practiced at telling lies because it has been forced on her and, in many cases, has been an unquestioned part of her family lifestyle. Even when she is fully aware that lying in her adult life leads to anger and troubled relationships, she may feel addicted to lying. This kind of self-perception leads to intense feelings of guilt, shame, and despair, and reinforces her experience of profound isolation. The secret thus becomes all the more compelling as a substitute for relationships with other people.

Until the TRS woman works out other ways to feel powerful and to relate to people, keeping the secret *is* positive. When she begins to achieve a healthier life, the functions of secret-keeping become less critical. Eventually, the powerful hold that secrets have on the TRS woman is diminished and they are no longer a necessity.

Disclosing the Secrets

There are arguments for confronting the TRS woman's history of silences and secrets. One is that the anger and fear attached to the untold secrets will fester, further sickening the woman's system and distorting her sense of wholeness and cohesiveness. Another is that telling the secrets is a powerful way of connecting victims with each other. The ritual of group storytelling legitimates both the person and the story, connecting the woman to a larger community. Adrienne Rich offers this from *On Lies, Secrets and Silence* (1979):

> In every life there are experiences, painful and at first disorienting, which by their very intensity throw a sudden floodlight on the ways we have been living, the forces that control our lives, the *hypocrisies* that have allowed us to collaborate with those forces, the harsh but liberating facts we have been enjoined from recognizing. Some people allow such illuminations only the brevity of a flash of sheet-lightning, that throws a whole landscape into sharp relief, after which the darkness of denial closes in again. For others, these clarifications provide a motive and impulse toward a more enduring lucidity, a search for greater honesty, and for recognition of larger issues of which our personal suffering is a symptom, a specific example. (p. 215)

While telling secrets may be frightening, sometimes the act of break-ing the silence breaks the chronicity of the fear. Most important, telling the secret of trauma allows the child victim to get protection and sup-port from a variety of sources, just as she will, as an adult, get more protection and support from helpers, partners, and friends.

In my own life, there was a long time when my memories of abuse were partially occluded. When early therapy experiences silenced my efforts to reconstruct the incest narrative, I found other ways of gradu-ally coming to terms with what had happened to me. There was the night of mutual disclosure with my friend Fiora. I heard her say the words aloud: "My father gave me drugs when I was a child. My father beat me. My father made me have sex with him." Then I heard her say, "Something like that happened to you, too, didn't it?" And I heard myself say, "Yes." This was the beginning of telling a story that was long overdue, the story that could gradually move out of the darkness and allow me to begin to live my own life, no longer overshadowed by my father and "our" secret.

In beginning to break the silence of my own trauma history, the most powerful tool was sharing stories of female oppression and empowerment with friends in the early women's movement. I heard variations of my own story in political meetings, in movies, in femi-nist writing. Some of the most significant moments of realizing my own power happened through political action. Healing through con-nection was the beginning of moving toward disclosure of my per-sonal history.

Unfortunately, there are also snares and pitfalls involved in disclos-ing the secrets of trauma and adult self-injury. Telling old secrets of a traumatic childhood may seem safer than telling the current secrets of self-harm, but both areas can be filled with hidden traps and disap-pointments. Adults, like child victims, can be injured by unsafe disclo-sure. In twelve-step recovery programs such as incest survivor groups and groups for the addictions often related to incest (Alcoholics Anonymous, Narcotics Anonymous, and Overeaters Anonymous, for example), the sharing of trauma secrets may create a sense of relief and connection to a community, but it may also constrict the telling of the story in order to fit a prescription for how the story should be told. The complex interplay of loyalty, fear, rage, and connectedness inher-ent in the abusive relationship becomes oversimplified. The woman telling her story—or perhaps the silent listener sitting in the last row—may be overwhelmed with feelings of isolation, and frightened by the thought that her perceptions and experience do not match those of others.

Those who promote the disclosure of childhood trauma or adult self-injury too soon fail to recognize how fraught with danger telling these secrets can be. They fail to understand that keeping the secret often serves a protective function for the victim. As I have already discussed, the victim of child abuse often needs to protect the abusive or neglectful relationship, just as the woman who hurts herself may need to protect the internalized relationship that her behavior represents. In many well-meaning but misguided attempts to aid the victim, the listener ignores or is unaware of the contradictions and confused loyalties that are part of telling the trauma or self-abuse story.

Connected to this phenomenon is the debate about whether some therapists actually create false memories in their clients. The psychologist Elizabeth Loftus is a memory expert who has been prominent in this controversy. In a recent article (Loftus, 1993), she raises significant questions about the incidence of childhood sexual abuse memories being completely repressed. Loftus believes that total amnesia is not as common as many experts in PTSD treatment and research claim. Loftus also questions how authentic some of these early childhood memories could actually be and how many details recalled by adults are really accurate. She suggests that some of these stories are more likely remembrances told to the child or adult by someone else, and not true memories.

Researchers studying repressed memory (Loftus, 1993; Ganaway, 1989; Watters, 1991) suggest that what people claim to remember is likely to be altered by various factors. According to these experts, the accuracy of the recollections of traumatic events is affected by such factors as suggestions made by a trusted family member or therapist, the age of the patient when the supposed event occurred, and the degree of terror involved in the repression of the original memory.

Many experts in the field of trauma disagree with this perspective. The researcher Karen Olio (1993) suggests that it is more to the point whether the memory retains essential veracity. She also states that "the possibility of implanting entire multiple scenarios of horror that differ markedly from the individual's experience, such as memories of childhood abuse in an individual who does not have a trauma history, remains an unsubstantiated hypothesis" (p. 2).

From my perspective as a therapist and supervisor, I can see that there are many reasons why therapists, as recipients of the trauma or self-abuse secrets, may inadvertently distort the client's attempts at disclosure. One problem is that we may try to impose our understanding on the woman who reveals her shame and pain, in both our language and judgments.

Trauma causes an enormous rupture in the basic sense of certainty about what one knows. It shatters language and our ways of conceptualizing the whys and hows of human behavior. Trauma strikes at the heart and soul and thus demands another kind of language. Our process of healing must incorporate these challenges. Those who really want to hear the TRS woman's story must learn to tolerate not knowing, to let go of inadequate explanations and interventions. While professional helpers cannot share their personal stories with clients, there is still a lesson to be learned from the twelve-step recovery movement's subjective ways of knowing. Listeners in twelve-step meetings achieve empathic attunement by hearing their own stories embedded in the speaker's story. The listener can never completely know another's experience of trauma, however. The continuously shifting experience of being inside someone's story because it is like one's own and then being suddenly outside the other's experience mirrors trauma relationships, where abuser, nonprotector, and victim move in and out of each other's empathic awareness.

Professional training can get in the way of hearing the client's subtext. Professionals are in grave danger of knowing too much at one level without knowing what is essential at another, deeper level. When we divide the players in childhood trauma into victim/perpetrator and good/bad dichotomies, we risk giving the trauma survivor the message that she herself is "bad," since the relationship with the abuser has become an internalized part of herself. The same pitfall exists when the listener seems to judge or condemn the TRS woman's report of self-injury. Such a listener reduces the complexities of the storyteller's experience, failing to understand how the trauma survivor or TRS woman can equate violence with love or perceive the abusive adult as nurturing or an important source of basic survival needs.

For the TRS woman, the listener's distortion of her story can be devastating. It is hard for her to break the silence and to begin to tell her secrets. It is therefore unendurable when the secrets are misused and the story misunderstood.

KAREN BETRAYED AGAIN

I tried to tell a counselor at my school, the nursing school, but she really didn't get it. I started saying how I thought maybe I should be telling someone about the stuff that happened with Dad. She said, "So you're telling me you are an incest survivor?"

"I guess so," I said. "I don't really think in those terms, but yes, I guess I am."

"So no wonder you seem so scared and angry," she said, like it was all so neat and simple. "Have you reported this to the police or told your mother?"

Now keep in mind that I was a twenty-one-year-old adult at this time. And of course I was not about to tell the police or my mother. What good would it have done? So I said, "Uh, no. Maybe I'm giving you the wrong idea here. It's not a big deal, really. I mean the whole world seems to be incest survivors and incest perpetrators these days. So my situation isn't so unusual, really."

The counselor leaned forward and said to me, in this really fake attempt at sympathy, "I know how much pain you are in. It's okay to cry. You're safe here."

So, like a jerk, I do sort of tear up a little. She's got the tissue box in my lap in an instant, and she said, "What your father did to you was terrible. He used you and took your innocence away from you. It's okay to get really angry. Just let it all out. You'll feel better."

I looked right back at her and I said, "How do you know how I feel? Are you an incest survivor or whatever?"

She pulled back into her chair and gave me this nervous smile. "I can't help you by telling you about myself," she said. "That's not part of the therapy relationship. My job is to be here for you." She tried to look compassionate again, but she didn't convince me.

"I loved my father," I told her. "I still do. I don't know if you can understand that."

"Of course you loved him," she shot right back, "because he coerced you and made you dependent on him. You had no choice but to love him." She gave me a stern look before she delivered her next comment. "But Karen," she said emphatically, "your father did not love you. Fathers who love their children don't abuse them."

"I'll have to think about that," I said, getting up and putting on my coat. I made an appointment to go back, but I never went. That night I binged and drank wine until I puked my brains out.

Many of my clients have been important to my learning to respect the functions and logic of secret-keeping for the TRS woman. By giving up their secrets, these women faced the loss of control and the loss of relationship with the abuse, which had protected each in her own way since childhood.

My experience with Laura illustrates my growing awareness of problems in disclosure (Miller, 1993). Laura began her first session with me by disclosing the paternal incest. Despite her nervousness, indicating that she felt little safety with me, Laura insisted on telling me as much of her childhood incest history as she could squeeze into the session. She came to me straight from inpatient and halfway house twelve-step treatment and had been advised that self-disclosure was the path to recovery.

I learned by my mistakes in allowing Laura's premature disclosure. What I observed was that telling the secret of childhood trauma was not initially healing. One problem with Laura's disclosure was that it was not framed within a relationship. I was as disconnected from her as any listener would have been if Laura had been telling her story on a talk show. Thus, the tales of sadistic abuse served only to stimulate in Laura feelings of guilt, shame, and violated family loyalty, leading again and again to self-punishing behavior. I was a helpless bystander, witnessing the excruciating reenactment of traumatic abuse, this time by her own hand.

Laura was acting on the belief, commonly held among professional helpers and the lay public, that the first step in healing the incest wound is to disclose the shameful, painful secrets. This was not the best way to begin. Her initial disclosure was potentially a repetition of earlier trauma dynamics, when neither her mother nor concerned teachers at school could (or would) intervene to protect her. She had also internalized her father's paranoid commands to protect their secret relationship. It was therefore very risky for Laura as an adult client to break the silence and to ask for protection by doing so.

Fortunately, Laura's story does not end in disaster. Despite the premature disclosure of the complex incest relationship, Laura and I together managed to create a meaningful and real relationship that ultimately made her disclosure a safe and trust-building experience. I gradually learned to work with her by learning the meanings of her symptoms (what she was reenacting) and the rules about family loyalty and alliances. Although it was difficult, I began to block her attempts to disclose the abuse stories; I explained why I was doing so, framing it as trying to protect her in ways she was not accustomed to being protected.

It was important for me to explain to Laura why we needed some time to develop mutual trust before she told me the details of her abuse. I told her I needed to understand more about her relationships not only with her father but also with her mother, her siblings, and other adults who were significant in her childhood. We had to establish a joint conviction that when she told me her story, neither she nor I would be overwhelmed. I had to know how she had felt unsafe in the past and who else, besides herself and her father, she might still be consciously or unconsciously protecting.

Laura's story represents the damaging effects of premature, unsafe disclosures. Laura was fixed on the idea that if she did not share her story in twelve-step meetings, she was being cowardly or not trying hard enough. My work with her needed to begin by understanding the negative associations specific to her childhood experiences of disclosure. I needed to protect her by waiting until we had developed a stable, trusting relationship before I tried to hear and understand her secret shame and suffering.

Laura's experience of "forced" disclosures in twelve-step meetings is somewhat similar to Karen's experience of having her disclosure distorted by the counseling center therapist. Each woman felt a sense of being invisible. Their stories were distorted by the listeners; the way they thought about their experiences remained misunderstood. Their descriptions of themselves and their relationships were judged to be "wrong," and instead they were told what they should think about the relationships.

There are hundreds of TRS women who hear the stories of other trauma survivors on TV or radio, or in magazines and newspapers, and wonder what is wrong with themselves. They feel marginalized or isolated because the stories they hear are all the same and do not seem to reflect the complexity of their own feelings about their relationship to the abuser and to the abuse. Moreover, what they are feeling is different from what they are told they should think. The child who is not protected sees her relationship to the nonprotecting caretakers differently from how others see it. Both the child and the adult survivor have complex longings and loyalties that color their perceptions of the mother or other adults who did not or could not protect them.

Among the nonprotecting caretakers represented in this book, there is a wide range of reasons for their incapacity to protect the children. The children have a range of stories they tell themselves about this failure to get protection. Later, the TRS woman creates new stories based on the childhood story and incorporating other feelings and information she has gathered through life experience. For Laura, her mother's incapacity to protect her has a different meaning from Karen's experience: Laura was actively trying to protect her mother from her father's murderous rage, while Karen felt both neglected by and invisible to her mother. Then there was Lee, both unprotected by her mother *and* abused by her. Finally, there are women like Nancy who may not believe that what happened to them should have been stopped. For Nancy, the abuse perpetrated by her grandmother was a form of affection and privilege, perhaps even protection, in her mind. Because of oversimplified and unprotected disclosure, many survivors tell only part of their story. It is no wonder that the TRS woman who cannot tell the whole story, or cannot find herself in the generic "victim–villain" abuse story, ends up feeling doubly shamed and alone.

Lee's process of silence, deception, and secret-keeping was different in some ways from Laura's. I was called in by Lee's therapist, Martha, to provide a consultation. One problem was how and where Lee's secrets, both past and present, could safely be explored. Working with Lee's therapist helped me further to understand the importance of developing a strong therapeutic relationship based on mutual trust and relative acceptance of each other's beliefs about loyalty, protection, and secrets. It became clear that this kind of relationship had to be carefully constructed before it was safe to move to the traumatic and complex memories of childhood incest and to confront the secrets of the adult's abusive behavior. It also confirmed the necessity of involving other people

in the therapy process with whom the client has a meaningful, supportive relationship.

In Lee's case, it was temporarily important to include her husband,
David, in therapy. David's presence served several purposes. It diffused
the apparently frightening intensity of one-to-one meetings with
Martha in which Lee might feel trapped and forced to reveal more than
she was ready to share. It allowed Martha to work with the couple on
the beliefs that kept them mutually stuck in dysfunctional patterns generated by the secrecy protecting the internalized incest relationship.
Martha also needed to look at areas of current functioning, and David
was able to provide an assessment of Lee's depression and potential for
self-harm as the secrets of her childhood trauma began to surface.

I had suggested to Martha and Lee that it might be useful to get
David's ideas about Lee's family and find out what he knew and
believed about child sexual abuse. It turned out that this was a more
significant area of investigation than we might have guessed. Given
David's capacity to ignore some disturbing aspects of Lee's behavior
and her family's peculiar dynamics, it was not surprising to learn that
David, too, had undisclosed secrets about incest in his family. With
some hesitation and a defensive introductory warm-up, David disclosed
that he and his younger brother were sexually involved over a period of
approximately three years during childhood. Since David's brother was
five years younger, this behavior was not simply children's sexual play
but constituted sexual abuse. The activities had included masturbating
each other and oral penetration of the younger brother. David had initiated genital fondling when he was nine and his brother was five. The
progression to oral penetration happened when the younger brother
was seven. David ended the abuse when he was thirteen.

David was ashamed of sexually abusing his brother, but he stated
that he thought it did neither of them any real harm. He believed his
brother enjoyed most aspects of it. When Martha explored David's
beliefs about why it had happened, David described his shame at being
small for his age. He was teased and humiliated by the other boys.
Abusing his brother made him feel powerful. He insisted that he could
see no reason to talk to his brother now about their childhood sexual
involvement or to go to therapy himself.

David's story served to create an opening for more of Lee's memories to surface. The secrets in Lee's past were allowed to emerge more
as reflections on or responses to parts of David's story. She felt more in

control of the material because she was participating in the construction of her partner's story as well as her own. She was therefore able to avoid the dynamics of blame and shame so common in women who fear disclosure of their self-abuse more than they do the disclosure of their victimization in childhood.

From consulting with Martha and Lee, I learned the importance of carefully allowing secrets to be uncovered at the client's own pace. For both Lee and David, the resulting awareness was that sexual involvement between children and adults is harmful on many levels. This gradual shift from denial of sexual abuse as traumatic to the realization of its damaging effects was achieved by working from the premise that disclosure of shame and trauma is healing only within the context of a noncoercive, carefully constructed relationship. David and Lee also learned together that the incest relationship is complicated for both the child and the abuser, varying greatly from one client to another. David was eventually able to enter therapy and work out some important issues concerning power and shame.

On the basis of my work with clients such as Laura and Lee, and my own experience as a client, I have developed a more careful, protective treatment approach in working with past and present abuse secrets. I emphasize the centrality of relationship in developing stages of self-disclosure. The secrets attached to the abuse relationship are complex and tenacious, and must be approached carefully and thoughtfully. Like the naturalist who successfully enters the habitat of a wild creature by both observing and being observed, the listener must find ways to create a relatively safe environment in which the TRS woman's secrets can be disclosed as part of a genuine relationship. I suggest that this work be done in stages, moving from a gathering of relevant family history, beliefs, and myths to networking with peer support groups and other helping professionals and finally to a one-to-one relationship in which the heart of darkness can open. No story of childhood trauma or self-abuse is exactly the same for one person as it is for another. A multidimensional approach can allow the various levels of complexity to be brought forth and explored.

It is important to establish a collaboration between the TRS woman and the helper or listener. The storyteller should continually be encouraged to seek self-determination, to view herself as expert in her own healing process. Her story should be heard with the reassurance that she is the primary "author," with the listener offering responses in much the same way a friendly editor would. TRS women should be encouraged to share their secrets and stories in a variety of healing relationships, including family, friends, partners, peers in recovery, and spiritual healers.

In the early stage of treatment, direct disclosures of trauma memories and related symptomatic behaviors are not the central ingredients of the narrative. As much as possible, I actively block the disclosure of abuse secrets and try to contain disclosures of current symptoms. At this stage, I do not yet have a clear enough map of the territory, especially of previous failed attempts on the client's part to feel understood, accepted, and protected in relation to abuse issues. In addition, my client has not had enough time to observe and assess my relational capabilities and to feel confident that disclosing the trauma and self-abuse would be safe.

The ideas I have incorporated in my approach to TRS have been profoundly influenced by my experience as a client as well as through moments of insight as a therapist. I have to make each exploration of shameful, secret memories and current confessions of shameful self-abuse directly connect to the therapist–client relationship. Each act of sharing is accompanied by questions for the client about her moment-to-moment feelings of safety. She must feel protected and loved throughout the terrifying disclosures of her shame and pain. The relationship at this stage of treatment is what makes everything possible or else pointless. For the disclosure to be healing, therapists must provide the context of a relationship that allows for the power of telling a story to someone who listens with knowledge, skill, and empathy, and that emphasizes mutuality between the listener and the self-abusive woman. Telling the secrets of childhood trauma and adult self-harm can be healing or can just as easily repeat childhood exploitation and betrayal.

For TRS women, there is a long journey between beginning to tell the secret and safely arriving at the place of connection and empowerment. The TRS woman must begin to experience wholeness within herself as one of the steps toward connection with others. In the following chapter, the problems of the fragmented self illustrate some of the obstacles the TRS woman must navigate.

4

Self-Protection

Among her legacies from childhood, the TRS woman has been left with an inability to protect herself or to maintain the boundaries necessary for self-definition. She longs to have inside herself the capacity to self-soothe and self-protect, but often she does not know how.

JUNE: RELAPSE AND SELF-BLAME

I wish I could understand why I end up like this over and over again. Maybe I'm just unlucky, or maybe I don't know how to stay out of bad situations. Maybe I'm like my son Tony Jr., who always gets himself into some kind of trouble and always gets caught.

It's like the last time I had a slip, fell off the wagon, so to speak. Things had just been piling up and I was feeling like I couldn't take another thing going wrong. So then my daughter gets suspended from school for a week for getting into a fight with some other girls. This I couldn't believe. I mean, my kid is a tiny little thing and she's quiet and even kind of mousy. So I call the school and tell them, very nice at first, that my Dawn could not possibly have gotten into a fight. They have an attitude, probably because it's me and we've had our differences more than once. One thing leads to another and I hang up, mad and ready to take her out of that school permanently. She starts crying, begging me not to send her to Catholic school, and then I lose it with her.

So then I feel so bad that instead of going for my daily walk with my neighbor Norma, something I count on for my sanity, I take Dawn shopping and use the money I was saving to get myself into an aerobics class. I blow it on this tacky jeans and jacket outfit for Dawn, even though it makes her look like a little tramp, to be honest with you. So, no aerobics class for me.

Later, I'm sitting in my parlor watching my program. I think, "June, you are such a goddamned fool!!" and I get up and pour myself a whiskey and soda and drink it right down as I'm standing there. So then of course I can't go to my AA meeting, and I'm crying and asking myself why, why, why did I do it?

It's kind of like what happened when I had the job at the supermarket and I had even gotten promoted to assistant manager. Then this Spanish lady got caught shoplifting and I felt bad for her, so I let her go. The manager, a boy, really, about twenty-two, comes up just as I open the door to escort the lady out of the store and tells me I have to call the cops and get the lady arrested. I tell him I won't do it and if he wasn't such a child himself, he would understand that she deserves another chance. He tells me again to call the cops. I tell him, "Go do it yourself." The chump starts to reach for the phone, and the poor lady is crying and praying in Spanish and she's tugging on my sleeve for protection. So I take the phone and I rip it out of the wall.

Well, you probably guessed it: I got fired. It wasn't fair, but I know I didn't look out for myself.

Oh God, I'm going to cry again. It's so stupid. I'm so stupid. Why do I let myself get caught like this? How come I can't ever keep myself safe? My girlfriend Norma would never begin to get herself into the kind of situation I'm talking about here. In fact, Norma's just the opposite. She knows how to protect herself. How did she get that way, so strong?

One woman told me about her favorite song as a child, from *Oklahoma*. Her family listened to the record often and she memorized the lyrics:

I'm just a girl who can't say no
I'm in a terrible fix
I always say c'mon let's go
Just when I oughta say nix.

This memory seemed especially poignant when I imagined the words sung in the squeaky voice of a nine-year-old girl, the victim of prolonged paternal incest. Saying no is often impossible for the powerless child, and continues to feel impossible to the adult survivor. Just as it is simplistic to think that ghetto teenagers will "just say no" to drugs, it is naive to believe that adults who have been sexually abused in childhood can easily choose healthy, nurturing lifestyles or relinquish self-harmful activities.

June typifies the TRS woman who can't say no. She continually "dries out" in her substance abuse treatment programs and then relapses. She cannot protect herself from the harmful effects and consequences of drug and alcohol abuse. She also has trouble saying no to her teenage children, to her partners, to friends, and even to strangers. Her job history reveals a series of situations in which she failed to protect herself.

Not only is June unable to say no to drugs or to people who make unreasonable demands on her, but, like many other TRS women, she is also unable to keep herself out of unsafe or unpleasant situations. While she may not sound like the child singing "I'm just a girl who can't say no," her voice, raspy from too much barroom smoke and alcohol, evokes the memory of Janis Joplin offering her lover a piece of her heart.

Janis Joplin represents the archetypal TRS woman. She was famous in the sixties not only for her incomparable voice and performance style, but also for her epic public displays of self-destruction. In what was often described as a continuous frenzy of wanting to be loved and admired, Joplin gave her body to a cannibalistic music industry and a voracious public by abusing drugs and alcohol, abusing her voice, engaging in endlessly risky behavior, and allowing her considerable financial earnings to be taken from her.

Women like Janis Joplin and June do not protect themselves. They have become cut off from the protective part of themselves. A severe

lack of self-esteem permeates their behavior and communications. They
are easy to exploit because they are so preoccupied with giving themselves to whomever or whatever may offer the love and admiration they
have never been able to develop within themselves. When they are as
flamboyant in their behavior as Joplin was, they are also blamed for
their exploitation because they appear to be "asking for it."

More covert symptoms such as eating disorders can sometimes keep
the TRS woman from being blamed as readily for her failure to protect
herself. Women like Karen Carpenter, a pop singer who eventually died
from the effects of chronic anorexia, are often viewed more compas-
sionately than the boozy, promiscuous Janis Joplin types. Neither
Karen Carpenter nor Janis Joplin, however, could protect her body, her
spirit, or her heart.

The Failure to Protect Boundaries

The inability to self-protect leaves all the TRS woman's boundaries
open to invasion. Frequently, she has a difficult time protecting the
boundaries of her body. In childhood, she was invaded physically. As
an adult, she is prone to continuing violations of her body, by others
and by her own hand. If she does not like to be touched in either casual
or intimate circumstances, she has difficulty accepting that it is okay to
feel uncomfortable or to express discomfort.

My own experience as a survivor is illustrative. I achieved a major
step in my recovery when I was finally able to say no to a client who
persistently requested a hug at the end of each therapy session. My vic-
tory was in saying no to something that made me uncomfortable and in
recognizing that I was entitled to my personal preference, even if it
meant saying no to what someone else wanted from me.

Karen is likely to become sexually involved with a new boyfriend
early in the relationship. She gives signals that she wants to engage sexually and actively pursues sexual contact if it has not been initiated by
the man. While she enjoys the physical closeness and tenderness of kiss-
ing and being caressed, she is often ambivalent about the genital stimulation that follows. She is more likely than not to find penetration
uncomfortable rather than pleasurable. She has, however, already

developed a pattern in the relationship of seeming to be the enthusiastic "take me, I'm yours" girl. When she has to decide if it's all right to say no, she finds that she can't.

Karen then doubts herself, blames herself, and feels increasingly anxious about who she really is. Her boyfriend has no way of knowing about her ambivalence, and so assumes she is enjoying sex with him. Karen begins to feel trapped and increasingly angry that he doesn't understand her, is insensitive to her, and is causing her to feel extreme anxiety and physical pain. She longs for him to be the tender white knight who will rescue her from this situation. Instead, unbeknownst to him, her experience is that her white knight is raping her.

When these feelings of being violated and shamed take over, Karen is overwhelmed by a sense of isolation and helplessness. She wishes for protection, but she has no idea how to help herself or to let anyone else know what she needs.

The TRS woman finds it equally difficult to protect her time and space. Her time is often subtly exploited. She may have an unclear sense of her basic needs, for example, not knowing if she herself needs to eat or to sleep or if she is responding to her partner's need. She perceives the needs of a partner or other family member as coming first, although they take up time that she may not really want to give. The pattern is the same as when she was a child, when the abusive adult had the power to take from her whatever time he or she wanted or needed, regardless of how the child might have wished to spend it.

TRS women frequently participate in activities that they may not enjoy but cannot allow themselves to question or reject, because they cannot separate their own needs and wishes from those of their partner, child, or friend. Lee watches hours of TV baseball, football, and basketball with her husband, David. She often feels depressed when doing so, but she insists that watching sports together is something they both enjoy. When pressed to explore this belief, she admits that she was never interested in sports, but got into the habit of watching with David so he would not feel lonely. If she were to continue her examination of this pattern, she would begin to feel anger at David, who falls asleep when they are watching movies she wants him to see with her. Rather than experience anger and disappointment, however, Lee convinces herself that it is her fault if she gets depressed during the ball games, instead of admitting to herself that she is bored and would prefer some other way of spending time with David. Even in her own mind, Lee has become a woman who likes to watch sports.

When the TRS woman does take special private time for herself, it may be to engage in self-abusive activity. Such behavior usually necessitates secrecy, so it is often a time when everyone else is sleeping or out of the house. Even single women who live alone may wait for their own "special" time to drink, binge, or cut, when the rest of the world is sleeping or relaxing. The time of the self-abusive behavior, therefore, often coincides with the time when the child was most often abused. In a strange way, the time she protects for this behavior may be when she feels most in control. It is time used the way she wants to use it. It is time when others cannot interrupt or insist that she meet their needs rather than her own. This is one of the many reasons it is so difficult for the TRS woman to relinquish her symptoms. It may be only at this time that she feels a real sense of personal identity.

Space is another dimension often invaded and exploited. The violation may involve physical, mental, or emotional space. When a child's physical space is violated, as Nancy's was by her grandmother's invasive caretaking, her right to that space is compromised. The child is never sure whether she can have private space in which to bathe, dress, or use the toilet. She does not symbolically experience having a room with a door. Now that we know Virginia Woolf was a sexually abused child, the title of her famous essay, "A Room of One's Own," takes on an additional meaning beyond the general lack of space that women can call their own.

Someone like June frequently gives up her mental space to accommodate the thoughts, questions, and conversation of her teenagers and various partners. To a certain extent, the more June drinks or "zones out" on drugs, the more she can protect her mental space. Because of the constraints on the TRS woman in expressing direct wishes or requests, she has a difficult time saying to anyone, "This isn't a good time for me to listen. Could we talk about this tomorrow?" Instead, she tries to protect her private mental and emotional space by getting high or through other self-abusive behavior.

Karen cannot protect her emotional space; she gives up her right to feel and express anger when she observes injustices in the hospital where she works. The only way she can claim space for her anger and sadness is to drink wine alone at night. The wine becomes her protector, giving her the space to cry and voice her anger.

Because the TRS woman has difficulty knowing what her boundaries are, she often feels as if she is merged with the people close to her. She has trouble identifying a solid sense of self. The question she unconsciously asks herself over and over is: "Where do I end and you begin?"

This blurred sense of self is often manifest in a confusion of thought: "I don't know what I think / your idea is undoubtedly better than mine / your thoughts overpower mine, so I don't remember now what it was I was thinking." This kind of thinking is a carry-over from the abused child's experience of being invalidated. When the child was abused, invaded, or neglected, her thoughts were frequently discounted. If she tried to articulate her distress or confusion about what was happening to her, she was told, "You don't know what you're talking about" or "You are imagining that—it never happened" or "Oh, how you exaggerate!"

At whatever age this kind of communication occurs, the child's sense of her own mental clarity and conviction is eroded. She cannot protect her sense of mental competence in the face of the adult correcting, belittling, or shaming her. Similarly, the adult TRS woman does not trust her own thinking and often trails off midstream in a conversation, contradicting herself and becoming somewhat incoherent. In extreme cases, she may sound almost psychotic. Although obscure communication may be self-protective in the sense of keeping secrets, it is also a form of dissociating from what is too painful or discouraging to bear.

Dissociation

As I explained in chapter 1, dissociation occurs when the mind cannot tolerate a traumatic event and responds by splitting off the experience from consciousness. In childhood, dissociation may be the best source of protection the abuse victim has; the child who is not adequately protected dissociates in order to survive the traumatic failures in her relationships with "all-powerful" caretakers. She splits off the bad parts of her experience with them, internalizing them as parts of herself.

Unfortunately, the processes of dissociation that were protective in childhood are what keep the TRS woman from achieving healthy self-protection as an adult. Even though the abusive and nonprotecting parents no longer have the same power to hurt her, the adult woman continues to dissociate, not having learned more appropriate and effective ways of self-protection.

Dissociation takes a variety of forms, one of which is analgesia: becoming numb, both physically and emotionally. A common form is amnesia; the loss of memory may be total or it may apply only to certain disturbing events or particular activities. Denial is a rejection of the painful realities of life. Cognitive confusion is a temporary state during which thoughts seem to be disorganized or don't make sense. Depersonalization is the sense of being outside oneself. Finally, identity disturbance includes the experience of feeling divided into separate personalities within oneself, the fragmentation that leads to the Triadic Self and its role in the reenactment of childhood trauma.

In order to understand the central function of the failure to self-protect in Trauma Reenactment Syndrome, it is important to clarify the ways these various forms of dissociation operate in the child and later in the adult woman. Sometimes only one form of the dissociative phenomenon is experienced. In other circumstances, a person engaged in dissociation can experience all of these effects, either simultaneously or in rapidly shifting sequence.

Analgesia

Analgesia can be experienced as physical or emotional numbing. The body may feel frozen or weightless. Often this occurs for trauma survivors during sexual activities and for TRS women during their symptomatic cycle. Many women who cut, burn, or otherwise mutilate their bodies describe being physically numb or not present, either before they hurt themselves or during the act of self-harm.

When Lee cuts herself, she is numb and separated from her adult body. She may not have a clear sense of self: that is, she may feel that she does not have a body. Or she may describe seeing herself cutting her body, but without feeling any sensation. Later, she describes the experience almost as if it were someone else doing the harm to her body.

The woman who dissociates may report feeling nothing or having no clear mental response to significant events or communications. Many of us have experienced this state of shock upon receiving deeply upsetting news, such as the death of a loved one or the sudden loss of a job or relationship. This state occurs much more frequently for TRS women, who often describe feeling nothing when everyone around them is having strong reactions to a frightening, saddening, or even joyous event. This lack of response can be misunderstood as a failure of empathy or a general incapacity to feel "normal" emotions or have "normal" thoughts. Because it is hard for the woman to explain what may have triggered the dissociative response and her peculiar absence of reaction, she is subject to negative judgment from others, who perceive her as cold or unfeeling.

An example of such a situation is portrayed by the actress Meryl Streep in the movie *A Cry in the Dark*. Streep plays an Australian mother whose infant is snatched from the tent one night when the family is camping. For a variety of reasons, the woman is wrongly accused of murdering her baby. She is in a state of shock, showing persistent dissociative signs of analgesia, and her flat, numb style is quickly construed by the public as a lack of feeling for her child. The manifestation of trauma in such a case obscures the expected responses of grief and rage, and the trauma victim instead appears cold and indifferent.

Amnesia

The TRS woman may develop amnesia (completely blocked memory) or occluded memory (disconnected fragments of memory that seem blurred, hazy, or confusing) about parts of her childhood abuse. This is the mind's way of protecting itself from unbearable fear or anger. Victims of serious car accidents, for example, often cannot remember portions of what actually happened.

Children may cope with their abuse and neglect by using the protective shield of amnesia. It is sometimes hard to distinguish between what the child is not allowed to disclose and what she actually has repressed. She may remember parts of her trauma at one time but not at others, or the memories of the same event may be different at different times. As I discussed in chapters 1 and 3, there is increasing controversy surrounding the issue of false memories of childhood abuse. The following remarks by the researcher and psychotherapist Karen Olio (1993) sum up how we might think about this controversy in relation to the repressed and fragmented memories discussed here:

All memories contain inaccuracies and distortions in the details that are recalled. For adult survivors of childhood sexual abuse, however, it is not the small details—e.g., the exact age, the number of incidents, etc.—that are essential. Rather, it is the validation of the reality of the abuse that is crucial. The question is not whether there are inaccuracies in memory, but whether memory retains essential truths. (p. 1)

As I explore the use of amnesia as a dissociative defense in the TRS woman, it is important to understand that her memory of certain details may be repressed for good reason. If and when she begins to recall previously buried memories, the protective function of her amnesia slips away, and she is likely to be understandably confused or contradictory in her reporting. For example, Lee's amnesia had served as a form of protection when she was a child. As an adult, it was harmful to Lee in some ways because she felt emotionally cut off from others, David included. She also had no idea why she did not want to have children. As the protective barrier of amnesia crumbled and she began the process of recovering abuse memories, she had to find new ways to keep the memories from flooding her and creating unbearable terror and pain.

Denial

The nonclinical word *denial* is another term for blocking out painful memories as well as distressing current events. A word familiar to all of us these days, it is most often associated with twelve-step recovery programs. Denial is another way to talk about dissociation. One can be "in denial" about the extent of a drinking problem or more generally about one's own behavior or the behavior of others. Some of the milder forms of dissociation would seem to be synonymous with denial. When the TRS woman tells herself and others that she feels fine or that her marriage is perfect, despite the suffering caused by her self-abusive behaviors, she is in denial about the problem or she is dissociated from the painful realities of her life. In their more extreme forms, dissociative thought processes are far more disconnected from reality than simple denial.

Cognitive Confusion

The clinical term *cognitive confusion* means that a person's thoughts seem fragmented or do not make sense. Sometimes cognitive confusion makes a person say or think things that seem to be "borrowed" from someone else. This form of dissociation happens regularly for most TRS women. It can even make them seem psychotic.

There is a difference, however, between the dissociative state of the TRS woman and the mental condition of a chronically mentally ill person. In the midst of extreme cognitive confusion, the TRS woman may seem to be losing touch with reality, but this is a temporary state. In an especially stressful or frightening moment, the TRS woman's inner experience may shift back in time to when she was being abused in childhood, so that she is thinking in the confused, dissociative way that was necessary then.

The act of abusing a child must be denied, even while it is happening, by both the perpetrator and the victim. The child joins the abusive caretaker in a state of cognitive confusion often employed by the adult to justify his or her behavior. Later, the child must reassemble her mind in some sort of "normal" structure so she can continue to function. Because this cycle becomes entrenched, the TRS woman frequently regresses to this confused state in the face of distressing events or thoughts. Many child abuse experts agree that an adult survivor can, at certain times, appear as if she is psychotic, when in fact she is only temporarily confused or disconnected from her usual thought pattern (Gelinas, 1983; van der Kolk, 1987; Herman, 1992).

One of the most discouraging aspects of the TRS woman's experience is how she is perceived by others in regard to the dissociative expression of her thoughts. The professional therapist, counselor, psychologist, social worker, nurse, or doctor may diagnose her as psychotic, paranoid, or thought-disordered. The nonprofessional may see her as crazy. For the TRS woman, these misperceptions are one more way in which she is isolated in her world of pain.

Depersonalization

LEE: OUT OF BODY EXPERIENCE

I am so peaceful right this minute. I am floating outside myself. I really feel like I have no self. There is no body, no feeling. I am mind. I can float out the window and up into the sky. I can hang suspended on the ceiling watching myself sitting down there in Martha's office with David.

It sounds crazy, but it doesn't feel that way. I know that I have a body and that I am sitting here on the couch next to David. But I'm also on the ceiling. I can hear Martha's soft, gentle voice and I can smell her perfume, both very comforting and familiar. David says something to me, but I can't seem to follow what he is saying. My mind slides away. I look at Martha's mouth and I want her to kiss me on the cheek the way my Aunt Lucy did.

I'm suddenly in Aunt Lucy's house. I don't know how I got there. It's strange, because when Martha asks me about my relatives, most of the time I can't really remember anything or anyone. But I can see Aunt Lucy, and I can see her kitchen with the flowered curtains and the tea cozy like a chicken and the yellow placemats. Aunt Lucy is making a huge cake. She gives me the frosting spoon to lick. I ask if I can live with her forever.

I can't remember what she answers. Her eyes are very sad. They are blue, like David's eyes. I can't see her eyes. I can see David's. He's looking at me, watching me, and so is Martha. They are waiting for something. "Oh," I say. "Hi." Martha looks worried. "I'm okay," I say. "I was just thinking of something, but I don't know what it was now." My voice sounds strange, as if I was talking in a tunnel. I wish I could have stayed wherever it was I went. I wish I could get myself back there.

"Are you feeling sad?" Martha asks.

"No," I say, surprised. I look at David. He has tears in his eyes. I wish I could feel something. Most of the time now it's like this. I can't feel anything. I can't remember things. I can't think clearly.

Lee seems to be moving into an almost psychotic state. This is not unusual for survivors of trauma, but it is not a permanent psychosis. When she was "floating on the ceiling," she was in a dissociative state. She was invoking her childhood skills of dissociation in the face of returning memories, achieving numbness and constricted emotions as a form of self-protection.

The abused or neglected child has a well-documented capacity to remove herself from being consciously present during traumatic episodes. Again and again, formerly abused children recall how they would "leave their bodies" and watch themselves during unbearable events. This is called "depersonalization" or "derealization" in clinical terminology. It is an adaptive, self-protective capacity that all people have that allows for effective functioning in the face of crisis or extreme danger. So, too, the TRS woman uses this defense mechanism, especially when she is engaged in self-harmful activities. She may also use this capacity to escape being fully present during seemingly nondistressing social interactions that have some hidden terror for her.

Identity Disturbance and Fragmentation

Everyone has the sense of having a unique identity, different from that of anyone else. We call this identity our "personality" or "self." Some people have a stronger or more cohesive sense of self. Some like to think of themselves as relatively simple, uncomplicated personalities: "what you see is what you get." Others see themselves as more complicated, changeable, or difficult to know.

Women, especially survivors of childhood trauma, are generally less likely to have a strong, cohesive sense of self than men. Most women, and TRS women in particular, feel that parts of themselves do not fit together. The TRS woman often feels as if she is not only one self; she has only a vague sense of who she is or how she is seen by others.

The TRS woman may be viewed by others as unusually complicated, confusing, or changeable. Whether these perceptions are communicated directly to the woman or are observations made about her, the variability with which parts of her self emerge can be problematic in ongoing relationships.

Lee is like many survivors of severe abuse or neglect, which virtually reshapes the child's sense of self. Lee split off the terrifying parts of her abusive mother and the intolerable emotions engendered by the trauma. She created distinctly separate aspects of herself. In extreme cases, these parts may become a cast of characters: the "alters" of Multiple Personality Disorder (MPD). (This and other clinical descriptions and diagnoses will be discussed more fully in chapter 6.) Although Lee is not quite in the category of MPD as it is usually described, she is close to that state. She is almost completely separated from her adult self when she goes into memories from childhood. When she "floats up to the ceiling" while in therapy, she is not really within the boundaries of that self who is sitting with Martha and David. When she is gripped by childhood memories, her voice sounds very high and young, not at all like her normal adult voice. Her face looks like a child's. And when she cries, it is the sound of a young child.

Lee's definition of who she is and who she was depends on other people's definitions of her. In childhood, she was defined by her family as a good girl, a pretty little girl, a sweet girl. As an adult, she turns to David to define her. In her ten years of therapy, she has colluded with her therapist in adopting the therapist's picture of her. Deep inside, Lee feels the panic of believing that she does not really exist except as defined by the needs and wishes of others. Often she finds herself desperately trying to control some aspect of her life in response to her growing panic that she is losing her self.

The splitting or fragmentation of self is a central feature of the TRS woman's profile. It can range from a relatively mild experience of feeling unlike one's "real" self to the frightening experience that one's body houses many selves. In true Multiple Personality Disorder, the fragmentation is so deep and chronic that the various parts of the self, the alters, are split off from each other to the extent that they may be unaware of one another. Most TRS women, however, do not have an entire cast of separate, well-developed personalities within themselves. It is more likely that the TRS woman is aware and partially in control of the separate parts of herself, but is unable to understand or accept how these often conflicting parts fit together.

For the abused child, the most common experience of fragmentation is the feeling of having a "good" self and a "bad" self. The good self is mystified or horrified by, or sometimes just disconnected from, the bad self. The TRS woman retains this differentiation of self, and it is the bad self that commits acts of self-injury, acts out sexually, or avoids close contact.

The concept of the child identifying with and internalizing the aggressor has its roots in early psychoanalytic theory (Ferenczi, 1932). It also is part of various object relations theories, including the psychiatrist W. R. D. Fairbairn's concept of the internal saboteur (Fairbairn, 1952). In psychoanalytic terms, this means that the child, rather than tolerating "badness" in the omnipotent parent, takes in the badness and incorporates it as part of the self. This splitting allows the parent to be all "good." In the best-known writings about Borderline Personality Disorder by the psychiatrist Otto Kernberg and others, splitting is a hallmark of the borderline.

There is controversy about whether the fragmentation we see in children and adults who have been abused is an exaggeration of the "normal" development described in objects relations theory ("splitting," as described by Kernberg, Fairbairn, and others) or whether it is a dissociative defense triggered by the abuse. Also, controversy continues among clinicians and theoreticians as to whether there is a sharp distinction between Borderline Personality Disorder and Multiple Personality Disorder. Often in this debate, the key distinction is between the splitting of the borderline personality and the dissociation of the multiple personality. The researcher Colin Ross, known for his work on the treatment of Multiple Personality Disorder, uses the concept of "splitting" synonymously with "dissociation" when describing victims of trauma (Ross et al., 1990). Ross has a broad definition of dissociation, referring to a continuum of mental processes defined by a failure to make normal associations.

The psychiatrist Frank Putnam, one of the foremost authorities on dissociation and the etiology and treatment of Multiple Personality Disorder, talks about the far-reaching effects of fragmentation and dissociation on the abused child's developmental process (Putnam, 1989): developmental tasks, such as the process of integrating parts of the self or the acquisition of control over emotional responses, are disrupted. The developmental milestones that a child should be helped to achieve through dependable, loving relationships with caregivers are unachievable for the traumatized child. The primary task for such a child is to escape from the trauma, which she does by dissociating.

According to the psychiatrist Richard Kluft (1993), alter personalities in MPD can sometimes be recognized as manifestations of the original abuser. These personalities, sometimes referred to as Internal Persecutors, can wreak havoc in the MPD's life and may inflict serious bodily injury in attempting to harm or kill other personalities. Kluft names common types of alters: Cross-Gender, Promiscuous, Administrator, and Obsessive-Compulsive (the latter two alters can be quite competent professionally and are the ones typically seen by coworkers). There are also Protector and Helper personalities to counteract the toxicity of the internal persecutors. Other alters might include substance abusers and anesthetic or analgesic personalities.

While we see all of these personality aspects in the TRS woman, they are not usually as split off and separated from each other as in the true multiple personality. Nonetheless, there is much to be learned from the emerging research on Multiple Personality Disorder that would help us understand the fragmentation of the TRS woman.

Gender Identification

Another aspect of severe childhood trauma affecting the experience of self is complicated gender identification. Gender identification difficulty can be traced to the discomfort a trauma survivor may feel in identifying with her mother. Whether or not the TRS woman was abused in some way by her mother, she almost certainly felt betrayed and unprotected by her. She may have grown up perceiving her mother as intrusive, invasive, punitive, or even murderous, or she may have seen her mother as weak, sick, incompetent, or powerless. Neither portrait is a pretty one. The daughter grows up either trying desperately to be as different as possible from her mother or believing that there is no other way to be a woman.

A TRS woman may follow in her mother's footsteps, loyally and hopelessly adhering to the "woman as doormat" role. She presents a hyperfeminine self, totally submissive, passive, self-effacing. She feels, looks, and sounds helpless and is often as ineffectual as her own mother was. The woman who chooses this role may hurt herself by overeating to the point of obesity or drinking herself into a quiet stupor. On the other hand, she may use a mood-altering activity such as drinking to unleash her rage. When she is sober once more, she is apologetic and often finds it hard to believe she has been verbally or physically abusive to others. The hyperfeminine woman may also engage in various forms of well-concealed self-mutilation. Bulimia is a favorite self-abusive behavior for the hyperfeminine woman; she can hide this behavior well, so her facade of being pleasant, attractive, and "normal" remains impenetrable.

Nancy was trying to outrun age, to be the perfect child who still belonged to her grandmother, the child created in her family's image of who she should always be. Nancy's ways of hurting herself—surgeries, diets, and pills—were influenced by her anxious attempts at hyperfemininity. Because there were poor boundaries between herself and her grandmother during childhood, and because she tried to be the "pretty little angel" that her grandmother demanded, Nancy had a very confused sense of how to be a mature woman.

As a child, Nancy was not allowed to assert her own definition of self: her child's body, her own preferences, fears, likes, and dislikes. Instead, she took on her grandmother's body issues, wishes, and preferences. Her parents were mythical figures, off on their travels or on their way to work or a party. In trying to become someone who could turn their indifference into attention, Nancy took on an identity that was impossible to sustain. Her TRS patterns in adult life revolved around her attempts to achieve the American ideals of femininity: a perfect and eternally youthful body that is both slender and firm, flawless skin, bright and glossy hair, eyes without age lines, and a dazzling smile. Never knowing who she really was, Nancy was frantic in her commitment to achieve a hyperfeminine perfection. She was trying to remain "Gram's and Daddy's pretty little angel," although she was a woman approaching fifty and her grandmother had been dead for more than thirty years.

Nancy's reactions and behaviors may be more extreme than some, but she epitomizes the TRS woman who exaggerates her femininity in a desperate attempt to be someone's angel: all "sugar" without the "spice" of an emotion such as anger. The various parts of Nancy include the Victim and the Nonprotecting Bystander, as well as the outer shell of perfection and the buried anger. The angry part of her was so unacceptable to the "pretty angel" self that she had to split it off. The angry, raging, and abusive persona failed to measure up to traditional feminine standards of sweetness and tranquillity, and certainly would not have been responded to favorably when she was a child. Nancy became conscious of the way she was splitting off a central part of herself only after she began to scrutinize her family stories in therapy.

The converse of Nancy is the woman who rejects the more feminine way of being a woman and takes on a more powerful, sometimes more masculine or androgynous style. A variation on this theme is the woman who presents herself as extremely sexual in the "tough broad" tradition. The most obvious example of this personality in today's popular culture is the pop idol Madonna. She has created an image for herself that is as gorgeous and voluptuous as Marilyn Monroe's, but with a tough, provocative edge. Madonna is all-powerful in her image as sexual predator.

While the TRS woman who chooses a "tough" or androgynous persona may seem to have escaped the negative legacy of her mother's helplessness, she will have other problems. Powerful, nonsubmissive women are often perceived as aloof, condescending, unapproachable, unfeminine (which can be translated as castrating or "man-hating"), and "unnatural." Thus, the woman who is already isolated by virtue of her secrecy, shame, and addictive behavior is even more the social outcast.

Another problem of gender identification may show up in the woman who takes on the characteristics of her abuser, whether this was a male or female adult. She may be cruel to her own children, her partner, friends, lovers, employees, or colleagues. Her symptom is most often alcohol or drug abuse. In many cases, the alcohol or drug acts as a disinhibitor; the part of her mind that usually controls the degree of unacceptable behavior stops working and her abusiveness escalates. She is hated and feared by many of those who live, work, and otherwise interact with her. She is also the hardest to reach for those who try to help.

Laura's story illustrates these problems of the fragmented self and the confusion in gender identity. Was she a male warrior figure, invincible and cruel like her father? Could she accept herself as female without experiencing this identity as powerless, the Victim, the helpless Nonprotecting Bystander mother?

Laura talked about these struggles six months after beginning therapy.

I can't do it. I can't give up the running, the pounding my head with my fists, the way I test my courage by calling them names and then running from them if they come after me.

My therapist keeps talking about "our relationship." Yeah, right. What relationship? She even has the stupid nerve to ask if I feel sad or lonely or abandoned if we miss our session. I'm not a child and she's not my mother. I find her insulting.

I can't stand women like her. She's not a wimp or anything. In fact, she's not really pretty or feminine. I mean, she doesn't wear makeup or dress up like some of the others I see coming in and out of the waiting room. But she's nothing like me either.

For some reason I can't help liking her voice. It's very warm and soothing. I like to imagine going to sleep listening to her talk because her voice is like a soft blanket. But I never would let her know I think about this. I don't want to like her, I don't want her to be my mother, I don't want to need her.

I certainly don't want to be like her. I like how strong and thin my body is. I hate her breasts. I hate her softness.

She asks me if I love my mother and what I think about her. Of course I love my mother. I took a hundred beatings myself just to keep him off of her. I let him do stuff to me so he wouldn't do it to her or to my little sister or brother. What do I think about my mother? I think she lost more than I did because she tried to love him. She was weak, trapped just like I was.

My therapist and my mother are sort of alike in some ways, but they're also totally different. I wonder if anyone ever beat up my therapist? I wonder how she could protect herself? I bet she couldn't. I wonder if she likes me? I don't care, but I wonder. Sometimes I think she does like me. That totally freaks me out. I can't stand the thought.

Anyhow, it doesn't really matter. I'm not going to keep coming to see her anymore because it's not helping.

Laura's ambivalence about me was complex. She clearly disavowed any attachment and refused to identify with me. She was afraid to be "soft" and yet she clearly longed for some form of maternal comforting. Her warrior persona kept her from accepting any kind of female vulnerability. She was afraid of any kind of attention from me or longing aroused by me, and her response was often expressed as panicky revulsion:

My therapist makes me furious. She says I'm being my father, beating up on myself. She even dares to say that I am loyal to my father and that I am still in a relationship with him. In my heart. No way. She's a fool.

Besides, I really don't think I have a heart. I'm not soft like that. I don't even know what the word *love* is supposed to mean.

Laura's mother had been so miserably abused and disempowered that Laura could not identify with her, even minimally. The development of trust and affection in later stages of therapy was important. It offered Laura the possibility of accepting herself as female through the process of attachment to me. She gradually began to understand that soft did not mean weak, and that "having a heart" would not necessarily mean that she would be victimized like her mother was. Through the successful development of positive relationships with women, whether therapists or peers, TRS women can begin to incorporate positive aspects of female identity as a new part of the healing self.

Laura's voice haunts me still as I think about the challenge for the TRS woman to tolerate trust and genuine affection in any kind of relationship.

The Triadic Self

Fragmentation of the self or personality is the traumatized child's means of protecting herself by dissociating, and it is also the foundation of the TRS woman's failure to protect herself. Fragmentation is the most distinct feature by which the TRS woman can be distinguished from other trauma victims, the most significant way she is different from women whose substance abuse or eating disorders are treatable through more direct, symptom-focused approaches such as twelve-step programs. It was my discovery of a nonprotective pattern of fragmentation in the women I was treating for addictions, eating disorders, and compulsive self-injury that led to my growing awareness of the configuration I eventually named the Triadic Self.

For a long time I did not fully understand how pervasive this configuration was among my female clients suffering from chronic addictions, eating disorders, excesses of dieting and cosmetic surgeries, or self-mutilation. Like most medical and mental health professionals, I viewed each cluster of problems as different, requiring separate treatment needs and skills. I referred alcoholics and drug abusers to chemical dependency programs and hospitals and women with eating disorders to groups and hospitals specializing in such problems. I gave feminist lectures to women who dieted and exercised excessively about society's pressure for women to be forever thin and glamorous. I hospitalized women who cut and burned themselves, hoping that the hospital staff would contain their behavior.

I also worked with most of these women on their histories of childhood abuse and neglect, helping them to uncover their buried memories and to experience a supportive therapy relationship. Some of them walked off into the sunset of total recovery, but many did not. I puzzled over the high rate of relapse, not only among my clients but in similar client populations seen by my colleagues as well. We were seasoned clinicians. We followed the rules for treating incest survivors, addicts, alcoholics, borderlines, and MPDs. What were we missing?

What I began to see in all these women was a personality configuration similar to Multiple Personality Disorder, but much less extreme. I started to examine what I perceived as a common personality fragmentation in all the different clusters of clients with high relapse rates, and recognized a reenactment of the original trauma through their process of self-abuse. The reenactment was identifiable as three parts of the self locked in a self-destructive performance that seemed unstoppable: the Victim weakly protesting the harmful behavior, the Abuser inflicting the harm, and the Nonprotecting Bystander who could do nothing to stop the cycle. I named this form of dissociative fragmentation the Triadic Self.

The Triadic Self reflects the relational patterns these women experienced in childhood as a central part of the trauma. The Abuser within, the Victim with, and the Nonprotecting Bystander within become a familiar part of the child's daily life. The child can't ask for help or even describe this experience of fragmentation, because she has no way of understanding that this is not a "normal" way of being. Unless she is so severely traumatized that her inner mental fragmentation becomes flagrantly psychotic, she may appear relatively "normal" to others.

When this child continues the pattern of fragmentation into adulthood, she repeats the trauma over and over. Self-harmful patterns of behavior are reenactments of harmful relationships. Through self-abusive behaviors like drug and alcohol abuse, eating disorders, and self-mutilation, the TRS woman reenacts the child's relationships with the abusive and nonprotecting adults.

The absence of self-protective capacities is critical in this process. In childhood, the trauma victim was afforded no consistent protection. Therefore, there was no way she could learn how to keep herself safe. She developed an internalized Abuser and an internalized Nonprotecting Bystander as a way to incorporate the "bad" parts of her caretakers, which were unbearable for the child to perceive in these all-powerful adults, but tolerable if she learned to perceive them as parts of herself.

She had no way to internalize a Protective Presence because that quality was missing in her adult caretakers. There was no supply of protective nurturance to take from these adults and incorporate as part of herself.

I owe a special debt to my client Laura, who was the first to help me discover the Triadic Self. Through telling her story of childhood trauma, Laura signaled to me the hidden parts of herself. The issue of complex loyalty was prominent in this case. Although Laura spoke of her father with scorn and rage, it became increasingly clear in our work that she had internalized her relationship with him to such an extent that his "voice" was often indistinguishable from hers. For example, he had convinced her that he was teaching her to be an invincible warrior through the vehicle of his sadistic behavior. As an adult, she had developed a belief that only through her self-inflicted torture could she remain safe or inviolable. His voice became the voice of this isolated young woman who feared closeness of any sort. Laura had developed a powerful and quite split-off part of herself, the internalized Abuser. By letting me get close enough to her to hear her painful story, she had broken his rule. She therefore punished herself through increasingly dangerous self-abusive behavior.

Laura's disclosures reenacted the central issue of her past failures to gain help or protection from those in parental or authority roles. I now think of this internalized part of Laura as the Nonprotecting Bystander, and I, too, was in that role when I listened to her story without knowing how to help empower her against the pain. Gradually I began the process of learning which parts of Laura represented the internalized Abuser, which was the Nonprotecting Bystander, and the Victim. Most important, I began to understand how essential it was for me not to fall into the role of the Nonprotecting Bystander myself.

Laura was frequently angry at me in sessions, especially when I interfered with her systematic plan for regurgitating her incest story. She could not understand why I kept getting in the way of her compulsive recitation. For quite a long time, we met in an atmosphere of mutual discomfort, combatants in a life-and-death struggle. Laura did not trust me because she perceived me as afraid to hear her story. I was uncomfortable with Laura because she seemed so provocatively out of control in her episodes of self-destructive behavior. She was also disturbing because she seemed so completely detached from both her behavior and her abuse history. Neither of us felt understood or cared for by the other.

The significant turning point in my work with Laura came one day when she was talking about her latest savaging of her body. I daringly suggested that she was doing her father's work for him. Laura was outraged. I persisted, pointing out that her father had taught his little girl that he was hurting her to make her strong, to make her a warrior. As an adult woman, she claimed she had to keep testing and strengthening herself by inflicting pain and confronting danger. She finally acknowledged that this might be a useful idea. Laura and I were then able to work toward identifying the fragmented parts of her personality and slowly integrating them in a healthier way.

There were several important lessons for me in this work with Laura. One was that I could inadvertently step into the role of Nonprotecting Bystander. Equally important was my growing recognition that the "wounded warrior within" had complicated allegiances; Laura, like other women who characterize the abuser as only "bad," had not been allowed to explore the complexities of her identification with and attachment to this central figure in her life. Perhaps the most important lesson that I learned from Laura was that it is not at all simple to stop self-harmful behavior. Even with the best support from twelve-step programs and the most empathic attunement to the client's trauma history, there is an entrenched struggle going on within a TRS woman that blocks traditional treatment approaches. There was a long way to go in working with Laura, even after we learned together how to identify the Triadic Self. Developing a strong enough relationship to nurture the development of an internal Protective Presence was an enormous challenge.

The shattered trust experienced by the abused or neglected child damages her ability to form attachments. She suffers from what van der Kolk (1987) has referred to as a "disorder of hope." Instead of perceiving herself as a whole person, connected to others who admire and love her, she experiences herself in fragmented connection to people. Because she allows only some parts of herself to engage with other people, her perceptions of being fragmented are reinforced in her experience of how others respond to her.

The effect of the fragmented self on relationships is drastic. When there is an absence of clear identity and firm boundaries between self and others, when the self is in pieces, when there is denial and dissociation in how the self reasons and communicates, when there is uncertainty about how to accept being female, relationships are troubled, challenged, or, in extreme cases, nonexistent. Most TRS women find that they are chronically distressed by relationship problems, and they become discouraged when all the advice they get from experts proves unhelpful. Why, they ask, am I stuck in the same old discouraging relationship dance?

The next chapter connects the pervasive war against the body, the role of secrecy, and the failure to self-protect that engenders fragmentation with the problems most TRS women experience in relationships. Through understanding these connections, the relationship problems so many TRS women share begin to make sense. What we can name and understand we can begin to heal.

5

Relationships

Relationships occupy significant background space as well as center stage in how Trauma Reenactment Syndrome gets played out. In the background, they are both the catalyst and the context for the repetition of the Abuser-Victim-Nonprotecting Bystander configuration of self-abuse. In the foreground, relationships become a central vehicle in the TRS woman's life for reenacting the dynamics of abuse and nonprotection, mirroring the dynamics repeated through bodily self-harm.

The symptoms play a dominant role in the TRS woman's relationship patterns. Binge-eating, drinking, drug abuse, starving, purging, and self-mutilation are all behaviors that have a major impact on her relationships. The symptoms serve to regulate distance, pushing people away while at the same time demanding involvement in the form of containment and caretaking. Also, by engaging in relationships that covertly or more openly repeat the dynamics of abuse and nonprotection, the TRS woman remains stuck in a vicious cycle of bodily self-harm and related harmful relationship patterns: the self-harm acts as both a response to and trigger for abusive, nonprotecting relationship dynamics.

TRS women often express disappointment and frustration resulting from childhood relationships as well as the effect of their self-harmful behaviors on current relationships. Karen and June voice several prominent themes familiar to most TRS women and those who know them: fear of abandonment, a longing to be protected, and a preoccupation with deception. I have often noticed an obsessional quality in the TRS woman's approach to relationships, which is not surprising when we think about how she had to organize her relational life as a child beset by danger and insecurity.

KAREN

I don't know what I would do if my friend Ellen gave up on me.

I used to freak out about how much I depended on Rob, my last boyfriend. I'd catch myself thinking about how everything would be okay once I was with him on the weekend. So then of course when I did see him, I'd feel too vulnerable. So I'd get us into a fight and that way I could push him away. My therapist and I talk about this a lot lately, about how I push people away because I'm so afraid to depend on them and afraid they'll abandon me. It's a control thing, I guess.

JUNE

You can't ever really trust anyone. It's sad to say, but it's true. Every man I've trusted has betrayed me. Ma was so religious, but kids weren't part of her religion. She talked about love, but her loving was all for God; it didn't go beyond the church doors as I see it. I used to hear her talk to the priest about what a good mother she tried to be and how she tried so hard to care for her family. And the priest would tell us how fortunate we were to have such a good mother. Then she would smile at us in front of the priest as if she really loved us and we were such a happy family. It was so fake. Two hours later she'd be yelling about how we'd wrinkled our church clothes or not picked up our toys and how miserable she was to have such ungrateful children. Then she'd send us to our rooms. No dinner.

You have to be really careful around people. They say that they love you, but it's a lie. You start believing it, that they do care about you, and you usually end up hurt. You have to be really careful about letting people in.

KAREN

I couldn't stop thinking about Rob. But I didn't even really love him. I get just as obsessed sometimes with thinking about my friend at work and how much I want her approval. But I can't be honest or open with her, so I can't really get close. I hate thinking about anyone all the time, whether I love or hate them or just want them to like me. I can't risk getting close to anyone because then I'll just get obsessed with them and it ruins everything.

Please love me. Please leave me alone.

JUNE

Each one of the guys I've loved, I've turned to him for a little kindness, a hope that he would cherish me and honor me and protect me. I guess I keep looking for some guy who is kind of old-fashioned and gallant, a gentleman. I read about them in romance books, and I keep hoping that one will turn up sooner or later. But in some ways I can't stand the idea of a guy always around, trying to help me, take care of me. Like Roy. I had to let him go because he got on my nerves. He was a sweet guy when he wasn't drinking, and he was great in the sack too, but he just drove me crazy with all of his interference in how I do things. He wanted to take my boys in hand, to help me out, you know? But I said no way.

KAREN

This is going to sound really silly, but I like to imagine my therapist taking me home with her to the nice cozy house in the woods I imagine is hers. And she would fix me hot soup and homemade bread, and then we would sit by the fireplace and she would hum to me and stroke my hair. Then I'd go to bed and she'd come into the room and she'd tuck me in under a beautiful soft quilt and sing me a lullaby. Then I'd wake up in the morning and it would be sunny and warm in her kitchen. That would be heaven. But of course it's just a fantasy. Even if she would offer it, there's no way I could let her be that kind of mother to me. I couldn't stand it, really.

Relationship dynamics can set off the symptomatic behavior waiting to happen inside the TRS woman. But just as the relationship affects the symptoms, symptoms affect the relationship. It is important to understand how this cycle is experienced by each person in the relationship. Lee and her husband, David, have very different ideas about how their relationship and Lee's self-harmful behavior are connected. After Lee's third serious episode of cutting, she and David went together to talk to her therapist, Martha:

DAVID: I am trying hard to understand Lee's behavior, but I just can't. Maybe if it didn't scare me so much I could tolerate it, but I can't understand it. I get scared, frustrated, because I can't make sense of it. I know she can't understand it herself. That is what I keep thinking. (To Lee) I think that it happened because I was feeling so close to you and I told you how much I loved you. So then you felt pressured by me. Was that what made you do it?

LEE: David, how could you think that your loving me could make me hurt myself?

MARTHA: What I'm guessing is that you felt guilty about not feeling sexual and maybe you cut yourself to punish yourself? Certainly you were not trying to punish David.

LEE: (Shaking her head) I had been in pain all that day because of what I dreamed the night before. It was really so weird, because, unlike reality, my mother told me how beautiful I was and how proud she was of me. All day I had been feeling sad because I wished so much that in real life my mother had loved me and been proud of me. David's tenderness made me feel a sudden burst of rage. I needed to cut myself. It was overwhelming.

This episode was understood and described by David, Martha, and Lee in three different ways. In understanding Lee's relationship with David, just as in understanding her relationship with her cutting behavior, it is important to be able to look at the patterns of interaction from several points of view. Otherwise we could oversimplify the cutting episode by blaming David ("You put pressure on Lee, which caused her to cut herself"), or by blaming Lee ("You felt guilty, so you punished yourself"), or even by blaming the internalized Abuser ("My mother hurt me, so my dream about her made me cut myself").

Relationship Challenges and Contradictions

In this chapter, I turn to the challenges the TRS woman faces in relationships with her partners, family, friends, and colleagues. As I noted earlier, there is no single model of how the TRS woman behaves in relationships. Moreover, like everyone else, each TRS woman is usually different in different types of relationships. For example, she may be competent and respected at work but helpless and dependent with friends and lovers.

Despite the variations both among TRS women and within each individual, certain issues frequently appear. The most prominent feature of TRS relationships is the relentless struggle for control. The TRS woman always feels as if her relationships are out of control, and she frantically tries strategies to gain control, even if it means avoiding relationships, destroying them, or fleeing them. Boundaries are also a major problem: for example, the TRS woman may inappropriately confide in her children about intimate activities or, at the other extreme, she may conceal from friends seemingly harmless or somewhat "public" aspects of her life. Another dominant theme is an intense longing for connection coupled with an equally intense mistrust of closeness. Other common relational difficulties include the invalidation or devaluation of the self, an inability to distinguish between personal needs and the needs of others, and difficulty with interpersonal conflict. These problems may be more or less prominent in each of the TRS woman's relationships.

In keeping with the variety of TRS symptoms, there is a wide range of relational "styles" among TRS women. Some are quiet and withdrawn and do not strongly engage in any of their relationships. Others are more extroverted and flamboyant. The more dramatic TRS woman is often referred to, both fondly and disparagingly, as "a real charac-

ter." Such women can be provocative, engaging in potentially enraging
behavior that serves to keep others at a distance or sorely tests
their commitment to her. She has an "operatic" world view and self-
presentation; events, behaviors, and conversations can all be larger
than life, so dramatic that they seem distorted. Sometimes this flamboyant style is entertaining, albeit exhausting. Still other TRS women are
characterized by intense depression, sullen withdrawal, or exaggerated
physical complaints. Their interactional style is less engaging and keeps
others as far away as possible.

Startling or mysterious mood swings are a problem for the TRS
woman. Although related to her self-harmful behavior, these moods
may be triggered by dynamics imperceptible to the observer. The TRS
woman herself may be mystified by these sudden shifts, which serve to
push others away, leaving her feeling abandoned or punished and thus
susceptible to active self-harmful behavior. The effect of this extreme
range of moods and behaviors on other people runs the gamut from
exasperated withdrawal to being helplessly drawn in or resentfully
engaged. The partner, friend, coworker, or family member experiences
a profound loss of control, which is exactly how the TRS woman herself felt as a child and how she still often feels.

The Need for Control

I have already described how the TRS patterns of self-harmful activity
reflect the need for control. This need often drives the TRS woman's
daily activities as well. For example, she may clean compulsively.
Always striving for control may make her unable to enjoy leisure activities or to function well at work. It is often at the root of her problems
with her children, other family members, and friends. It pervades her
efforts to seek help from professionals and peers, which she then rejects.

In the struggles around control in relationships, Trauma Reenactment Syndrome creates a generalizable pattern in which the TRS
woman alternates between avoiding social contact and then frantically
clinging to partners, friends, family members, and sometimes colleagues. The results of this pattern are horribly uncomfortable for her.
She feels unhappy and anxious when alone, but then equally unhappy
and anxious when with others. She endures seemingly endless cycles of
restlessness and discomfort. This pattern is an important part of her
inability to establish or maintain intimacy.

Bette Midler, playing the role of Janis Joplin in the movie *The Rose*, pushes everyone away and then cries out in a moment of desperate, lonely intoxication, "Where is everybody?" The TRS victim's ambivalence about her need for nurturance and her need to control creates a contradictory communication to all those involved with her: "Where is everybody?" and "Why don't they leave me alone!" This rapid shift between asking for help and then rejecting it exhausts others. Both personal and professional caretakers withdraw in exasperation. The TRS victim may experience this withdrawal as rejection, reinforcing her mistrust of relationships, and so the cycle escalates.

Extreme reactivity marks the TRS woman's behavior and is often a clue to her history of abuse. Because she has experienced relationships as both unpredictable and unsafe, she is quick to imagine snubs and criticisms. She may question the motives of everyone around her. She is also hypervigilant, a clinical term used to describe anyone who is always on guard, always watchful, quick to perceive any incipient danger, whether real or imagined.

KAREN, AS A CHILD

I always sleep on the floor of my room, not in my bed. I wake up if someone comes in my room. I keep my light on even though I get punished. I need to see if everything is where I put it when I went to sleep. My teddy has to be right next to me, just like this. If I move him, something will happen.

I know how to make Mommy's coffee for her just right in the morning. I know if she's going to be nice or mad by how she takes the cup from me when I bring it to her in bed. I know it's very important to be neat and clean and brush my hair before I bring her the coffee. I know how much Mommy loves me. That's why I have to do things right.

I know if Mommy is mad at Daddy by how she gets ready for him to come home at night. If she waits and has her first drink with him, she's not mad. If she tells me to make her a drink before he comes home, I know they'll fight. It's my fault they fight, but I can't figure out what I do wrong.

I am in the first grade. I'm always a very good girl at school.

My teacher says I'm trying to be too good. She says, "Go have fun, Karen," but I don't know how to do that.

Going to Extremes

Boundaries are problematic in many different ways for TRS women. The definition of the self in relationships is affected by both the weakness and rigidity of their boundaries. Karen offers a good example of the problem with rigid boundaries:

> My friend at work, Julia, keeps talking to me about her AA meetings. She tells me at lunch all about how she used to get high, how screwed up her life was. She seems so comfortable talking to me about this stuff. Julia even talks about really embarrassing moments like when she was still married and she would be so high she would get into sexual situations with other guys.
>
> Then there is Alice, another one of the girls I eat lunch with at the hospital. She'll talk about her period or tell funny stories about birth control and what happened with some guy she's seeing. I just can't get over being amazed by what these other nurses talk about so openly. I feel shocked, but sometimes I also envy them.
>
> They give me a real hard time about what a clam I am. "Hey, Karen," Julia says, "why are you holding out on us? I know you're seeing someone, so what's going on?"
>
> I feel angry and also really scared when they tease me about this. I know I'm secretive, but I just can't trust anyone enough to be different.

When she first began therapy with me, Karen was locked inside of herself, her armor a pleasant and sociable exterior. For example, when I asked standard questions about where she lived, who she lived with, and what her friendships were like, she hesitated before answering. Her answers were very brief and told me little about her.

Karen was also extremely reluctant to share any information with me about her intimate life. I asked her if she was dating, if she was sexually active, and if she had any sexual issues. She finally told me that she was angry because I seemed to feel entitled to such personal information. When I explained that these were questions I often asked when getting to know a new client who presented relationship problems as the reason for entering therapy, she was clearly astonished that anyone would answer such questions.

As I got to know Karen better, I learned that she was such an intensely private person that even her closest friend, Ellen, knew very little about her intimate relationships. Although Karen professed a willingness to try to share more of herself with Ellen, she had a difficult time doing so.

Because of rigid personal boundaries, Karen and other TRS women experience chronic loneliness and a sense of being both different from others and invisible. It is therefore logical that they also feel unloved and unlovable.

Some TRS women manifest rigid boundary problems in an extreme avoidance of normal social or physical contact. One of my clients left her house only to go food shopping or to a weekly twelve-step meeting. She could not go to work because she felt unsafe in any situation that involved flexible social contact. She also stopped seeing her friends and would not answer the telephone or the doorbell. Her contact was limited to a noncommunicative relationship with her husband, who worked an afternoon/evening shift, and her eighteen-year-old son, who was at work or with his girlfriend most of the time. The only reason this woman could tolerate her weekly AlAnon meeting was because it was highly structured and therefore predictable. She was not really able to make the program work for her, however, because she could not make use of the essential ongoing social support outside of meetings. She was stuck, refusing to go to additional twelve-step groups because that would mean going to a new place and meeting new people.

This kind of pattern, when it becomes severe enough to render the person dysfunctional, is called "agoraphobia," or fear of open spaces. Although it is considered a serious disorder in its own right, it is one of many possible symptoms of Trauma Reenactment Syndrome. In extreme cases, an agoraphobic is completely unable to leave her home under any condition. Mental health professionals often treat agoraphobia as an anxiety disorder, using behavioral conditioning and medication. When I encounter it in TRS women, I approach it as part of an understandable response to trauma, and I attend to the client's need to develop the capacity for relational attachment.

June's relational patterns represent the other extreme of boundary problems: loose or diffuse boundaries. Her personal boundaries are not only diffuse, but unpredictable. One day she may scream if her daughter comes into the bedroom without asking permission (even though the door is almost always open), and another day she will leave the bathroom door open when she is in the shower and tell her daughter, or even her teenage son, an intimate sexual episode while she dries off, fully visible through the open door.

Nancy manifests inappropriate boundaries in another way. She is careless, in fact indifferent, in regard to divulging personal details about her clients at the travel agency. When one client complained that Nancy had chatted with another about the financial and personal details of his trip, Nancy was genuinely bewildered by his outrage.

Love

Related to the problem of underinvolvement or overinvolvement in relationships is the inability to trust. Because of her childhood experience of violated trust, the TRS woman has difficulty trusting others. Coupled with this lack of trust is an equally powerful wish for protection. This creates a pattern of eliciting help and then rejecting it, asking for closeness and then destroying the longed-for relationship. Although the woman herself may initiate the breakup, she is paradoxically consumed by her fear of being abandoned.

Fearing abandonment becomes so habitual for the TRS woman that she organizes her life around the fear. There are two usual ways by which she can do so. One is to be willing to do anything required to hang on to the relationship, even if it is overwhelmingly masochistic. The other is to be the one who does the abandoning, or at least provokes it, so that it will not be done to her.

Both June and Karen represent the latter choice in their relationship patterns. Karen's style is more easily identifiable. She begins relationships and then suddenly breaks them off. Her overt reason for leaving is generally that she becomes extremely critical of the other person and can no longer tolerate anything about him or her. The covert reality is that she cannot endure the possibility of being vulnerable to abandonment, so she acts to preempt that potential outcome.

June's pattern is more confusing. Although she appears at times to behave like a doormat, allowing anyone and everyone to invade her space, time, and thoughts, she uses her wild drinking and drugging episodes to disengage from loved ones. By pushing people away in moments of drunken belligerence, she creates a safe distance and keeps relationships from becoming close enough to hurt her.

Devaluation of the Self

Because of their perpetual self-blaming, TRS women see themselves as the locus of responsibility in relationships, although that sense of responsibility is passive. It is a repeat of the childhood voice: "It's all my fault, but I'm trying really hard and I can't figure out what I'm doing wrong." Bewilderment and helplessness shadow every description of another failed relationship, and even when the TRS woman blames someone else, she is always perplexed by her feelings of inadequacy.

Although many women feel responsible for the quality of their relationships and blame themselves if a relationship fails, the scenario is amplified for TRS women. The self-harming cycle makes the TRS woman feel disgusted and angry with herself. She imagines, or knows firsthand, that her self-harming behavior will be viewed negatively by others. She incorporates what she perceives to be their censure or revulsion and begins to judge herself negatively, creating greater distance between herself and others and simultaneously magnifying her angry disgust toward herself. The atmosphere around her becomes increasingly difficult for others to penetrate, and so her solitude confirms her feelings of being unlovable and unacceptable.

The relationships of TRS women are often permeated with shame and fears of humiliation. The primacy of shame in relationships begins in childhood. Many writers in the mental health field have addressed the transmission of shame from parent to child, but the psychotherapist Sebern Fisher (1985) has written an especially lucid article about the process of transmission when the child's mother is filled with shame because she was abused, unloved, or neglected in childhood. Shame creates distance and loneliness, so the shame-bound mother is often very isolated emotionally, even if she is surrounded by other people. Her child becomes her great hope to feel connected, loved, and cherished. Unfortunately, because the mother cannot let go of the shame, it gets split off and located within the child. Thus, the child experiences herself as "bad" and takes on a shame identity.

The situation is far worse if the mother also abuses or neglects her child. The shame dynamics are then amplified. A child like Lee is filled with shame and self-blame, believing that she should understand why her "badness" is making her mother so unhappy and angry. The child who has been abused by someone other than her mother may also incorporate shame dynamics from the mother, who is ashamed for not protecting her child, or from the abusive adult, for example, a father who abuses his child and is filled with shame because of his behavior. The child makes this shame a permanent part of herself and becomes a shame-bound adult.

Because the TRS woman feels ashamed, she may feel a general sense of being humiliated in her relationships, especially if she is in a vulnerable position. She is more likely to feel humiliated in her work relationships or in an intimate relationship if she is in a clearly less powerful role.

The self-abusive behavior is a powerful trigger to activate shame and humiliation. When the TRS woman engages in self-harm, she is wracked by intense shame that serves to disconnect her from others, deepening her isolation. Because women are socialized to be centrally involved in relationships and even to be defined by them, it is doubly shameful to feel isolated and disconnected.

As a child, Lee was obviously made to feel pervasive shame, and she still carries her mother's shaming voice and part of her mother's own shame that was passed on to her. Lee is ashamed about being disconnected from others, especially David, and, most of all, ashamed about her acts of self-injury. Coupled with the shame are feelings of humiliation. As Lee began to remember more of the sadistic childhood abuse she suffered, her experience of humiliation was vividly recalled. It was also reenacted when she confessed her self-abuse to David and her therapist.

People who devalue themselves do not consider their ideas, thoughts, comments, wishes, or questions to be legitimate or worthy of other people's attention. TRS women frequently portray themselves to others in a negative light, coming across as apologetic and belittling their accomplishments in relation to other people's.

In my own recovery process, I became increasingly aware of how many times "I'm sorry" entered my conversation. Despite being well evaluated in my workshop presentations, public speeches, and class-room lectures, I persisted in the belief that I was really not very smart and therefore an impostor, and I expected to be exposed at any moment, like the naked monarch in "The Emperor's New Clothes." Minimizing my accomplishments and apologizing caused various rela-tionship disappointments and rifts. Giving the message that I didn't have much to offer and apologizing for everything I did or said created discomfort in others. Either they had to keep reassuring me, which put them in an anxious state of mind, or they would perceive a subtle rejec-tion, a kind of distancing, which would cause them to keep more sepa-rate from me than I really wished. Furthermore, I remained stuck in the isolation of my own self-critical fortress.

In looking back over the journey I took to move beyond that isola-tion, I realize that the support to do so had been offered to me over and over; I just could not hear it. It took the love of my friends, partner, colleagues, and therapists to open my eyes to what was right there. For many TRS women, being open to such love and validation is one of the last steps in the recovery process.

The Needs of Others

TRS women vary greatly in their ability to balance their own needs and those of others. Their symptomatic activities play a significant role in how this balance is tipped. For example, drinkers or drug abusers are often literally unable to meet the needs of others. Other TRS women like Nancy or Laura have difficulty perceiving or responding to the needs of others because they were not given the opportunity to develop that capacity in childhood. Still other TRS women—often those with eating disorders or other symptoms that do not render them completely unavailable—have trouble extricating themselves from the needs of others. Whether the women in this latter group are relating to partners, friends, family members, or coworkers, they are compelled by their need to be needed. A woman like June, having little awareness of her own needs, may work to induce dependency in other people because she needs so desperately to be a caretaker. As a partner or mother, she is prone to be smothering, giving of herself whether the recipient wants it or likes it. When the TRS woman is at the other end of the spectrum, she is a neglectful mother. If she is not attuned to the needs of her chil-dren, she is unable to provide adequate nurturance, protection, or enthusiasm, not because she is cold, unloving, or selfish, but because she did not experience having her needs nurtured or protected in childhood.

For TRS women, the failure to distinguish between their own needs and those of others becomes an obstacle to successful relationships. Nancy, for example, is sometimes unaware of the economic differences between herself and her friend Babs, with whom she owns the travel agency. Babs is divorced and has been living on the income generated by the agency. For Nancy, the business is more like a hobby. Because Nancy grew up in a family where she was unable to separate her own needs from her grandmother's, who was her primary caretaker, she is genuinely out of touch with what Babs needs financially, even though she thinks of Babs as her closest friend. Whatever she experiences as her own needs she projects onto others. Consequently, when Babs is hurt and irritated by Nancy's refusal to work enough hours to keep the business profitable, Nancy is mystified by her friend's anger.

Nancy's frantic demands for attention from her many doctors can be seen in the same light. Though less brutally abused than some of the other women in this book, she was scarred by the pervasive invasion of her personal boundaries, physical, mental, and emotional; she was never allowed to have her own needs or perceptions. It is no wonder, then, that she barrages the doctors with her demands until they agree in exasperation to a medication or surgical procedure that is not really necessary or in Nancy's best interests. Her insistence that her perceived needs be instantly accommodated sets her up both to misperceive what her actual needs are and to be exploited by medical personnel who are fed up with her.

Interpersonal Conflict

Conflict is a natural and inevitable part of any significant relationship. Women have historically avoided and feared conflict. Whereas most men are socialized to expect and even sometimes enjoy conflict (in philosophical arguments, sports-related aggression, and "friendly" physical and mental sparring among peers), most women are the opposite. We commonly feel bad if we lose our tempers, get into arguments, or yell at our children. To be a "man" often means having the capacity to fight; for women, fighting is usually considered unladylike or unfeminine.

The problem of women's socialization is compounded by childhood abuse. The TRS woman experienced powerlessness and often hopelessness in her childhood conflictual transactions. She believes that she will never get anything like justice in these types of interactions. How she responds to the social injunctions against conflict, and to the more individual messages she received in childhood, varies from woman to woman over a wide range of anger-related behaviors. She may be prone to sudden bursts of rage that are out of proportion to the triggering event. Or she may repress her anger. She may use constant bickering to avoid more direct and heated confrontations.

"I'm not angry!" snarls the smiling woman through gritted teeth. We have all seen this caricature, in others and in ourselves. For the TRS woman it is no joke. Many believe that they cannot be fully, powerfully angry at others, so they turn the anger inward. Anger, more than any other feeling, is the fuel for self-abusive behavior.

Despite the claim that women have "come a long way" in rebelling against the constraints of ladylike behavior, anger is still deeply unacceptable when expressed by women. When a man raises his voice, curses, or uses or threatens to use physical violence, it is unremarkable, even if (at least in some circles) it is not socially acceptable. When a woman does the same, she sets off deeply negative reactions. She may not be feared as the man is, but she is condemned and subtly shunned in many social settings. When she yells, curses, or hits, she is called a "bitch," a "harpy," a "ball-breaker." The man, it should be noted here, is called a "*son* of a bitch."

By turning their anger against themselves, TRS women comply with family and societal rules about silencing anger and protecting others. Even when the anger is expressed directly—when it has built up and then exploded—it is often ineffective because it is an overreaction to the event that triggered it. More often, the TRS woman's anger remains subterranean: it takes the form of self-abusive behavior.

Anger is problematic in all of the TRS woman's relationships, although it takes various forms. What makes it so deceptive and destructive is that it is often disguised as something else. Anger can easily masquerade as sadness, reluctance, aloofness, or even overcompliance. It affects how the TRS woman distorts her perceptions of herself and how others distort her.

Lee avoids conflict and seems to repress her anger almost completely, savaging her own body instead. It is not surprising that she is unable to connect her self-abusive behavior to rage.

Karen, too, is perceived by others as always remaining calm and

never getting into a conflict with coworkers or patients. As we have
seen, Karen *does* know that she is angry. She experiences herself as
seething with anger but never being able to express it directly. When
Karen and I first began our work together, she could make the connection that her self-abuse was fueled by rage, but she felt helpless to do
anything about it. Her fantasies of inflicting bodily harm on the doctor
at work remained split off from her actual interactions with him. When
she began to express anger directly to him, to coworkers, to friends,
and, finally, to boyfriends, she was well on her way to recovery from
directing rage at herself.

Nancy is most likely to express her conflicts through bickering. She
criticizes her husband, children, friends, and doctors in such a way that
she is often engaged in a defensive mode of communication. Because
bickering is so much a part of Nancy's daily life, she can easily avoid a
more profound and productive level of conflict without ever noticing.
Many people report that they are frequently irritated by Nancy, but no
one ever really engages in significant conflict with her.

When I first knew June and Laura, they were both likely to express
rage and engage in conflict. Unfortunately, they were no more successful in their efforts than the conflict-avoidant TRS women. Laura's style
was to move through life in a cloud of perceptible rage. Almost everyone, no matter how casual the relationship, could feel Laura's anger,
even though they were generally mystified as to what might have war-
ranted it. Laura's rage worked like a magic cloak of noxious fumes to
keep everyone at a distance. When people tried to reach out to her, they
were coldly rebuffed. Whatever conflicts could have been worked
through and resolved simply vanished, along with the many people
who kept a wide space between themselves and Laura.

June's conflicts were more intermittent and less mysterious in their
origins. She was apt to lose her temper frequently, launching into dia-
tribes against the object of her rage. June would "lose it" as readily
with coworkers as with her children or partners. She would engage in
appalling and offensive name-calling and make outrageous accusations
that were not retractable. June kept others permanently defensive and
withholding in their relationships with her. When she would finally
calm down, she would be demonstratively remorseful, but it was often
too late to repair the relationship.

In all the relationship areas described so far, the TRS woman repeats the trauma-bound childhood relationship. She reenacts the various dynamics of what was done to her, recreating the Abuser, the Victim, and the Nonprotecting Bystander in her current relationships. Those with whom she is currently involved experience what it was like for her in the traumatic relationships of childhood.

Lovers and Spouses

One of the most problematic areas of relationship for the TRS woman is the domain of intimate partnerships, marriages, and sexual romances. The problems she has modulating closeness and distance generally escalate in relationships involving sexual vulnerability. Many TRS relationship problems could be generalized to all women who were traumatized in childhood. The differences between TRS women and other trauma survivors occur in situations where the symptomatic behavior plays its own particular role in relational dynamics. One major distinction for TRS women is how the Triadic Self enters the picture. Another difference is demonstrated in how others respond to the TRS woman's self-harmful behavior: this factor is woven into the fabric of all her involvements, but especially her intimate involvements.

Some TRS women completely avoid intimate relationships. More often, the TRS woman engages in relationships, sometimes lasting and sometimes not, that are beset by chronic frustrations and failures. She may avoid sex or she may engage in dangerous sex or promiscuity. She may exhibit extreme mistrust of her partner. She is likely to hold expectations of betrayal, disappointment, and exploitation. In some cases, TRS women are chronically engaged in conflict.

Some relationship issues are especially difficult to comprehend, both for the TRS woman herself and for those who care about her. If she has learned to equate violence with connectedness, for example, she may engage repeatedly in apparently humiliating and sometimes dangerous relationships. The TRS woman's identification with whatever and whomever is "bad," which began in childhood, may lead her to doubt that she is valued by her partner. She may view her partner through a distorted lens, seeing the "dark side" as magnified, or else denying that her partner has any negative attributes.

Lee's sexual restrictions were connected to her self-harmful behaviors. Her sexual activity with her husband was constrained by the injuries she inflicted on various parts of her body, by her shame at the scars on her body, and by prohibitions against anything reminiscent of what had been done to her as a child. All these restrictions meant that she could engage sexually with David only in the dark, only if she felt in control, and only if she was the one to initiate the sexual interlude.

Nancy also avoided sex. She worried so much about any bodily imperfection that the time was often "just not right" to make love with her husband, Chip. She was oblivious to any connection between her sexual relationship with her husband and her childhood relationship with her grandmother. She would engage in lengthy cosmetic preparations getting herself ready to make love with Chip; often he would fall asleep by the time she emerged from the bathroom. She would wait for Chip to notice some new detail of her wardrobe or hairdo and withdraw in sullen disappointment if he did not, later emphasizing her disappointment by refusing any sexual overtures from him. The problem with her tactics was that they reinforced the TRS cycle: if he fell asleep waiting for her or did not continue to pressure her to have sex, she would be convinced that she was unattractive to him and would launch into a new round of self-improvement and avoidance of intimacy.

For many trauma survivors, especially TRS women, sexual pleasure is often interrupted either by memories of the abuse or by flashbacks, a more fragmented and emotionally overwhelming reexperiencing of the abuse. TRS women with a history of neglect are less prone to flashbacks, but they can experience similar interruptions of sexual pleasure because of intrusive shame anxiety. Such images, memories, and feelings often create a general anxiety about sex or a more specific anxiety or dread during certain sexual activities, and in some cases an inability to achieve orgasm with a partner.

Sexual problems of this sort add to the distress many TRS women already feel about body image and their failure to achieve sustained intimacy in relationships. The memories and flashbacks triggered by sexual activity may lead to overwhelming internal pressures for the TRS woman to harm herself. When she responds to sex in this way, the self-harming cycle leads her to increasing self-hatred and avoidance of closeness, thus precluding further sexual engagement. Also, seeing sex lead to escalating self-harm often causes her partner to pull back from further sexual encounters, whether from compassion or dampened ardor. The woman then feels rejected and her self-hatred and despair increase.

To the TRS woman, it can seem that the only way to engage sexually, given the snares and pitfalls she will likely encounter, is to fall back on her childhood skills of dissociation. She uses the defenses of numbing, distancing from herself, or moving into a different "self" in order to get through sexual episodes; however, she then feels alone and, often, used because she does not feel connected to her partner. Another tactic, if she is a substance abuser, is to engage in sex when she is intoxicated or on drugs. Women who use eating disorders or self-mutilation as their preferred form of self-harm describe the secondary gain of these symptoms as keeping would-be sexual partners at a distance.

Somewhat more surprising, perhaps, are the many TRS women who are extremely sexually active. These women engage in compulsive sexual activities, sex with strangers, unsafe sex, sadomasochistic sex, and other varieties of risk-taking sex. They are often misunderstood and condemned, even by therapists. It is easier to feel sympathy and support for the sex-avoidant abuse survivor than for the sexually unconventional or compulsive survivor. My experience with TRS women is that this latter style is one of the most difficult areas to explore, because the woman so harshly condemns herself. The various forms of sexual extremism may lead to escalating self-hatred and strong negative responses from the TRS woman's partners, friends, and helpers.

The sexually wild TRS woman suffers the consequences of her behavior, even if she does not have a consistent partner or keeps her behavior well hidden. One of my clients was terrified that someone would find out that she regularly engaged in risky sexual alliances with virtual strangers. On the surface, she was "not the type" to lead this kind of lifestyle. She was embarrassed by her double life and deeply discouraged, believing that her compulsive sexual risk-taking prohibited her from sustaining a lasting, friendship-based relationship with a partner.

"Why do I do this?" she asked me repeatedly. As a survivor of incest, she thought that it made no sense for her to be sexually "promiscuous" (as she labeled herself). She hated the memory of sex forced on her by her uncle, and she believed that as a result she ought to hate sex. A central part of our work together was to help her understand the logic of her sexual patterns. We were then able to help her develop more satisfying ways of being sexual without having to give up the companionship and love she wished for in a more enduring relationship.

The preoccupation with control discussed earlier in the chapter plays a significant role in the TRS woman's sexual activities. The determination to be in control sexually is frequently at the root of "acting out" sexually. Not surprisingly, the TRS woman may have a strong wish to feel sexually ruthless and dominant. She may feel a sense of mastery or even revenge in choosing to be sexual with partners she does not really know or like, or in flaunting a provocative, flamboyant sexual lifestyle. She may feel that she is in the role of the aggressor, dominating her victim, and thus reversing the position forced on her as a child.

Some TRS women engage in sadomasochistic sex. If she is in a submissive relationship with a partner whom she fears, she may endure such sex because she is afraid to say no. In this case, she is directly reenacting her childhood abuse. In other cases, the woman may not be coerced to engage in rough sex; in fact, she may enjoy it. She may feel a sexual thrill at being in the masochistic role in a mutually consenting sexual relationship. This pattern can be very upsetting or at least puzzling to the TRS woman, as well as to her partner or therapist. It is one of the many apparent contradictions in the TRS woman's personality and behavior.

There are several ways to explain this behavior. One is that she is continuing to seek sexual pleasure in a way that recalls whatever excitement or pleasure—in addition to fear, pain, shame, anger, and revulsion—she may have experienced in her childhood sexual episodes. Another explanation is that she is attempting to master the childhood trauma by repeating it over and over. This pattern, which tends to show up in many aspects of the TRS woman's relationships, is parallel to the experience she creates for herself when she engages in her self-harmful behaviors.

Many TRS women have a tendency to either find or gradually create a partner who is similar to the abusive parent in terms of behavior, personality, beliefs, and ways of being in a relationship. She replicates the abusive dynamics, albeit unconsciously, because of her loyalty to the abuser and to her family in general. The abusive relationship is oddly welcome because she is familiar with the dynamics; she knows what to expect and how to be a victim. The role of the internalized Abuser is critical to how the abusive relationship gets replayed; the internalized part of the self that the child originally split off from the abusive parent and incorporated within herself is projected onto the partner. Again, the idea that violence equals connectedness organizes the TRS woman's perceptions of intimacy and becomes an integral part of the couple's dynamics.

Illicit relationships with forbidden partners may also be part of the TRS woman's sexual pattern. She may pursue sexual liaisons with married men or women, workplace supervisors, or unethical therapists. In the worst case, therapists who are themselves inadequately treated TRS victims may become involved with their clients. Illicit relationships may replicate the excitement and intensity of the secrecy, the power dynamics, the illusion of "specialness," and the pain of the TRS woman's childhood experience.

Power

The TRS woman's need for control may go beyond sex to pervade the couple's entire relationship. Power struggles are common in the areas of time, money, social activities, and household tasks. Friendships are also a frequent subject of control: for example, who the couple will spend time with, who among the partner's friends is acceptable, and whether the TRS woman is "allowed" to have her own friends.

All these areas may be characterized by undercontrol as well as overcontrol. The partner and not the TRS woman may be overcontrolling, sometimes to the point of abuse. At the other end of the continuum, the partner may have no involvement whatsoever in negotiating a mutual set of expectations or arranging daily life.

In a related aspect of power dynamics, the TRS woman often engages in overpossessiveness, as well as a cycle of provoking betrayal so that she gets hurt. She may provoke a partner so that he hurts her, rejects her, or appears to deceive her. Without being conscious that she is doing so, she may even choose partners who are most likely to hurt or betray her. She may become trapped in conflict because her partner is overly controlling and possessive, or she herself may be obsessively concerned with her partner's fidelity.

One of the problems of such jealousy may be that the TRS woman cannot allow herself to trust a partner or even someone with whom she is more casually involved. Consequently, she may have affairs, thus communicating that sexual and emotional fidelity are not valued. However, she often becomes wildly upset if her partner also sees other people. She may be less openly provocative, seeing other people secretly, living the kind of hidden life enacted in her abuse relationship in childhood, but this time more in the role of the perpetrator.

Repetition of the original abuse dynamics, played out in the TRS woman's choice to have secret affairs and thus enact the role of the abuser, would seem to be one way to "act out" rather than "act in," or hurt herself. In my experience, however, it does not seem to be an either/or choice. The TRS woman may be active in multiple affairs, secret or otherwise, and still continue her self-harmful behaviors. I believe that she continues to harm herself even while she appears to be externalizing the Abuser because she feels deepening guilt and shame and thus punishes herself even more harshly.

Caretaking

Codependence is a word that we may hear too often these days. Sometimes when a concept is overused, it loses its meaning, and I think this is what may have happened as codependence has become a buzzword in the media. However, some elements of the idea of codependence are relevant to the TRS woman's relationship problems. The concept of codependence was developed by the twelve-step movement to describe the relational patterns of many partners of people with addictions. My brief definition of codependence is that the partner devotes herself so totally to the alcoholic or addict that she submerges her own needs and becomes addicted to meeting the other's needs. She performs many caretaking acts, often at a cost to her own desires, needs, and self-esteem.

The TRS woman may be hyperactive in regard to her caretaking role in the relationship. She may choose a partner who requires unusual amounts of caretaking, or she may take over many caretaking functions so that the partner becomes less and less capable of normal adult self-care. She may take on her partner's feelings, anticipating every need so quickly that her partner may not even have time to perceive his or her own needs.

June's history of childhood neglect compelled her to try to be Supermom to her own children. When they were young, she tried to give them every minute of her attention, often neglecting her own needs completely. The inevitable result was that she would feel miserably uncared-for herself. Her exhaustion and emotional depletion would then lead her to plunge into a drinking binge. The children never knew whether to expect "Dearest Mommy" or "Mommy Dearest."

The TRS woman is unlikely to give her family or friends clear messages concerning her own need to receive caretaking. Such self-neglectful concealment occurred regularly between Lee and David. She wanted David to get the message without having to tell him. Lee liked David to bring her coffee in bed on lazy Sunday mornings, but because she could not tell him directly how much this meant to her, he would sometimes disappoint her. This situation grew into a small nightmare. Lee would wake up in the morning, imagining that she smelled coffee brewing. She would wait in delighted anticipation for David to appear in the bedroom with a tender good-morning kiss and her cup of coffee. When David did not make the longed-for appearance, she would slip into a state of inner-directed fury that would trigger a period of total avoidance of David. He, in turn, would be mystified as to why she was so cold in their casual contacts throughout the day.

If one was not sensitive to Lee's history, it would be tempting to judge her as too sensitive or a pampered wife who expected her husband to read her mind. While David never thought these things about her, he was hurt and puzzled by her inexplicable rejections and aloof behavior.

Alternative Choices

Some TRS women choose to avoid the replication of relationship dynamics from childhood by avoiding intimate relationships completely, as Laura did. Karen, in another variation of avoidance, had a series of brief relationships that she ended before she became too vulnerable. Some TRS women opt to have relationships that are sexual but not especially affectionate or even friendly. June goes through periods in her life when she "gets laid" frequently, but stays out of any relationship that could have emotional significance. A fourth avenue is a marriage like Nancy's, in which Chip is almost completely disengaged from Nancy emotionally, not even sharing a semblance of a friendly, companionable relationship. Although Chip and Nancy do have a sexual relationship, it is perfunctory.

The choice to be in lesbian relationships is sometimes related to the wish to avoid replication of a childhood abuse experience. A lesbian lifestyle may be a positive, pro-woman choice and at the same time a way to avoid being dominated, betrayed, or exploited by a male. For women who were abused by males during childhood, there may be an understandable incapacity to respond sexually or emotionally to men. For such women, a lesbian lifestyle may be an adaptive alternative. Many therapists who work with incest survivors report that there seems to be a somewhat higher instance of incest history among lesbian women than among exclusively heterosexual women.

There are complications, however, in how a lesbian lifestyle is related to childhood abuse. I have been saddened by the number of lesbian clients I have worked with over the years who have been TRS women. Living and being intimate with a female partner does not heal all the wounds of childhood abuse and neglect. My lesbian TRS clients have been in even greater distress, at times, than their heterosexual counterparts. They feel even more disturbed by their inability to stop their self-harmful behavior, because they feel that not stopping betrays the pride they feel in affirming their lesbian lifestyle. They also feel greater disappointment when their female partners are unable or unwilling to rescue and protect them from their self-harmful patterns.

One woman I saw for therapy was chronically disappointed that her partner could not magically become her Protective Presence. The client had lived with rage and sorrow for many years, longing for the mother she had never had because her own mother was alcoholic and emotionally distant. She had been involved with men for some years before changing her sexual preference to women. "I never expected much from men," she told me, "but it kills me when women let me down." Her eating disorder had escalated since her relationship with her partner, Mary, had started. She wanted Mary to help her stop bingeing, but was furious with her when she tried. It took a long time in therapy before she was able to let go of her rage at Mary, rage that was much more relevant to her relationship with her nonprotecting mother.

There are also lesbian TRS women who were abused primarily by their mothers. Although it would seem that being intimate with women would be an unlikely choice for victims of maternal abuse, it makes sense if we think about the internalization of the Abuser and the compulsion to repeat the abuse dynamics that many TRS women manifest. As we will see in part II, on treatment, for these women, working out the dynamics of the internalized Abuser when she is the same person as the Nonprotecting Bystander is a sizable challenge.

Friendships

Over many centuries and across many cultures, friendships between women have been understood as a primary source of support and validation. It is especially tragic, therefore, when the TRS woman's capacity for trust and mutual empathy is limited even in nonsexual, nonpartner friendships with other women and men. Trust issues, feelings of envy and resentment, and the experience of devaluing the self and therefore collaborating in the devaluing of all women are perplexing issues in the friendships of TRS women.

The TRS woman may not trust female friends to be loyal, to understand her, or to value the friendship. In concealing her self-abuse symptoms, she creates a more pervasive problem, having to hide, distort, and lie about many aspects of her life. Her incapacity to be open and honest with a friend may make her feel so much shame about her own untrustworthiness that she perceives her friend, correctly or not, as not trustworthy either.

Surprisingly, trusting male friends may be easier than trusting female friends. For some women, the betrayal by the female parent was more internally wounding than the betrayal by the male parent. When this is so, the TRS woman expects less of men and is therefore less vulnerable to them, while the intensity of her longing for a woman's love and loyalty makes her fear that any closeness to women will inevitably hurt. Other TRS women, however, cannot overcome the mistrust of men engendered by childhood trauma. These women avoid relationships with men in general, occasionally allowing an individual man to become the exception, a sort of "good brother."

Competition and envy between women in general is not unusual. Hand in glove with female competitiveness is the TRS woman's tendency to devalue herself and all women. Since the TRS woman has trouble feeling strong and safe in her gender, and since her mother failed her as a role model, it is easy to see why she may automatically devalue other women. Often she is not conscious of this tendency, and therefore it is harder to identify and begin to change such patterns.

The longings for protection, validation, and positive identification with a maternal figure become central in the friendships of many TRS women. Failures deliver a crushing blow, and of course there are failures when expectations are so great. When a TRS woman is disap-

pointed repeatedly by female friendships, she begins to infuse them
with approach–avoidance dynamics, as she does in other relationships:
the TRS woman forms close friendships, then withdraws. When friends
respond by becoming more cautious or even leaving her, she is
wounded and thus likely to escalate her behavior in subsequent friendships.

A peculiar bonding around shared symptoms can happen when two
TRS women form a friendship. Sometimes an intense connection occurs
even when only one of them suffers from the syndrome but the other is
a survivor of childhood abuse or neglect. Self-abusive behaviors as reenactments of childhood trauma, even when not identified consciously,
function to initiate and maintain the friendship. The bond can create a
normalization or denial of the symptoms. On the other hand, it can also
create mutual empathy and strength to fight the symptomatic behaviors.

In hindsight, my friendship with Fiora was deepened by our shared
symptoms as well as our shared history as incest survivors. We felt a
powerful bond of identification, the thrill of being truly seen and understood by one another. It was perhaps even more compelling a bond for us
back in the late sixties than it would be for women today, who are more
accustomed to talking with their friends about both incest and self-abuse
behaviors. Female friends can undoubtedly play a central role now, as
then, in helping to articulate the experience of childhood trauma and in
trying to help each other relinquish self-harmful activities.

TRS women's friendships have the capacity for many strengths. The
suffering of the TRS woman can make her exquisitely attuned to a
friend's experience. She can offer empathic support in times of stress.
She can show tolerance for problems, weaknesses, fears, and shortcom-
ings. When the friendship provides steadiness and nurturance unparal-
leled in the TRS woman's previous relationships, she can respond with
powerful loyalty and affection.

The Family of Origin

The TRS woman faces a complex and difficult set of relationships with
her family of origin. Each relationship has some unfinished business,
some shadow of an internalized dynamic. Not only is the TRS woman's

relationship to her abuser distorted by fear, hatred, unresolved love, and longing, but so is her relationship to the nonprotecting parent and other family members in caretaker roles. In addition, her relationships with siblings can be affected by unresolved bitterness, guilt, and resentment.

Parents

The TRS woman's unresolved longing for love and validation may keep her overinvolved with either or both of her parents or with her primary caretakers. She may be excessive in her caretaking responsibilities or, conversely, her parents may still be taking inappropriate responsibility for her. Nancy's father, for example, still pays her traffic and parking tickets. Karen, on the other hand, is unable to extricate herself from being both parents' principal confidant.

The TRS woman may continue to need permission from a parent for decisions, activities, and opinions. Perhaps more frequently, a parent turns to the adult woman for such permission. Karen's mother asks her what she should do about financial problems, management of her home, and her health care.

By being emotionally involved in this manner, the TRS woman remains in bondage to her parents or her mental representation of them. She may need their approval to validate her own thoughts, or she may need to continue to care for them to confirm her self-image as a caretaking person. The caretaking functions embodied in her beliefs about herself are paradoxical: the TRS woman harms herself as a re-enactment of parental abuse or neglect, and she cannot protect herself from self-harm because she was not taken care of by the nonprotecting parent, yet she plays the role of caretaker to her parents.

Loyalties are extreme in families where there has been abuse, so the TRS woman may be unable to talk to anyone about her abuse or neglect. She is intent on protecting both her abuser and the parent who could not protect her. In the same vein, she may also protect her family from any problems in her current life, instead of asking for support and sympathy.

The protection of the TRS woman's mother seems to be an especially complex dynamic. Many therapists and other trauma experts try to avoid holding the mother responsible for abuse by the father, boyfriend, uncle, brother, or grandfather. Unfortunately, this can obscure the problem for the TRS woman when she needs to address her mother's incapacity to protect her. Loyalty to her mother kept the child from demanding protection from her during childhood. In adult life, it binds the TRS woman to her mother, even if only in her mind. One of my clients, Molly, courageously began working on her trauma and self-abuse issues for the first time in her early sixties. She had a very difficult time with her eighty-year-old mother, who told her that her weight problems were caused by a lack of willpower and nothing else. My client protected her mother by not confronting her when she began to connect her eating disorder with her childhood history of maternal neglect and paternal incest. She refused to talk to her mother about her childhood, even when her mother berated her for being "weak" and "greedy," and for creating her own problems.

Over time, Molly and I worked out various ways for her to begin to make demands on her mother and stop protecting her. A turning point came when Molly told her mother that the ample amount of money her mother continued to hoard should be shared with her daughter. Molly had been living very frugally, working two stressful jobs in order to pay her bills. She had almost no time to do things she enjoyed, and eating became her vehicle for both self-soothing and self-harm. Molly felt powerless to stop her binges and was in profound despair, even after she became more clear about whose voice (abusive father) directed her to keep eating and whose voice (mother) refused to help her stop. When Molly was able to demand some long-overdue financial support from her mother, she was able to work fewer hours and to begin taking better care of herself.

The TRS woman may experience some confusion about where she stops and where her parents begin. In childhood, she developed an internal identification with the abuser and another identification with the nonprotecting parent. These parts of her parents were split off and incorporated as parts of herself during the process of trauma-related internalization. Even if she is able to understand that she carries these representations of her parents within herself, it may be very unclear to her which parts belong to which parent. Because she cannot name or separate these parts, she remains completely unconscious of, or confused by, the internalized parts of her parents that influence her to do or say what she does. Nor does she generally understand how these forms of identification are imposed on her by her family.

The negative effects of such internalization can include a range of problems in dealing with her family of origin. Because she has over-identified with both the abusive parent and the nonprotective care-taker, she may be unable to see that the dynamics in her ongoing relationships with them are still the same. She may also continue to internalize her parents' "bad" actions, ideas, or communications, perpetuating the patterns of childhood trauma.

Siblings

The TRS woman's relationships with her siblings may not have changed much since childhood. There may be both overt and covert jealousy among siblings. If she was the primary victim of childhood abuse, the TRS woman may be bitter and jealous of the sibling or siblings she perceives as having been better treated or favored. The reverse may be true: the TRS woman may be the object of sibling jealousy because she is perceived as having received more attention—even if the attention was negative—or as having been better loved or "special." Both the TRS woman and her siblings may experience ongoing survivor guilt, which may force them apart, make them feel isolated, and leave them in pain.

Abuse perpetrated by a sibling also creates ongoing problems in the adult sibling relationships. Unless they have had help talking through the abuse and have come to understand the family and social contexts that produced it, there may be a complete break between the abuser and the victim or, at best, there may be unspoken or unprocessed tensions, guilt, uneasiness, fear, or anger.

The TRS Woman as Parent

In my work as a family therapist, I have had extensive experience in dealing not only with TRS women but with their families as well. Unfortunately for TRS mothers, achieving a nurturing, positive parenting relationship seems as difficult as achieving a loving, trust-based relationship with a partner. The self-abusing woman did not experience good parenting, and without such a model, she often struggles to avoid being a negligent or abusive parent herself.

Parenting styles often get passed down through many generations. Dysfunctional patterns of family abuse and neglect cannot be discussed openly and become part of the family's collective denial. It is important for everyone involved with TRS women, as well as for TRS women themselves, to keep the multigenerational patterns of abuse and neglect in mind, so that it is possible to achieve a more compassionate stance in relation to the TRS woman's parenting failures, even while holding her responsible in her role as a mother. It is a challenge to avoid the mother-blaming that pervades the literature on abusive families and self-harmful mothers. My hope is that through trying to understand why the TRS woman sometimes fails to be a good parent, the reader will develop more, rather than less, compassion for her.

Because it is important for the TRS woman to stop blaming and hating herself, it can be difficult to explore the problems of parenting. My work in therapy includes reminding the woman and those who love her that she may be accountable for parental tasks without having to feel blamed or bad for what has gone wrong.

One problematic aspect of parenting for the TRS woman is that the consuming and secret life created around her symptomatic behaviors interferes with her ability to be a consistent parent. Also, the TRS woman experiences herself as fragmented, partly because of her childhood trauma and partly because her TRS behavior can subsume much of her personality or psyche. Her lack of a cohesive self creates difficulties in parenting. She may feel shame about not knowing how to be a healthy parent, for example, to set appropriate limits, to modify angry behavior, or to offer consistency. She may be unable to experience comfortable emotional or physical closeness to her children. This distancing may be more pronounced with one gender than the other. Some women project their anger at men onto their sons, and are critical of and harsh to them, while other TRS women project self-hatred onto their daughters or fear that they cannot protect a girl. Gender aside, the TRS mother tends to be either overprotective or underprotective.

Because of her history and her own unresolved sexual issues, the TRS woman may be extremely uncomfortable with her children's developing sexuality. She may therefore exhibit undue harshness or intrusiveness toward their sexual behavior, or she may not provide openings for them to explore sexual questions or behaviors. When her children are at the developmental stage that corresponds to the time in her own childhood when she was abused, she may become punitive, rejecting, controlling, or overprotecting around sexual issues or more generally.

The TRS woman sometimes turns to a daughter (less frequently, a son) for intimacy and protection when she is unable to get them from an adult partner. This creates an unfair burden for the child and is also ultimately frustrating for the mother, since the child is incapable of providing these adult functions.

Working as part of a parenting team may be problematic. See-saw behavior around control is likely; the TRS woman may vacillate between feeling totally responsible for her child and rejecting any responsibility. Because she often avoids conflict, she is also likely to fail to work through important differences in parenting styles or beliefs with her partner. She may fail to trust the coparent because of her hopelessness or incapacity to expect parenting abilities and commitment from a male partner.

The TRS woman is also hampered by her fear of getting too close, of being eaten alive or swallowed by her children. Conversely, she may be paralyzed by the fear of engulfing or smothering her children. She often has difficulty encouraging autonomy and the development of self in her children, because in her own childhood she had no role models for doing so.

A TRS mother may have difficulties finding a way to involve grandparents with her children. The problem may be her lack of autonomy from her own parents or a childlike fear of them that she communicates to her children. She may completely cut off herself and her children from contact with the grandparents.

Whether or not she stays connected to her parents, the TRS woman is reminded of them as she struggles with her own children. She may find that she is overcome with grief as well as rage when she recognizes in the eyes of her children her own vulnerability as a child. She may find herself wondering repeatedly, "How could they have done such things to me?" as she experiences the trust and fragility in her children's relationship to her. When feelings like this get stirred up, she may be unwilling to subject her children to any form of contact with their grandparents. Even more important is that in reality she may not be able to trust her own parents with her children if they were abusive or neglectful to her. Because they may not be safe, grandparents are often not a good resource to help the TRS woman with parenting.

The TRS woman's involvement with professionals, including health care providers, child protective services, the legal system, and the school system, can interfere with her parental autonomy and competence. The role played by professionals in this kind of situation is parallel to that of her parents: the children see their mother as disempowered and often feel a combination of contempt and protectiveness toward her. Seeing her failures reflected in the eyes of her children may trigger increased self-harmful activities in the TRS mother.

Despite all the challenges that TRS women face as parents, it is possible for them also to be extraordinarily empathic and devoted to their children. They understand a child's vulnerability and capacity for suffering and may therefore be slightly better attuned to their children. When they recover from TRS, they can be excellent role models, teaching both sons and daughters how to be strong, self-confident, and loving, as they have learned these lessons themselves in adult life.

Work Relationships

Some TRS women are rendered so dysfunctional by their symptoms that they work only sporadically, work at jobs beneath their abilities, or cannot work at all. Other TRS women may appear to function very well in a job context. Work relationships may seem less troubling than other types of relationships. The TRS woman may hide the self-abusive behavior and her often chaotic personal and inner life. There are, of course, problems in this domain, whether hidden or not.

The TRS woman may take on more than her share of work or more than she can manage. Overextending herself is perhaps the most common problem for the TRS woman. She takes on too much responsibility without being aware until it is too late, because she cannot assert, or does not know, what she wants or needs. In many cases, she was "parentified" in childhood, that is, given adult responsibilities for housework and child care, and may also have been the confidant, caretaker, or "wife" to one or both of her parents. Thus, in adult life she is unable to assess when too much is being demanded of her, or if it is appropriate to her work role. Even when she realizes that she is unhappy about all the extra or inappropriate tasks she has taken on, she has an extremely hard time asserting herself and saying no. This pattern holds true even when she is her own boss and sets her own schedule and agenda. She also may work compulsively in an effort to either avoid or atone for her self-abusive behavior. If she misses work regularly or has botched some aspect of her work because she was engaged in self-injuring activities at work or at home, she may overwork to correct anything she has failed to do perfectly or to convince an unhappy employer that she can make up for her failures.

Depending on where she works and the context of her work, she is susceptible to participating in dual relationships because of her boundary problems. She may try to mix evaluative roles with vulnerable friendships, or she may make inappropriate demands on employees or those she supervises. Even in more egalitarian situations, she is likely to sabotage professional relationships by mixing roles, as Nancy does in her partnership with Babs.

At the other end of the spectrum is the TRS woman who stays distant and aloof from others. She is seen by colleagues as unfriendly or arrogant, unapproachable, and unable to have allies and work friendships. Lee is perceived by those who work in her video stores as aloof and unapproachable. Unfortunately, this distance denies her the resources of a social network and a support system that many women enjoy in the workplace. Laura was a dependable, competent worker, but was fired from several jobs because she refused to interact even minimally with her associates, which made everyone extremely uncomfortable in her presence.

Despite the various problems encountered in work settings, many TRS women are more comfortable and more successful in job relationships than in others. The structure of these relationships and the relative distance and lack of intimacy combine to make the work domain an easier place for the TRS woman to be connected to others. This makes work an important part of the recovery process that I explain in part II.

PART II

THE HEALING
JOURNEY

6

Misunderstandings and Mistreatment

Understanding why women hurt themselves is an important step toward healing. Equally important is understanding the components of good treatment: what works and what doesn't. "The Healing Journey" begins by showing how Trauma Reenactment Syndrome has been misdiagnosed and how these misunderstandings have led to mistreatment. Unfortunately, misdiagnoses continue to be significant in the pattern of relapse experienced by many TRS women today.

Women who are self-abusive have traditionally been described in pejorative ways by both their peers and mental health professionals. Those who choose alcohol, drugs, or food as their self-destructive weapon are viewed as "weak" or having no "willpower." Those who self-mutilate or torture themselves with extreme diets or compulsive cosmetic surgeries are pitied as "masochistic" or "self-destructive." The women also usually think about themselves in negative terms. They accuse themselves of being "crazy," "codependent," "disgusting," "hopeless," "incompetent," "unlovable," "bad," and "undeserving." Many people who are involved with these women use the same negative labels, describing them as "wild women" who are "bad" or, in mental health jargon, "acting out," "manipulative," or "borderline."

Historically, the mental health profession has used various diagnostic terms to categorize and distinguish among the types of women who hurt themselves. Before Freud and the advent of modern psychological theories, women who hurt themselves were thought of either as saints or as possessed by demons. By the end of the nineteenth century, they were routinely considered to suffer from hysteria, a problem for doctors rather than priests. In more recent times, these women have been diagnosed as schizophrenic, depressed, obsessive-compulsive, narcissistic, histrionic, borderline, multiple personality–disordered, alcoholic, anorexic, bulimic, drug-addicted, or suffering from more unusual compulsions such as trichotillomania (compulsively pulling out hair).

It is hopeful that now, for the first time in history, many women who hurt themselves are able to name themselves as trauma survivors. It is also useful that they can identify themselves as suffering from the disease of addiction: they describe themselves as addicted to food, alcohol, drugs, or relationships. Women of all socioeconomic classes, ethnicities, and sexual orientations, from young adults to the elderly, are seeking help in psychotherapy and recovery groups. Their treatment programs are designed to address depression, self-esteem issues, sexual problems, compulsive behaviors, and "healing the wounded child within." The language of trauma and recovery has become as much a part of contemporary culture as the terms "adult child" and "codependent," also quite recently incorporated into common language.

Most of the women who hurt themselves can make the connection between their self-abusive behavior and their history of childhood trauma. Beyond awareness lies the need for a more comprehensive understanding. Just as they seek help for their addictions by attending twelve-step meetings and reading self-help books, many of these women are also in treatment for their childhood trauma history and are diagnosed as suffering from Post-Traumatic Stress Disorder (PTSD). Treatment focusing on childhood abuse may include individual psychotherapy, hypnotherapy, group therapy (both therapist-led and peer groups), inpatient hospitalization, couples therapy, and family therapy. Other forms of recovery from PTSD may include spiritual groups, reading, meditation, wilderness activities, massage therapy, movement therapy, psychodrama, and self-defense courses.

Being aware of the link between the symptomatic behavior and the trauma history, however, is not sufficient. Despite all their hard work, many women remain entrenched in chronic self-abusive behaviors and relationships. A major therapy insight or a lull in the symptomatic behavior may seem to signal that the problem has ended. All too often, however, the behavior recurs, or a substitute behavior begins, making the woman and those who care about her feel discouraged or even hopeless. When the self-abusive woman has worked hard in therapy on her trauma history and has been faithful to her addiction recovery program, she feels betrayed and doomed when she finds herself once again engaging in self-abusive behaviors. Professionals, partners, and friends may also feel like giving up on her. This atmosphere of discouragement and blame increases her feelings of self-hatred and isolation, and may add to her reasons for repeating the familiar cycle of self-harm.

The labels she has been given do not seem to help her choose the right treatment. The treatment that she has been assured will help does not seem to work. Why, we might ask, has she been mislabeled or misdiagnosed?

The label or diagnosis that a TRS woman is given by most therapists is likely to be based on the self-harmful behavior she exhibits. Secondarily, her personality characteristics are categorized and clustered to indicate her diagnosis. Her relationship patterns are also considered, but many clinicians do not use them as primary information. Even when a therapist with a more systemic view concentrates on her relationships and her place within the system they create, it is not enough to help her stop her patterns of self-injury.

The woman who hurts herself will not necessarily choose to identify with a psychiatric diagnosis, but she will look for a description that seems to fit, offered either by the media (talk shows, self-help books, magazine articles) or by her peers. She may be more likely to choose an addiction-related label or, more recently, a PTSD-related description. If in fact she is suffering from the additional complex problems encompassed by Trauma Reenactment Syndrome, she will be misunderstood—by herself and others—and she will not achieve lasting recovery, regardless of which description and treatment protocol she chooses.

The diagnoses, labels, and treatments that I describe in this chapter are those most often applied to TRS women. I review the reasons why parts of each description seem to fit many TRS clients. By analyzing what does and does not apply to TRS clients, I hope to avoid the either/or polarity of diagnosis. Rather, I present an inclusive and comprehensive way of examining how description and protocol relates to the understanding and treatment of Trauma Reenactment Syndrome.

Borderline Personality Disorder

Because the TRS profile has many similarities to Borderline Personality Disorder (BPD), many mental health professionals assume that the TRS woman should be diagnosed and treated as a "borderline." Patients diagnosed as borderline are generally women, and a high percentage of them are survivors of childhood trauma (Herman and van der Kolk, 1987).

The following list of characteristics is included in the guidelines for diagnosing Borderline Personality Disorder in the *Diagnostic and Statistical Manual of Mental Disorders* (DSM III-R), published by the American Psychiatric Association (1987) and used by clinicians to diagnose clients: (1) unstable and intense interpersonal relationships; (2) impulsiveness in potentially self-damaging behaviors, such as substance abuse, sex, shoplifting, reckless driving, binge-eating; (3) severe mood shifts; (4) frequent and inappropriate displays of anger; (5) recurrent suicidal threats or gestures, or self-mutilating behaviors; (6) lack of a clear sense of identity; (7) chronic feelings of emptiness or boredom; and (8) frantic efforts to avoid real or imagined abandonment.

Self-mutilation is a symptom generally associated with this disorder, as long as the wounds are self-inflicted and not made for cosmetic purposes (for example, piercing, tattooing, face lifts, breast implants or reductions, tummy tucks, or buttocks tucks). When someone makes a suicidal gesture—that is, superficially cuts herself or overdoses minimally so that it does not seem that she was really trying to kill herself—she is also likely to be diagnosed as borderline.

Self-abusing behavior is often seen as an attention-getting device, one of the ways by which a borderline attempts to draw the focus of others to herself. For that reason, this diagnosis is perhaps the most troublesome of the various ways TRS women are labeled. If the clinician sees the abusive behavior as a form of manipulation rather than as an expression of anguish, what hope does the TRS woman have of understanding why she does it? Understanding the self-harmful behavior as the reenactment of childhood trauma, rather than as manipulation, is central to distinguishing between the borderline and the TRS woman.

In the following description of BPD and its treatment, it is evident

how it could fit many TRS women. To avoid misdiagnosis, it is important to see the overlapping characteristics and behaviors from an interpersonal, trauma-centered perspective, rather than as fixed, unalterable
personality traits.

One of the standard descriptions of the borderline personality is that
she "splits": she rigidly separates everything into extreme categories of
good and bad. In dealing with professionals and others, it means that
she views people as all good or all bad, and tends to set them up against
each other. For example, a woman who constantly seeks out medical
help may very likely tell Dr. Wonderful that he is the only one who
understands her, and that Dr. So-and-So has not given her the treatment she requires. Dr. Wonderful then feels like the avenging rescuer
and believes the patient's story that Dr. So-and-So refused to give her
the necessary medication. In actuality, she may have told both doctors
the same story, so that she ends up with a massive supply of the medication she is seeking. She may lose later on, if both doctors discover
how she set them up.

When professionals get angry at clients for splitting, they may have
little inclination to try to understand the reasons for the client's behavior. Yet exploring both the meaning of the medication for the patient
and the significance of provoking doctors' anger can communicate
much about the patient's childhood history. Learning why the client is
acting out in this particular way could enable the helpers to see her as a
TRS woman in need of understanding and patience, rather than as an
"acting out" or "splitting" borderline who needs "tough love" or aloof
containment.

Another feature of the borderline personality is a pattern of unstable
relationships. In *The Rose*, Bette Midler, playing Janis Joplin, portrays
the archetypal borderline. She is passionately and impulsively seductive,
creating an almost instant intimacy with a soldier she picks up one
night. By the end of the night together, she has told him her most intimate and shameful story, about being gang-raped by her high school
football team. She persuades him to go AWOL from the army to go on
the road with her, but she ends up exploiting his devotion to her. He
tries to rescue and protect her, only to be capriciously screamed at,
physically attacked, and rejected when she is in the throes of a drug-
induced rage. Her pattern of cajoling and adoring him and then attacking, humiliating, and rejecting him finally pushes him away. When she

realizes that he has finally given up on her, she plunges into an abandonment panic that leads to a lethal overdose.

Although this is an extreme portrayal of the borderline personality, it has all the components of the push–pull dynamics that characterize this variety of relationship disorder. When seen as part of BPD, such relationship patterns are viewed as pathological and also somewhat intractable. At best, the clinician will teach the client how to predict and control this dysfunctional behavior. If the relationship patterns are seen through a TRS lens, however, they can be linked to the Triadic Self. The internalized Abuser drives others away, while the Victim calls out, "Please don't leave me." In the TRS analysis, it is the Nonprotecting Bystander who gives voice to the woman's hopelessness about her capacity to maintain healthy relationships.

Another characteristic of the borderline personality is persistent impulsivity in areas of behavior that are self-damaging, such as spending too much money, sexual promiscuity, reckless driving, and shoplifting. Although impulse behavior per se is not enough to warrant the borderline label, if it is seen with some of the other patterns previously mentioned, it will act to alert the mental health professional to the possibility that the patient is borderline.

Instability of moods is considered a hallmark of Borderline Personality Disorder. Sudden depression, anxiety, or irritability can occur and just as rapidly disappear. Anger is the most troublesome of all the mood swings, perceived by others as inappropriate, out of control, or overwhelmingly intense. The borderline is frequently angry and will even express it physically, breaking things and sometimes assaulting people.

TRS women are also frequently impulsive and can have very unstable moods. These patterns can be understood as reflecting past trauma and expressing internal conflict.

Uncertainty about self-image, long-term goals, and ethical values are all associated with the borderline diagnosis. Another central characteristic of the borderline is persistent identity disturbance. Laura, who could have "earned" a borderline diagnosis on the basis of her self-injuring, impulsivity, and intense anger, also exemplifies a lack of self-definition that would clinch such a diagnosis in the eyes of many traditional clinicians. She reveals a confusion of gender identity and sexual orientation, and a shadowy, incomplete sense of self common to many TRS women who are misdiagnosed as BPD:

How can I know who I am? I look at myself in the mirror and I see a thin, scared-looking female, but inside I think sometimes that I am as cruel and hard as any man. I prefer thinking of myself like that. I am a sexless man, but I can't be opened up like a woman.

My therapist asks me if I have ever felt attracted to other women. What a weird question! I don't know what "feeling attracted" is. I don't want anything from anyone, certainly not sex. The thought of sex with a woman disgusts me, and the thought of sex with a man makes me want to kill.

She asks if I have any moral feelings about any kind of sexuality being wrong, whether it is sex with men or with women. Another flaky question. What makes her think there is any such thing as moral feelings? I don't know what my values are. Maybe I don't have any values.

I tried to tell her I didn't have values, but she said she didn't buy it. She pointed out that I told her I would do anything to protect my mother or my younger brother and sister. "So?" I said.

I feel empty inside most of the time. If I'm empty, then there really isn't a "me" in there to have values, or be attracted to men or women, or even be a woman or any kind of human being. But I go on acting as if I have a me, a body, a heart. What I do know I have is guts. I am my fierceness. That's all I am. Tough. Guts. Hard as iron.

As I have noted, some of the criteria for the diagnosis of Borderline Personality Disorder may fit many TRS women. There are disastrous problems in diagnosing a TRS woman as borderline, however, particularly because of how she will be treated.

The woman with a borderline diagnosis, more than any other type of client, is viewed as causing problems for herself and is often blamed for her interpersonal failures.

Friends, colleagues, and loved ones are invariably exasperated by many of the so-called borderline behaviors, and will often get angry and pull away when the behavior becomes too upsetting. Their withdrawal creates even greater anxiety for the TRS woman, who already has an intense fear of abandonment and ambivalence about closeness, and the TRS cycle escalates.

Mental health practitioners are more likely to have negative reactions to supposedly borderline clients than to any other group. Borderlines are called manipulative, blameful, rageful, sexually provocative, unstable, messy (in terms of suicidal and self-injuring behavior), and splitting (known to set up professionals against each other). Many mental health professionals believe that the damage done to the borderline's sense of self is irreparable. They consider these women unable ever to achieve mutually satisfying relationships or to live stable lives. Treatment of borderline clients is often doomed to failure, therefore, because the clients are blamed and disliked for their "resistant" and "provocative" behavior. Their prognosis for recovery is seen as extremely low. They do not respond predictably to any category of psychiatric medications and they are difficult to "manage" in groups. They exhaust the patience of most hospital staff and private practitioners. They often leave treatment before any real change can occur.

Perhaps the most damaging aspect for the client who is diagnosed as borderline is that she has been labeled as someone who is not nice to therapists or to anyone else trying to help her. She will typically overvalue and then devalue her professional helpers. Unlike the typical male client who devalues people who try to help him, the borderline woman will engage intensely with her helpers, so that her anger and rejection are unsettling. Also, because of the gender double standard, most people have higher expectations that women will be pleasant, accommodating, and even complimentary to professional helpers; when a man is rude or contemptuous, it is less surprising. The TRS woman who behaves in an unpleasant manner with helpers is likely to be blamed, judged, and referred from helper to helper, or simply forced to contain her feelings. Just as she was misused and silenced in her traumatic childhood, she is misunderstood by the adult world. This empathic failure exacerbates the problems of the woman who should be understood as TRS rather than borderline.

There are ways that the borderline diagnosis could be of use in identifying certain aspects of the TRS woman's life. Even some reconceptualized aspects of borderline treatment could be incorporated in treating TRS women. More and more frequently, clinicians of various persuasions are beginning to both explore and challenge the borderline diagnosis and how it is used to determine the treatment of female clients

(Benjamin, 1993; DiCello, 1993; Herman, 1992). In 1990, I was a speaker, along with three other psychologists (Anne Alonso, Marsha Linehan, and Lorna Benjamin), at a conference titled "The Borderline Dilemma: Women on a Condition of Women." From our various professional perspectives, we explored the problems and solutions this diagnosis creates for women. We all felt that the diagnosis is often used to signal to other clinicians that the client is difficult or even unmanageable and has a poor prognosis. Why is it that this diagnosis is given to so many women and to so few men, we asked?

Several possible explanations have been offered for this imbalance. Leaders in the field of trauma treatment (for example, Herman, Perry, and van der Kolk, 1985; Landecker, 1992) believe there is a high correlation between a history of child sexual abuse and the Borderline Personality Disorder diagnosis. Because significantly more girls than boys are sexually abused, according to the researcher Diana Russell (1986) in her ground-breaking study of self-reported sexual abuse—a fact that has since been confirmed by the majority of child abuse experts (for example, Herman, 1992; Courtois, 1988)—it would be logical to expect more women than men with the borderline diagnosis. The four of us debating the borderline dilemma agreed with this perspective linking childhood sexual abuse to the borderline diagnosis, but we had other ideas as well.

Another way of looking at the use of the diagnosis is to suggest that the characteristics it describes, including a high incidence of self-mutilation, feelings of emptiness, fear of abandonment, inappropriate anger, and a chronic sense of victimization, are reactions of women to childhood trauma because of gender socialization. The man who has been abused in childhood is likely to turn his anger outward rather than inward (van der Kolk, 1987; Kreisman, 1989). He is not allowed to express fear of abandonment, just as he is not allowed to portray himself as a victim, and his expressions of anger will be less likely to be viewed as inappropriate. When a man loses his temper and curses at or hits someone, his behavior is seen as relatively normal; when a woman shouts curses at another adult or hits, she is seen as out of control and not normal. Such gender distinctions help to explain why there seems to be this special diagnostic category (BPD) reserved almost entirely for females who have been traumatized by childhood abuse.

There have been important contributions to the professional literature on positive uses of the borderline diagnosis and related treatment approaches (Benjamin, 1993; Linehan, 1993; DiCello, in press). My position is perhaps more skeptical than that of my colleagues, however. I question whether we can safely condone the use of the borderline diagnosis at all. While I have found it to be a useful means of briefly identifying a cluster of behaviors when I am consulting with other mental health professionals, I continue to have serious questions about whether the very existence of the diagnosis may cause us to mislabel patients and thus approach treatment in a damaging way. When I think about the need of the TRS woman to be understood from a perspective of exploring her self-harm, rages, and relational turbulence, I worry that the traditional treatment protocol of "containing" the borderline client will be used to silence the TRS woman as long as the diagnosis continues to be used. The following case history illustrates my attempt to move clients away from this potentially damaging diagnosis.

BJ was another client who helped me understand more about the misdiagnosis of Trauma Reenactment Syndrome. She was twenty-five years old when I first met her. Already she had a chart as thick as a city telephone directory at the local hospital's psychiatric unit and emergency room. BJ was the youngest daughter among five children. Her grandmother, who had raised her, was also known to the psychiatric unit, where she had been hospitalized frequently.

BJ was assigned to me for "maintenance" visits as part of my caseload. I was instructed simply to "manage" her medication check-ins with the psychiatrist and periodically to fill out forms enabling her to get permanent disability support from the state. I was also warned that BJ was prone to aggressive behavior toward her female therapists and had a bad temper and a tumultuous history of relationships with both male and female partners. When I looked at her chart, I saw that she had been involved in the mental health system since she was sixteen years old. Her diagnosis was Borderline Personality Disorder and she was also flagged as a substance abuser.

Unlike many clients with a borderline label, BJ was well liked by most clinicians because she had a flamboyant, histrionic style that entertained them. BJ was, in fact, a very intelligent young woman who instantly engaged and also scared me. I could understand why her behavior toward her previous therapists kept professionals at a safe distance from her. Still, I was disturbed to think that at age twenty-five she would be written off as essentially incurable, incapable of achieving a stable and happy relationship, and unable ever to work or be free of the mental health system.

When I first met her, I was struck by the contrast between the Greenpeace sweatshirt she wore, which had an endangered baby seal with huge, vulnerable eyes on it, and her dark glasses, punk hairstyle, and scowling face that confronted me with sneering contempt. As I got to know BJ better, I learned that the contrast was expressed in many different ways. BJ did not have a clear picture of herself. She was perpetually trying out various personas: tough, helpless, seductive, assaultive, adult, child, raging, withdrawn, nutty, sane.

BJ's story became an important one as I learned how even the most loving and benign of professionals can obstruct the recovery process of the TRS woman through misdiagnosis and misinformed treatment. The doctors, nurses, psychologists, social workers, and emergency room workers who came into contact with BJ seemed genuinely to care about her, so the borderline label did not result in the punishment that it does for many other clients. Yet she was not treated as having the capacity to change her role from chronic mental patient to ever-changing, potentially healthy human being. As in most treatment of borderline clients, the approach to her concentrated on containment. Rather than exploring her history of childhood abuse (which was well documented by the mental health system), or trying to change her way of relating to professionals, or helping her become more independent of the system, people treated her as though she were a lovable but recalcitrant two-year-old. The message from the system seemed to be a monotonous litany of what she should and should not do. No one tried to engage her in couples therapy; no one tried to get her various medications reduced; no one explored her childhood trauma history with her. What surprised me most was that no one had actively addressed her obvious problems of substance abuse.

My first stage of work with BJ was to discuss with her the diagnosis of Borderline Personality Disorder and to see if she thought it was correct. I explained as benignly and tactfully as I could what the disorder entailed. The very next week, BJ appeared with a book on diagnosing Borderline Personality Disorder, which she had read cover to cover. Needless to say, she was not pleased with her diagnosis. I suggested that she could instead be given a substance abuse diagnosis and that she could actually achieve recovery if she were willing to work hard at it. I also began seeing her with her current partner, a woman who was threatening to leave if BJ could not control her episodes of violent rage.

I began to explore with her what she was feeling when she occasionally became sexually aggressive and obnoxious in our individual sessions. The first time she made a sexually aggressive move, I told her I would treat her like a sane, competent adult and call the police to arrest her if it happened again. After that, she confined her sexual acting out to assaultive verbal provocations. We were gradually able to work on some genuine feelings of vulnerability. Rather than simply instructing her on how to contain her unacceptable sexually aggressive behavior, I invited her to explore its antecedents with me. What had I asked her that had triggered feelings of vulnerability and hence her attempts to push me away? What did her feelings about me have to do with her feelings about other significant people in her life, both in the present and the past?

BJ's case illustrates how the borderline diagnosis can infantilize a client who should instead be understood and treated as a TRS woman. While I was not totally successful in my efforts to help her explore her feelings and her childhood abuse, I did help her to feel that she was not destined to remain a child of the mental health system forever and that she was capable of making important changes in controlling her adult life, with all its pleasures, privileges, and responsibilities. I was also able to help her focus more on her identity as a substance abuser, a diagnosis with more hope for recovery than BPD.

I often wish I could be working with BJ in therapy now, because I have more fully developed my ideas about TRS women. I would like the opportunity to change her diagnosis again, this time to Trauma Reenactment Syndrome, and to engage her in the treatment approach that has evolved since I was her therapist. I would also have liked to work more with her, and the larger treatment system, on her substance abuse, another area in which the TRS woman often receives only partial help.

Substance Abuse and Eating Disorders

Substance-abusing women have always been viewed with distaste and condemnation by the professional helping system, as well as by society at large. Reactions most frequently express fear of the woman as "out of control," which translates into "unladylike" or "unfeminine," and rage triggered by the sexual provocations associated with female drug use. Although female addiction is now met with greater understanding by professionals and the public, the TRS woman still suffers from being diagnosed in terms of her addiction alone. Of course, if she is abusing alcohol or drugs, or if she is starving or bingeing and purging, the addictive pattern is an important part of her description, but it is only part of the picture.

Being identified as addicted does have some advantages over being seen as psychotic, like Fiora, or borderline, like Laura and BJ. Most important, recovery is seen as possible. Rather than living with a chronic stigma, pathologized by the mental health system and consigned to permanent dependency on that system, addicted and eating-disordered women know that they are not considered hopelessly mentally ill. They learn that they will not have to be involved with the mental health system or psychiatric medications for life and that they can join many other successful, nonstigmatized women who have found recovery in twelve-step or other peer support programs. These women are given hope in their recovery from addictions.

Addiction support groups such as the twelve-step programs are very effective when used as part of treatment for the TRS woman. Twelve-step recovery groups offer an experience of community that is central to the survival of the woman who hurts herself. Becoming free from the addiction and the relationship patterns it has created brings great relief. Perhaps an even greater relief comes from telling one's story of shame, pain, and failure to others who have shared similar experiences. Such sharing of stories in groups is an important part of what makes the recovery movement work, especially in groups that focus on alcohol, drugs, eating, gambling, and other behavior-focused addictions.

Unfortunately, the TRS woman, even while working toward recovery, still may not achieve lasting freedom from her pain. She may engage wholeheartedly in a program to address her addiction, succeed in complete abstinence from her addictive behavior, and create a support network to help her maintain her abstinence. But she is likely to find herself wondering if she is the only one in her recovery meetings who continues to feel unbearable fear, rage, or grief, who continues to feel unsuccessful in her most significant relationships, and who is tormented by a childhood she cannot understand or put to rest. June voices this distress:

So what's wrong with me? I don't get it. I go to my meetings, I stay on the wagon, sometimes for a year or more at a time. I call my sponsor when I'm feeling tempted or discouraged about myself. I help others in the program. I even get myself to do the things they tell you, like about getting exercise, turning it over to your Higher Power or praying, not hanging out with the crowd you used to drink with.

How come I feel like I'm going to explode right out of my skin sometimes I'm so tight? How come I keep losing it with my kids? How come I couldn't make it work with Roy? How come I go crazy and let myself make it with guys I don't even like sometimes? What's wrong with me?

What is wrong is that June is not being given all the help she needs to explore and rework the long history of pain and trauma she endured both in childhood and adult life. Addiction-focused treatment does not encourage people to focus their attention on memories of childhood suffering, except to delineate the general patterns of growing up in a dysfunctional family. The addict is not encouraged to remember the many reasons she may have had for using substances for solace. Instead, she is encouraged to stay with the present. She is urged to concentrate on achieving and maintaining abstinence and a more productive life here and now. Although dysfunctional interpersonal styles are addressed as part of recovery, there is a strong emphasis on taking responsibility for one's own choices. Twelve-step recovery programs emphasize detaching from those relationships that are harmful, and turning one's agonies, doubts, and questions over to a Higher Power.

This goal of trusting a Higher Power is often hopelessly unattainable for women who have no experience in trusting anything or anyone. There is a central paradox common to all the treatments that fail to help TRS women to achieve full recovery: when a woman has had no consistent experience of being protected in childhood, she has no internalized capacity to trust or self-protect as an adult. To be able to entrust one's whole self to a support group, a Higher Power, or a psychotherapist requires the gradual integration of parts of the self. The problems created by the experience of repeated childhood abuse and neglect keep this integration from happening. Without being helped to identify and understand her fragmented self, the TRS woman does not have a clear sense of self-definition. She has no grasp of her own power and autonomy, her experience of personal agency. Without an awareness of the Triadic Self and the larger contextual patterns in trauma-based systems, without having had intensive relationally centered psychotherapy, the TRS woman cannot really be in a relationship with her Higher Power.

There are other pitfalls for women who have felt controlled by others all their lives. The TRS woman may acquiesce too readily to turning over her personal power again to a paternal image of authority. She is then potentially repeating a deeply dysfunctional pattern without understanding why it is that she continues to feel so out of control and without self-definition. In the addiction-focused support group, she may also be blocked from talking about her trauma experiences, another repetition of the abuse dynamics. She is given the message that her feelings of pain and loss of control can be turned around by changing something that is wrong in her, by owning responsibility for her addiction patterns. She is offered the support of others in doing so; she does not have to face the agonies alone, as she did in childhood. But she is still asked to view her pain as existing in the present, something she must evict from her heart, mind, and body. She is explicitly instructed to stay in the present and not dwell on the painful past. So her story of childhood torture or neglect must stay buried or relegated to a split-off consciousness, a separate part of her life. She is given no map or language to make sense of her fragmented and secret life.

Despite the problems of the addiction approach to TRS women, there are several positive aspects of this paradigm. One mentioned earlier is that, unlike the borderline diagnosis, there is a strong belief in the capacity for recovery. The woman who is working on her substance abuse or eating disorder as an addiction will be helped if she believes that she can achieve healthy relationships, a cohesive sense of self, and control of her moods, impulses, and behavior. To achieve these goals, she can focus on her abstinence from addictive behavior and work with others in following the twelve-step guidelines for attaining full sobriety in her thoughts and interactions.

However, drawbacks to this approach remain: the TRS woman is mislabeled as simply an addict and thus not helped to uncover traumatic childhood experiences or to learn how to repair the damage and fragmentation of the self that keep the TRS woman stuck in her self-harmful behavior.

Depression and Anxiety

Some TRS women have been diagnosed as clinically depressed, others as having anxiety disorders. The woman who is most likely to be characterized as suffering from depression or anxiety symptoms is one whose relationship behavior is less flamboyant or provocative than that of the borderline patient, whose verbal and emotional presentation is not psychotic, and whose life is not centrally organized around a particular addiction behavior such as substance abuse or bulimia.

Lee was the kind of woman likely to receive this label, despite the fact that she was cutting herself (which, without other information about her symptoms, could put her in the borderline category). To her therapist, Lee seemed typically depressed. She had low energy, showed little interest in sex, and was progressively seeking more and more solitude, escaping into long hours of sleeping. Unlike the borderline's behavior, she showed little evidence of overvaluing or devaluing others and she was not given to dramatic outbursts of anger. Unlike an addict, Lee was not characterized as manipulative in her interactions, nor did she overtly organize her daily life around her symptomatic behavior, as substance abusers and eating-disordered women do. Her subtle process of dissociating when cutting herself, or during conversations with David or Martha, was not obvious or extreme like the more flagrant hallucinations characteristic of the multiple personality.

As a "depressed" client, Lee would be viewed as a suicide risk. Depressed women, like addicted and borderline clients, sometimes engage in life-threatening activities, most often overdosing on pills, cutting their wrists, or inhaling toxic fumes. While all types of TRS women are capable of successful suicide attempts, it is more likely that the chronically depressed TRS woman will have intended to end her life, rather than doing so by accident. The borderline or substance-abusing TRS woman is more likely to miscalculate, taking a lethal dose of pills instead of the dose she intended as a way to numb her pain. However, all TRS women are self-destructive in potentially fatal ways and therefore should be taken seriously as suicide risks, whether the intention to die is conscious or not.

The depressed TRS woman is a client many therapists dread. The monotone narrative characteristic of the depressed person's communication and the entrenched pessimism and lack of pleasure or interest in daily life make this woman difficult to engage. Therapists, like anyone else, have a hard time sustaining their own energy, pleasure, or hopefulness in the company of a depressed person. Perhaps because talking with the depressed client is so difficult, the preferred treatment for clinical depression is likely to be medication and support therapy to help the client become more active in the world. While these treatment components are useful, they are not enough to penetrate to the layer of the self where the effects of the trauma are entrenched. With them, depressed TRS women can achieve more involvement with others and a higher level of vitality, but without a more fully integrated treatment approach, they remain self-destructive, still isolated inside themselves and at higher risk than others for suicide.

In contrast to the depressed TRS woman, a woman like Nancy, if she were to be given any mental health label at all, might be seen as having an anxiety disorder. Her anxious mood and hyperactive attempts to stay busy, social, and playful while trying to outrun the aging process fit the pattern of a person suffering from anxiety. TRS women who are most likely to be viewed by professional helpers as anxious are also most likely to be given medication as the primary form of treatment. They are also likely to be treated for specific behavioral problems, such as phobias and sleep disorders. While the medication and behaviorally focused treatment may give the TRS woman temporary relief from her particular anxiety symptom, her underlying experience of isolation and emotional turmoil continues.

Many TRS women are either depressed or anxious. Some are in therapy, some are on medication, some are even involved in twelve-step recovery groups because of addiction issues. Others, whose lives appear to be more manageable than those of the substance abuser, the alcoholic, the eating-disordered woman, or the borderline-type woman, are not in any kind of treatment. The types of treatment usually offered to women diagnosed as depressed and anxious are medication, nonspecific individual psychotherapy, symptom-focused support groups, and behavioral therapy. These treatments for depressed or anxious TRS women are not comprehensive enough, though. The untreated TRS patterns continue and the woman feels a deeper sense of depression or anxiety because she does not know what is wrong with her and senses that her helpers do not know either.

Multiple Personality Disorder

Various forms of dissociative disorders have been the focus of the misdiagnosis and incomplete treatment of TRS clients. In the late nineteenth century, Freud's treatment of women who were survivors of childhood sexual abuse and other doctors' hypnosis work with dissociative manifestations of early trauma represented the medical establishment's view that women with dissociative behaviors and communications were to be diagnosed as suffering from hysteria. While this was an improvement over seeing these women as possessed by demons, it still unduly stigmatized the victim of childhood trauma. Until recently, dissociative episodes were likely to result in diagnoses such as schizophrenia, manic-depression, or other forms of major mental illness. Now that childhood trauma has been understood to stimulate dissociative patterns in children that last into adult life, there has been significant development in the mental health field. The trauma researcher and psychiatrist Bessel van der Kolk has developed a new diagnostic category to assess the various types of dissociation related to early trauma not specified as part of other diagnoses. While this is a hopeful step toward more precisely understanding and describing the effects of trauma on dissociative phenomena, there is still much mystery and confusion in this area of diagnosis and treatment.

Multiple Personality Disorder (MPD), an extreme form of dissociation, has become enormously interesting to clinicians and the public over the past few years. Many women whose behavior seems relatively normal yet who are strangely withdrawn, isolated, or difficult to relate to are now being diagnosed as suffering from this disorder. The MPD client has several distinct personalities, or alters, as a result of dissociative patterns developed during trauma experiences in childhood. These parts of herself are split off from each other and have separate, fully developed personae. One personality may be a child; another may be an adult woman very different from the woman as she is known to the world; another may be a male alter; and so on. The alters do not necessarily communicate with each other. The primary task of healing is generally assumed to be the integration of these various parts of the self into a more unified and better functioning whole self, or at least improvement in coordination of the various selves.

Women with this disorder are being seen in therapy far more frequently today than in years past. The discovery that MPD seems more prevalent than professionals had assumed seems directly linked to the recent evidence that child sexual abuse is more widespread and more damaging than had been thought. There is increasing pressure to believe the mental health professionals who say that Multiple Personality Disorder is a relatively common response to severe abuse.

Treatment of MPD is still evolving and there is no "usual" protocol for working with this disorder. It is generally accepted that rather lengthy individual psychotherapy is necessary. The therapist and client work together to bring forth as many of the personalities as possible, getting acquainted with each part of the fragmented self. They then begin the work of integrating the alters, so that the client can have a more cohesive self and manage her life more effectively. Not much is yet known about how medications or support groups may work to aid the psychotherapy treatment.

MPD women can include Trauma Reenactment Syndrome among their problems. They are likely to engage in self-destructive behaviors, ranging from self-mutilation to addictions and eating disorders. They are slightly more complicated than other TRS women in how they communicate, however, because only some alters seem to be responsible for the self-destructive behavior. Theoretically, this factor could make treatment much easier, because the particular part of the self that does the damage to the body has already been split off and identified. One could work directly with this alter on the self-harming patterns and then either persuade the alter to stop the behavior or integrate the alter with the parts of the self where there is more capacity for self-protection. In practice, however, this is not easy. The destructive alters are more accountable for the self-harmful behavior than the Abuser–Victim–Nonprotecting Bystander fragments of the Triadic Self, but they are not easy to communicate with or to neutralize. The non-MPD TRS woman may be less aware of the conflict within herself than the MPD woman. However, once she develops an understanding of how the Triadic Self operates, she generally has an easier time developing a Protective Presence to stop the Abuser's self-harm.

A positive factor in connecting the MPD diagnosis with TRS is that the problem of dissociation resulting from childhood trauma takes center stage. All those who work with, or are in any form of relationship with, the TRS woman need to become familiar with the centrality of dissociation and fragmentation. The problems of the fragmented self for TRS women are on a continuum. MPD is at one end of the contin-

uum; at the other end is the Triadic Self, a less severe form of fragmentation. The attention being given to MPD should make the road
smoother for a better understanding of all TRS women and their problems with fragmentation and dissociation. The preoccupation with
MPD can get in the way, however; because they are distracted by the
novelty and drama of MPD clients, clinicians and other experts may
lose sight of the fragmentation problems presented by other trauma victims. Professionals may also exaggerate the simpler triadic version of
fragmentation so that it becomes a false MPD diagnosis.

Post-Traumatic Stress Disorder

Most recently, as the mental health system and the public have become
aware of the prevalence of childhood physical and sexual abuse and
neglect, TRS women have been given the label of Post-Traumatic Stress
Disorder (PTSD). Originally developed as a diagnosis for war veterans
and survivors of natural disasters and violent crimes, PTSD describes a
cluster of responses to traumatic events. Using this diagnosis implies
that the problem does not originate within the individual's personality,
but rather that an external event has created lasting but not incurable
symptoms or reactions. The PTSD diagnosis is now extended to survivors of child abuse, as well as to women who have been battered or
raped.

In *Trauma and Recovery* (1992), Judith Herman describes trauma in
this way:

> Traumatic events are extraordinary, not because they occur rarely,
> but rather because they overwhelm the ordinary human adapta-
> tions to life. Unlike commonplace misfortunes, traumatic events
> generally involve threats to life or bodily integrity, or a close per-
> sonal encounter with violence or death. They confront human
> beings with the extremities of helplessness and terror and evoke the
> responses of catastrophe. (p. 33)

The TRS woman's experience of both childhood trauma and the current trauma of self-injuring is accurately represented in this description.
Herman and others who specialize in the study and treatment of

trauma have provided a valuable map for understanding the suffering of women who were previously misdiagnosed and whose treatment suffered as a consequence.

The PTSD diagnosis identifies the genesis of the damage to the patient rather than describing the patient. This is an important distinction. When a TRS client is given a label such as borderline or alcoholic, a set of expectations is established in the minds of everyone who interacts with her. Especially with a label such as borderline or chronic depression, she may not be given the opportunity to be seen as a whole person or a person who is capable of change. But when a client is given the diagnosis of PTSD, she is seen as having undergone a severe trauma, and her symptoms or problems in living are recognized as having resulted from trauma. Compare "I am a bulimic" or "she is a borderline" with "I am recovering from PTSD" or "she is in therapy because of PTSD." Clearly there is a difference in how the whole person is portrayed. PTSD implies that there is more to her than the part that is represented by the trauma history.

Because of this major shift in awareness, not only in the professional world but in the media as well, many women with trauma histories are receiving more useful and empowering treatment than previously. While their particular symptoms may still be of concern, they are also offered the opportunity to explore their traumatic childhoods through psychotherapy and various kinds of healing groups. The PTSD-diagnosed woman works toward recovery by concentrating on the trauma itself: remembering, reliving, and then, when the trauma has been ventilated, reworking her self-image and her relationships. The recognition of PTSD as a major diagnosis, and its more sympathetic and holistic treatment protocol, represents a giant step toward recovery for TRS women.

Unfortunately, even the PTSD approach to treatment of the TRS woman is likely to be problematic. While the PTSD diagnosis is preferable to Borderline Personality Disorder, for example, it still does not adequately distinguish between those trauma victims who do not harm their bodies and those women who manifest their history of trauma through self-injury. It also does not describe the TRS woman's complex levels of behaving, thinking, and feeling as they are translated into relationships, especially as those relationships pertain to treatment. Furthermore, the scope of PTSD is too limited. The types of trauma that point to a PTSD diagnosis are generally understood to include childhood sexual abuse, adult rape, battle trauma, and natural disasters. This definition does not include such childhood traumas as physical abuse, severe neglect, or invasive caretaking of the more benignly motivated sort. Because clients with these types of traumas are omitted from the PTSD population, many women who hurt themselves are still left without an appropriate diagnosis.

Another increasingly problematic aspect of the PTSD label is that it tends to be overused and too generalized, somewhat like the term "codependence." The degrees of childhood trauma are difficult to measure and thus many different experiences may be covered by the catchall term PTSD. References to adult experiences of trauma may be even more careless and thus confusing or disturbing. For example, the rape victim has a very different experience of her own security and personal power in the world than does the exhausted graduate student who says she is experiencing "trauma" when she gets negative feedback on an important term paper.

Although the PTSD diagnosis is a step forward, it is still necessary to distinguish between all survivors of childhood trauma and that subgroup among them who are TRS women. The complexity of what has happened to create the pattern of self-destructive behavior is not adequately contained in most diagnoses or treatments of PTSD. In treatment, for instance, simply disclosing the details of the trauma or even reexperiencing it through flashbacks, supportive therapy, or group sharing is not enough. June, for example, could produce her recitation of childhood neglect memories, religiously attend twelve-step meetings, and successfully abstain from drinking. Yet she was far from feeling whole or capable of achieving success in interpersonal interactions.

When TRS women disclose their trauma histories, they are often bewildered that they do not feel substantially healthier. It is maddening for many of them to recognize that the process of disclosure may actually exacerbate their symptoms, as well as make them feel more alone and more out of control. This creates a cycle of feeling betrayed by those who were supposedly going to rescue or stand by them. In addition, they feel an escalation of self-blame because they assume it must be their fault that telling about the abuse did not lead to a healthier, more open experience of living.

One aspect of PTSD treatment that can increase the TRS woman's loneliness and rage about feeling different is the tendency to frame the story of childhood abuse in polarized terms. The abuser, referred to as "the offender" or "the perpetrator," is cast as the villain of the story. He (or she, in cases of maternal incest) is portrayed as all bad, often as evil. The nonprotecting mother is also cast in a bad role, blamed not for the abuse per se but for failing to be an adequate, nurturing mother. Then there is the child herself, the victim, blameless and powerless. Discussions in the popular press and on talk shows generally take this oversimplified position, and groups for survivors often adopt this victim/villain frame for telling stories. Even in individual psychotherapy, the therapist may coerce this point of view as the only correct description.

When the survivor is coached to tell or understand her story this way, she feels shaken. Because she has internalized these complex primary relationships, she is filled with confusion and shame. If she completely renounces her love or loyalty in relation to either the abusive or nonprotecting parent, she may feel as if she is renouncing and even hating a part of herself. If there is no space for her to question and explore this web of complexity, she shuts down, or blames herself, or increases her experience of fragmentation.

Responding to the distress of feeling different, unseen, and misunderstood, the TRS woman often escalates the frequency or seriousness of her symptom. She is blocked from integrating her understanding of the symptom with her trauma history because those who focus on the symptom may want her to stop probing and hurting herself by exploring her childhood; this treatment approach is telling her to stop thinking about the past and to learn to contain her dysfunctional behavior. In short, the PTSD treatment approach urges her to remember the trauma, but not to rework it in a way that might lead to lasting recovery. It is no wonder that many TRS women become increasingly hopeless about themselves, despite the possibilities for healing offered by the advent of the PTSD treatment movement.

Approaches to trauma treatment continue to become more varied and more sophisticated. Judith Herman (1992) has introduced a new diagnosis, complex PTSD, which makes important distinctions between adult-onset or one-time-occurrence trauma and trauma such as child sexual abuse that is sustained over a prolonged period, is perpetrated by someone in a caretaker role in the child's life, and tends to be more damaging. This kind of differentiation allows for a broader scope of treatment requirements. Many therapists and researchers continue to explore the complex responses of the survivor to her childhood trauma experiences; Bessel van der Kolk (1987), Judith Herman (1992), Lisa McCann and Laurie Pearlman (1990), Shanti Shapiro and George Dominiak (1992), Ronnie Janoff-Bulman (1992), and Denise Gelinas (1993) are all experts in the trauma treatment field who recognize that the therapy needs of the child abuse survivor are far more complex than simply recovering and reworking the trauma memories. Many theorists and practitioners of more general psychotherapy also recognize that there are more complex ways to work with trauma survivors than the oversimplified "remembering/catharsis/confronting/rebuilding" formula for PTSD treatment. Still, there is an absence of focus on the specific needs of the TRS woman in the literature to date. These needs are fully addressed in the multilevel model described in the following chapters.

The Family Therapy Perspective

Mental health professionals have too often ignored the importance of exploring the family system in their treatment of teenage girls and adult women who hurt themselves. If a TRS woman is viewed as depressed, the problem is most often seen as biologically based; if she is diagnosed as borderline, her current behavior becomes the focus of treatment, rather than the story of her family life, where the behavior began. Treating the intricacies of the family system's dysfunctional patterns may even be neglected when the symptom of choice is drug or alcohol abuse. In the past, when a young woman like Fiora entered the mental health system, the use of drugs or alcohol was attributed to her weak character and poor peer associations; clues were not sought in the family. At best, in more recent years, other family members' substance use may be explored and the individual's chemical abuse attributed to family patterns, but the underlying pain that engendered and maintains the abuse goes undetected.

Family therapy would probably have made a significant difference in how Fiora's life turned out. There was no referral for family therapy then, because very little family therapy was being done when Fiora was a teenager. Even today, there are several reasons why family therapy does not always happen, even when the TRS woman is still a teenager living at home. Fiora's father's ability to manage a smooth, educated, middle-class presentation, coupled with his eloquently stated concern for his daughter, protected the family from scrutiny. His behavior would have been less likely to escape notice if the family had been stigmatized by poverty, obvious substance abuse, or neglect. Abused, neglected, or invaded children and adults are less likely to receive protective services or agency protection when they are from middle-class, outwardly successful families, especially if the family is white and part of the dominant group in the particular social setting. Children from poor, nonwhite, minority families—most of all from single-parent families—are the likeliest to be seen as victims of their families.

Despite being likelier targets for professional intervention, children from families of lower socioeconomic status may still be mistreated. They may be moved from one dysfunctional family system to another, or a superficial intervention in the family may put them at greater risk of further abuse. Rather than working intensively with the family or removing the child permanently, the helping system too frequently moves in only long enough to accuse and threaten the family. When the dust settles, nothing is changed, and the family is better able to cover its tracks by knowing how to conceal ongoing abuse.

June had such an experience as a child. There were several investigations by children's protective services because June and her siblings showed signs of neglect. June remembers that a teacher once questioned her, asking her why she was falling asleep in the classroom, whether something was wrong at home. June was too young then to conceal what she later learned to cover up, and a social worker came to their apartment along with a truant officer. As June remembers it, her mother convinced the visitors that she would supervise June and her siblings more carefully. Later June was punished severely by her mother and told that if the social worker ever came back, June's cat would be permanently injured.

In other families, such threats are not necessary. The shame of revealing family secrets such as a mother's alcoholism, a father's inappropriate sexual behavior, or a neglectful home life can be enough to silence the child or teenager. Because the relationship with the abuser has become internalized and is felt by the victim to be a part of herself, she is often as fiercely unwilling to admit the parent's abuse as she is to reveal a wrongdoing of her own.

Another reason that the family system perspective may not be properly used is the distortion of the family history when seen through the PTSD lens. As I noted, the TRS woman in PTSD treatment is encouraged to tell her story in extreme terms in which there are victims and villains—a two-dimensional portrait of parents, siblings, and other significant family members that may not feel accurate to her at all. If she tries to explain her more complex picture of these people, with whom she lived and whom she loved in some way, she is often told that she is denying reality.

There are certainly problems with addressing TRS from a family therapy approach. Often the TRS woman in family therapy will be viewed only in her role as part of the family or couple system. Her individual symptoms and sense of fragmentation may be overlooked or minimized. Her problem of feeling disconnected and isolated, as manifested both in her self-harmful cycle of behavior and in the more general way in which she copes with relationships and life stresses, can be buried.

Family therapy has been vigorously criticized in the past for its failure to look at issues of power and domination in terms of gender, class, race, and age (MacKinnon and Miller, 1987; Goldner, 1987; Luepnitz, 1988). In the attempt to understand and respond to all members of the family, many family therapists have ignored the terrible realities of child abuse and woman battering, or refused to take an active role in intervening in ongoing interpersonal violence. More recently, family therapists have been more direct in taking a position on such problems and exploring ways to use family systems thinking and therapy techniques to approach these kinds of situations.

Family therapists such as Marsha Mirkin (1990), Jo Ann Krestan and Claudia Bepko (1985, 1990) Virginia Goldner, Peggy Penn, Marsha Sheinberg, and Gillian Walker (1990), and myself (Miller, 1989; 1990a; 1990b) have addressed problems of the violence-affected woman. Nonetheless, family systems writers and practitioners have not concentrated much attention on the structure of the individual self and the fragmentation that is a critical element in understanding the TRS woman. In my work, the family therapy approach is useful in the early stages of developing an understanding of the context that engenders and supports the TRS woman's patterns of self-harm and relationships.

*   *   *

The major diagnostic categories I have reviewed as most frequently applicable to TRS proceed from the most to the least potentially disastrous. The borderline diagnosis is the most unforgiving in its approach to clients. The opportunity to investigate the narrative meaning of self-harmful behavior is lost and the client is pathologized. She is taught to identify her patterns of thought and behavior only in order to control and contain them.

At the other end of the spectrum are the PTSD and family systems perspectives. These are the least potentially destructive to the TRS woman because they address her situation rather than her personality or moods. Both these perspectives see her as having been harmed by traumatic or dysfunctional family dynamics. They help her by changing the way she sees herself and teaching her to behave differently in relationships.

The addictions approach leans toward the more hopeful end of the spectrum because it also views the woman as capable of major change. Although she is viewed as an addict forever, she is educated as to how she can change her behavior and relationships by changing her ideas about herself and her habits of daily life.

The diagnoses of depression, anxiety, and MPD are in the middle of the spectrum. While they allow for more exploration of the connection between the woman's history of trauma and her current suffering than does the borderline diagnosis, they also trap her. These diagnoses imply serious, possibly permanent impairment. Treatment too often centers on long-term medication or unrealistically long-term intensive psychotherapy.

All these diagnostic categories offer useful pieces of conceptual wisdom or treatment strategies in dealing with the TRS woman's four major problem areas. The war against the woman's own body is interrupted by the abstinence approach of the addiction focus. This area is also targeted by some of the medications used to treat anxiety and depression, as well as the behavioral techniques of the better work with borderline clients. The pervasive problem of secrecy is also addressed by some of these categories. The PTSD approach, for example, elevates the breaking of silence to a center point of treatment. Addiction-focused treatment also emphasizes the importance of dislodging toxic secrets, as does most family therapy. The concepts of dissociation and the fragmented self are central in working with MPD and in many approaches to PTSD. Dissociation explains the person's problems in living and can be treated and healed. Finally, the problems that TRS women have in relationships are addressed in all the diagnostic categories reviewed in this chapter. However, how the relationship problems are to be understood and healed remains imperfect in each category, although some part of each approach can be incorporated in treating TRS, as I will show in subsequent chapters.

7

The Outer Circle

Because the symptoms of TRS are so complex, treatment must be comprehensive and carefully planned. It is necessary to understand not only the history that initiated the self-abusive symptoms and the context that perpetuates them, but also the function that they serve. The journey toward healing must integrate different theoretical perspectives and types of treatment, and must be based on the certainty of a safe, supportive therapeutic relationship in order to bring about lasting recovery.

In the remaining chapters, I concentrate on my own approach for working with women who hurt themselves. Of course, it is not the only good model for working with Trauma Reenactment Syndrome. However, understanding my model should be helpful in developing general guidelines for a multilevel, integrated approach to TRS. Chapters 7 through 9 are written for women who hurt themselves and those who love them, and also for the therapists who work with them. I have used descriptive language that I hope will be familiar to therapists and at the same time accessible to nonprofessionals, especially TRS women themselves. What is important for the reader to consider is whether her treatment approach includes the levels of intervention I describe.

I use the image of three concentric circles to represent the TRS woman's journey toward healing. Each circle represents the relative distance between the client's hidden, injured self and all the people in her life, especially her therapist and other helpers. The concentric circles also represent the distance the client and her helpers must travel to recover and heal that injured self.

No story of childhood trauma is exactly the same as any other, and because the ability of the client to tell her story in her own way is central to healing, my treatment approach is narrative-centered. Throughout treatment there is major emphasis on the power of self-disclosure, or storytelling, and on the importance of establishing collaboration between client and therapist. The client is continually encouraged to seek self-determination, to view herself as "expert" as she tells her story of childhood trauma and self-abusive behavior.

In the first stage of treatment, the "Outer Circle," I gather information about the context of the historical abuse and the current self-abuse; family rules, myths, beliefs, and stories provide information necessary to construct a new, more complex narrative about the individual in her current life. This process helps to develop a safer environment for the later stages when powerful, long-held secrets are shared.

In the "Middle Circle," when the client's story of her childhood trauma still has not been fully disclosed, her current problems and symptoms are addressed more directly. The beginning work of sharing shameful secrets about current self-harmful behavior happens primarily through group support. Clients are helped to connect with peer support groups, such as twelve-step recovery programs, and relevant professional systems, such as addiction-focused or trauma-focused hospital units. When necessary, the legal system, the child protection system, relevant school personnel, and supportive friends, family, and colleagues are also involved at this stage of the recovery work.

What is perhaps most important about the Middle Circle stage of treatment is that it builds a support system. The client and therapist are not left alone with the terrors and tribulations that inevitably emerge when, through telling the long-concealed and deeply shameful secrets, the client remembers, relives, and reworks the trauma story more deeply in the third stage of treatment.

In this third and final stage, the "Inner Circle," each exploration of shameful, secret memories and each disclosure of current self-abuse becomes linked to the deepening connection of the therapist–client relationship. Each act of sharing must allow the client to feel protected and accepted throughout the terrifying disclosures of her shame and pain. The Inner Circle therapy relationship is what allows the client to develop the capacity to protect herself from self-harming behaviors and to learn new ways to connect with others.

At the beginning of therapy, in the Outer Circle, the helper makes a connection with the client and explores the possibility of a relationship.

The central challenge in beginning to change patterns of self-abusive behavior is telling painful secrets. The secrecy surrounding childhood trauma has a long and important history that deserves careful attention. It is important for both clients and counselors to understand the tension between the need to hide the trauma story and the related symptoms and the need to tell the story. This tension must be respected if the therapy relationship is to feel safe.

A vital component in enabling the victim of abuse to tell her story safely is the development of a working relationship with someone who is expert in guiding women through this process. Much of the initial building of the safe relationship is based on mutual surveillance. Earlier, I used the metaphor of the naturalist and the wild creature in describing the beginning of therapy with wary, mistrustful clients. The therapist assumes the position of a naturalist, approaching slowly, observing, and allowing herself to be observed by the client over time.* It is important to note that the good naturalist succeeds not only by remaining quietly in the wild creature's habitat long enough to observe the creature, but also by being observed by the animal long enough for it to have some sense of what to expect from this potentially dangerous human.

Early conversations at the beginning of therapy should purposely avoid details of childhood trauma, even if the client has disclosed a history of childhood abuse, violation, or neglect. One reason for delaying the retelling and reexperiencing of the trauma history is that the self-abusive symptoms are likely to increase when this material is explored. The new therapist does not yet know the client well enough to help her through such a period effectively. The therapist should allow the client to observe her and get to know her, so that the client can make more informed decisions about how safe it feels to discuss trauma memories or current self-abuse. The therapist also should learn the client's story as it pertains to the issue of retaining control of secrets. The use of secrecy as a form of protection is of special interest for conversations in the Outer Circle. This topic must be explored carefully so that the TRS client does not feel accused of or blamed for her need to keep secrets. The client is indirectly teaching the therapist about her experiences of

---

*I use feminine pronouns to refer to the therapist, but this work certainly can be done as well by sensitive, gender-aware male therapists.

shame and fear. The therapist is also learning how close other people can come to the client without overwhelming her and taking control away from her.

In a carefully seeded therapy, a nonintrusive, nonjudgmental context is established in which the client is allowed to determine how to tell her story safely. The therapist should not impose her view of the problems being explored or the story being unfolded. She needs to understand enough about the client's beliefs and history to know what it means for this particular individual to take the first steps toward her.

The following story illustrates the impasse that often occurs in the Outer Circle if the client is silenced and misunderstood by the therapist. It also illustrates the way the client and therapist can cooperate when the therapist learns how to listen to her client. It is a story about my own learning as a therapist and supervisor.

The family therapist Betty Carter, in talking about the challenges facing therapists, commented, "We have all participated in the fog of not knowing" (1990). Angela's story shines forth out of the "fog of not knowing." This case was a milestone for me as a supervisor, an experience when much of my previous professional training and clinical experience was not useful. I was pushed into the uncomfortable abyss of not knowing what to do, and then forward to the experience of empathic awareness that gave me a new understanding of myself as well as of the client.

Angela came to the community health center with her older sister, Carmen. They were assigned to the family therapy training team I was supervising. The therapist I supervised was repeatedly overwhelmed by Angela and Carmen.

Angela was a low-income Greek-American woman in her early fifties. She had recently discovered a horrifying piece of family history: Frank, Angela's sixty-year-old husband, many years earlier had sexually abused one of their daughters. The abuse had begun when the child was eight and had continued until she was fifteen. The daughter had kept this secret for twenty-five years; she finally disclosed the incest to her Aunt Carmen at a family gathering. Carmen immediately told Angela. After this shocking revelation, Angela waited almost six months before she came to the mental health center, urged by Carmen to get treatment for herself and her family.

Angela appeared for the first therapy session with Carmen. She looked small, frightened, and considerably overshadowed by her older sister. Carmen was a large woman who sat sternly erect in her chair throughout the session, refusing to take off her coat, her handbag planted firmly on her lap. She frequently interrupted or answered for her sister. She was openly irritated with Angela, who wept softly throughout most of the session.

Angela had responded to the disclosure of the abuse with a mixture of powerful rage toward her husband and overwhelming guilt about her own role. She stated repeatedly that she had never suspected the incest, yet she continued to blame herself more than she blamed Frank. Both Carmen and the therapist asserted that Angela was not responsible for Frank's abuse of their daughter, that mothers and children do not cause men to abuse their children. Angela could not seem to take in these attempts at reassurance and wept inconsolably.

The therapist and I were puzzled and increasingly frustrated by a question that Angela asked persistently in each session: "Was it a love affair?" The therapist and Carmen took turns explaining patiently, and then less patiently, that the sexual abuse of children is not about love. "It's an abuse of power, a violation of the child, an act of violence," explained the therapist.

"It's sick," Carmen summarized.

It didn't seem to matter what anyone said. Angela would change the subject or weep even more copiously. Sooner or later the question would reemerge. "Was it a love affair?"

I felt helpless in my role as supervisor, baffled by why we could not seem to move the conversation along. I was troubled by my growing anger, which seemed to be spreading to include Angela, Carmen, and even the helpless therapist. Then something out of my growing clinical desperation jiggled loose a feeling, a memory fragment connected to my own personal history, that told me something about the question of love. It occurred to me that we needed to try harder to understand Angela's question. We were not really listening to her.

As is common practice in training students, I had been observing the session through a one-way mirror. I phoned Angela from behind the mirror, introducing myself by name and telling her that I really wanted to understand what she was asking. "Angela," I said softly, "I can't stop thinking about your question. I wonder, suppose it was a love affair . . . what would that mean?"

Angela stared at the one-way mirror, almost seeming to look through it and meet my eyes. She stopped crying and sat up straight, a posture we had not seen previously. She appeared to think a while about my question. Finally she answered me. "Well," she said, "if it was a love affair, the abuse my husband was doing to my daughter, then why? Why didn't I love her enough? Why didn't Frank love me? Did he love me enough? Do you think he was in love with our daughter? Do you think he's in love with her now? Still? Is she still in love with him?"

The questions poured out. She gradually became angry. Her voice got louder. She was still crying, but the volume was turned up, and she was soon raging against Frank, against her daughter, against all of her children. Then the rage turned toward her family of origin. Carmen tried to interrupt Angela, but the balance of power had clearly shifted. Frail little Angela had disappeared and Angela the lionhearted had emerged.

From that point on, Angela's question about the love affair framed the therapy. She told the painful, compelling story of growing up the youngest girl in a large family of first-generation Greek immigrants. It was the story of a victim, a scapegoat. Her mother and older siblings had been physically abusive to her. Her father lived in her memory as a kind but ineffectual figure, humiliated in the outside world because he could not find steady work. Angela had longed to be loved by her mother and to be protected by her father.

As an exhausted young mother, feeling alone and incompetent, Angela had taken on the abuser role and had been verbally abusive to her children. She recalled that she was especially abusive to the daughter who was sexually abused by Frank "because she was the one most like me. I could see myself in her. Sometimes I hated her. Maybe that's why I was so mean to her."

She had been blaming herself and feeling guilty since Carmen told her of the sexual abuse. "Maybe Frank abused her because he was trying to comfort her and protect her from me. Maybe he loved her and she loved him because I didn't know how to love her or him. Maybe he went to her for the love affair because I didn't want him. I used to push him away in bed because I didn't want any more babies."

At long last we began to understand the history underlying Angela's insistent question, "Was it a love affair?" Once we began to listen closely to her, Angela's story continued to unfold. We gradually developed a language rich enough to explore together the many levels of affective experience in her history. She drew us into pictures of herself as a child, a young mother, a middle-aged mother with adult children, and Frank's wife. Having made this connection with Angela, we were able to move into a phase of therapy that allowed her to explore some of her own issues of abuse and self-harm.

The lesson that Angela taught me has stayed with me. Angela helped me see the difficulty many clinicians have in finding ways to listen to clients who express contradictory, confusing, or unfairly self-blaming ideas, especially ideas connected to a history of abuse. Her therapist and I needed to understand the context in which Angela was asking her question: who she was, both in the present and in the past. In struggling to understand Angela, we also had to suspend temporarily all the rules we had learned about the treatment of child sexual abuse and to listen carefully for what she was really communicating. It did not work to argue with Angela about who was responsible for the incest. Nor did it work to accept her tenacious self-blame as the Nonprotecting Bystander. Angela needed to explore the question of love. It did not matter how many experts insisted that sexual abuse has no relationship to love. Angela needed to feel uniquely heard and understood. Stating the realities of power dynamics in the incest relationship was not initially helpful in providing the opening Angela needed. She continued to make her own individual, historical connections about what this disclosure of incest meant to her, working until she found a way to make us listen.

I learned from Angela the importance of listening for the unusual, the unexpected, the seemingly incomprehensible. What may be the most subtle and yet the most potent area of power dynamics is how the therapist listens to the client. Therapists and others who impose their own ideas about abuse (both child abuse and self-abuse) may distort the essence of the client's experience.

The capacity of many TRS women to communicate has been severely interrupted or impaired. Their power of speech has been so distorted that they are often communicating in a language of fragments, self-abusive behaviors, or painful silence. The narrative may be fragmented to the point of incoherence, confusing both the therapist and client. The therapist may feel incompetent when such a client presents her with an unbearably painful story, or frustrated by the client's silence, hostility, or self-harmful behavior. The therapist's frustration may then trigger her need for control and lead her to interpret the story or educate the client about it, rather than waiting and listening for the client's own understanding to emerge.

An especially confounding dilemma for the therapist–client process of attunement occurs when the client experiences herself as containing the abuser's secrets and shame as well as her own. When the client has developed a strong sense of self-as-abuser through the internalization process, or when she is actively abusive to others such as her children or her partner, she is often rendered mute or incoherent because of the degree of her shame. Therapists can easily miss this level of the story and leave the client feeling alone with her pain.

Creating Safety

Fear, shame, and pain are perhaps the most central features of the TRS woman's daily life. Although she may desperately long for relief from her self-harmful behavior, these feelings, and her history of nonprotective relationships may make it difficult for her to begin therapy. Therefore, the initial work needs to involve three critical components: recognition of secrecy as self-protection; exploration of what may be the most difficult dynamics in the therapy relationship; and creation of a trust-based relationship. It is vital for anyone who is going to be helpful to the TRS woman to begin by learning how to create a trust-based relationship with her. This safety needs to be felt by the TRS woman before she begins to explore her symptoms or trauma memories. The dynamics of power and control must be explored in the construction of the relationship, so that both client and helper understand how their roles are interdependent. The centrality of shame and self-protective secrecy must also be addressed in the early stages of treatment as therapist and client begin to make healing connections.

In order for the TRS client to begin to develop a feeling of safety within the therapeutic relationship, the therapist needs to understand the critical importance of the timing and pacing of the disclosure of shameful secrets. Premature disclosure of childhood abuse or current self-injurious behavior forces many TRS women to drop out of therapy and self-help support groups after only a few sessions because they feel exposed, judged, or threatened. For the adult survivor who abuses her own body, secrets represent many levels of experience. As I discussed in chapter 3, the TRS victim may be afraid of being punished, shamed, or shunned because of disturbing aspects of her symptoms. She may also keep the secrets of both her childhood trauma and current symptoms as a form of loyalty to and connection with the actual abuser. Related to the TRS woman's fear that disclosure will separate her from the actual abuser is her more powerful, unconscious fear that disclosure will separate her from her own internalized abuser—a more frightening prospect because of the threat of loss of self.

TRS women also experience a sense of control by keeping secrets. The woman who hurts herself can exert control by keeping herself and her secrets hidden from anyone who represents authority or perceived danger. She may even feel a sense of empowerment through keeping her symptoms secret from those who care about her and genuinely want to help. Good therapy should emphasize moving very carefully in the initial stages of treatment, so that the power of the secret and the client's need for control are always respected. For the disclosure of the abuses to be healing, the client must feel safe about revealing the dark secrets of her childhood and her self-harmful behavior. Therefore, therapists must listen with knowledge, skill, and empathy in the context of a significant relationship. Good therapy emphasizes a relationship of mutuality between client and therapist (Jordan, 1990) and an understanding that telling the secret can be either healing or a repetition of the experience of exploitation and betrayal.

My approach is different from most other models of treatment in regard to my avoidance of initial questions about abuse. The more traditional process for working with abuse survivors and self-abusive women is to request full disclosure of painful and often shameful details of past trauma as well as present abuse patterns. One rationale for being so direct is that the denial must be confronted or the client will continue to hide her secrets and remain unable to begin the process of recovery. Another rationale is that if the therapist blocks the client from talking about trauma memories or current issues, the client experiences a repetition of her childhood experience of being silenced when she tried to disclose the abuse. These are both sensible, logical rationales.

Why is it that the direct approach seems so often to fail? My experience with TRS women suggests that many feel exposed if they disclose abuse material too soon. Even worse, they may feel that they have to lie because they do not yet feel safe. In either case, the therapy relationship starts off on the wrong foot, with the client feeling frightened, ashamed, and angry at the therapist's invasive questions. Worse still, she feels guilty and disconnected if she is "forced" to lie. Thus, the problem of lies, secrets, and silences is perpetuated. Some TRS women simply give up on getting help because of this initial disruption in the fragile new relationship. When a woman gives up on getting help, she retreats to the isolation of pain, concealment, and mistrust.

The problems initially discussed in therapy should move quickly from the client's report of her self-abusive behavior to questions about seeking professional help and what this means to her. Beliefs about medical and mental health professionals should be explored thoroughly, including the influence of the client's personal experience and of her partner, friends, and colleagues on those beliefs.

The role of the family, gender, power and control dynamics in relationship to authority figures, the relationship between sex and love, and ideas about closeness and intimacy are issues that should be explored in a general way, both in terms of the client's current world view and in the historical context of her family.

Loyalty to parents and other childhood caretakers should be assumed, and questions about these important figures should be neutral in tone and content. Even if the TRS client perceives her childhood caretaker as abusive, neglectful, or nonprotective, it does not mean that she is ready to hear this person judged or blamed by others. Ideas about the locus of responsibility for the trauma should be carefully explored, because at some level the TRS woman still blames herself.

Family of Origin Beliefs

In beginning to work with a client, I elicit an outline of beliefs, behaviors, relationships, events, and feelings that developed through the client's childhood. Some of these beliefs and bits of family history remain problematic because of how they have become internalized and because of how they may be related to the client's current self-abusive behaviors. For example, a problematic belief may be embedded in the client's history with authority figures. She may have grown up in a family where anyone with a middle-class education, privilege, and power was mistrusted. Doctors, for example, may have been viewed by her family as exploiting their patients, discriminating against poor families, or being generally insensitive to the lifestyle constraints of poverty. One of my clients was mistrustful of doctors because in her experience they were harsh in their responses to women like her who weighed "too much." They ignored the reality of the predominantly starchy, high-fat foods that low-income people are often forced to eat and were oblivious to the difficulty for such a woman as my client to get the kind of exercise they recommended. "How am I supposed to get out for a 'brisk walk' every day when I got four kids, two of them still in diapers? How am I supposed to eat fresh vegetables, fresh fruit, and fish when my assistance check and my food stamps barely cover milk, cereal, spaghetti, and Pampers for the kids by the end of the week?" she asked disgustedly.

For a client who grew up with a deep mistrust of middle-class professionals, there may be unspoken fears that the therapist will need to explore gently and skillfully. Obviously, if a client is afraid to be open and vulnerable to anyone of middle-class status, she cannot readily tell such a professional that she is unable to trust her. This paradox is much like the classic command ordering the tense person to relax. An indirect approach is needed for the professional helper to determine what kinds of beliefs and myths color the client's expectations of her.

Rather than asking the wary client, "How do you feel about psychologists?" or "Please tell me if you feel you can be honest with me," I prefer a more indirect route to assess the potential for connection. The kind of questions I ask are designed to reveal the client's ideas and those of her family about disclosing "family business" to an authority figure. I may also explore stories from childhood that demonstrate examples of family loyalty or perceived betrayal by middle-class professionals. I inquire about the client's ideas about power: who has it and how is it used or abused? Again, the way I ask is nonthreatening. I might inquire about various family members' opinions about lawyers or doctors, for example, rather than asking more direct questions about the client's own opinion of psychotherapists. Questions about gender and power or status may be very revealing. If the TRS woman has grown up in a family where men were always given more power and higher status than women, I can expect that she has complicated feelings about herself and her lack of entitlement and about me as a female with power.

Even the form of the question I ask is indirect, rather than straightforward or confrontational. I might ask, "Who in your family would have been most likely to ask for help from a neighbor or a friend or a professional rather than from someone inside the family?" Or, "If

someone in your family were ill, were either of your parents confident
about getting medical help, or were they more likely to wait to see if
the problem would go away by itself? Which one of your parents
would have opposed going to a doctor for anything except a serious
medical emergency?"

Attitudes Toward Authority Figures

The myths and beliefs about authority figures, professionals, or anyone
else outside the family who may be seen as an "invader" are important
to investigate (Imber-Black, 1988; Miller, 1983). Most of us have experienced being asked to reveal personal, private information when we
had no way of knowing why the question was being asked or how
someone would receive our answer. This happens routinely in a minor
way when we are meeting with a doctor for the first time or being
admitted to a hospital. It happens on a grand scale when guests on TV
talk shows are asked to reveal their most shameful life events to an
audience of thousands.

In families where there are frequent encounters with the police, protective services, or the legal system, there is usually a bluntly stated
view of outsiders as invaders and a sense of family solidarity around
their own identity as outlaws. Many families, however, are less
straightforward in their views; there may be an undercurrent of mistrust toward all those who are outside the family or community, or
there may be isolated pockets of mistrust and defensive hostility.

One woman who came from a wealthy family that prided itself on
being respected in the community told me about the family history of
acute alcoholism, neglect, and sibling violence. This family socialized
with doctors and lawyers, and, as powerful members of the community, they were never in trouble with the police. However, because they
needed to keep their alcoholism and neglect of the children concealed,
they found many ways to keep a critical distance from the school system. The children grew up hearing contemptuous dismissals of their
teachers. When they had school problems resulting from the neglect
and violence at home, the parents refused to meet with teachers or
guidance counselors, blaming the school system for the children's class-
room problems. In working with this client, it was important for me to
keep in mind that her attitudes toward psychologists were covertly

reflective of her parents' attitudes toward teachers and guidance counselors.

By asking questions about how the family thought about outsiders and authority figures, the therapist can explore the client's attitudes about receiving help (Imber-Black, 1988). These explorations might be framed by such questions as: "If someone in your family got sick or lost his job, whom would your family tell? Whom would they think might help? What did your family think about mental health professionals such as social workers, school counselors, psychologists, and psychiatrists? Did anyone in the family ever use mental health services? Who else outside the family knew about this? Was the experience helpful or harmful? In whose opinion?"

If these areas are not explored early in therapy—in the Outer Circle—the therapist and client may bump up against boundaries or break long-standing internalized family rules about outsiders without realizing it. Even when the TRS woman feels positive about going to a counselor or therapist, there are likely to be some underlying anxieties, fears, or mistrust carried over from childhood that this kind of exploration can open up.

Karen can now talk about how nervous she was to begin therapy with me, although when we started, she was not fully conscious of where her anxiety originated:

You would think that because I'm a nurse, I wouldn't have had any trouble going to therapy. Like, it's cool to be in therapy, nothing to be ashamed of, anyone could benefit from it, you know. . . . And you would also think that my father, being a lawyer and all, I wouldn't have been prejudiced against professionals. But surprise, surprise . . . Oh, wow, was I ever wrong to think I wasn't totally freaked to be going to a therapist!

At first I don't think my therapist really got it. You know, I was very together on the surface. I said how being a nurse I knew that I needed professional help and I wasn't ashamed of getting it. And on and on, like that. Then she asked me a question about my mother. I think it was whether or not my father or anyone else tried to get help with my mother's alcoholism.

Well, I said he was always calling my aunt—my mother's sister—
and telling her he couldn't handle it and what could she do to help
him with my mother?

"What about getting help from a doctor or taking her to an
AA meeting?" my therapist asked me.

"Forget it!" I said. My father and the family doctor were golf
buddies and went fishing together. They even did things together,
you know, the two couples. The doctor's wife used to be at our
house playing bridge with my mother and the other ladies and
they would *all* be getting buzzed. And forget AA! My mother
used to get so upset sometimes and she'd be crying and asking me
to help her. I was only a kid, but I heard about AA at school and
from some friends. So I asked Mom if she would go to AA.

You know what she said? She said my dad would kill her if he
ever found out she had gone and talked about her problems in
public like that. She told me to never even tell him I had suggested
it to her.

So my therapist didn't know yet that my father sexually abused
me. She didn't know what I was doing to myself, like the vomiting and everything. The only thing she knew was that I had trouble with relationships.

I remember the moment she asked me if I ever tried to get
someone to help me when I was a child, like someone outside the
family. I burst out crying. I couldn't stop crying and I couldn't
even explain it. It wouldn't have done any good, I was sobbing.
No one could have done anything. I was all alone and no one
could help me.

She just sat there, not saying anything for a long time. Then
she said, "You're not alone now, even though it still feels that
way." Well, she was right. I did still feel alone, but it felt good to
have her say I wasn't. She was there and she wasn't pushing me to
explain what I meant. That felt good.

Karen and I were beginning to create a context in the Outer Circle
that would allow for the reliving of old trauma memories and the
process of recovery. In this early phase of developing the therapeutic

alliance, however, the emphasis was on developing the rules and expectations surrounding our continuing communication. My goal in the Outer Circle was to help both myself and Karen to think differently about her story, all the while purposely avoiding premature disclosure of the emotionally charged aspects of her past.

Family Myths: Love, Sex, and Gender

I am interested in understanding the client's beliefs about power differences among men, women, and children. Related to this topic is my interest in the process of sharing information within the family. In my exploration, the emphasis is on the patterns of communication and secret-keeping, rather than the content of the secrets themselves.

An important area for the therapist and client to explore is the client's attitudes toward love, sex, and gender-influenced relationships. Beliefs and myths develop in the family of origin that later are carried into adult couple and family dynamics. These beliefs range from how to be a good mother or wife to how love and sex are connected. These are important beliefs because they underlie the story that the TRS client has constructed to make sense of what happened to her in childhood and why she is living the life she does now.

Again, a direct approach is less likely to be successful than the more circular questions I prefer. A woman from an abusive family learns in childhood to be cautious, to lie, and to be secretive when necessary about the subject of sex. She also may have heard that she was being beaten or sexually violated in the name of love: "I have to do this because I love you. . . . If you love me, you will let me do this. . . . I love you, so this will never happen again." If this has been the case, it will be difficult for the woman to be open and direct when asked about her views of sex and love. The kinds of questions that can more easily be answered are, for example: "In the family you grew up in, if you wanted to know something about sex, would you ask your mother? What would have happened if you asked your father or brother or grandfather?"

A question about love and parenting might be: "When you were a child, did you think that all kids got beaten by their parents? Did adults talk about punishing children because they loved them? Did you worry that someone might take you away from your parents if you told anyone about problems at home?"

Gender-related questions about love and sex are also important to explore. I often ask clients to talk about the differences they were taught about men and women in their attitudes to sex. Did they hear that men "have to have" sex, but women learn to "just put up with it"? Did they feel ashamed of their bodies when they entered adolescence? Did they think their brothers (or males generally) also felt ashamed of their bodies? Did they ever hear that they (or women generally) were "asking for it"? Did anyone explain "the facts" about their bodies, reproductive functions, arousal, names of body parts?

When I was first getting to know June, I found that the questions we explored together about sex, gender, and intimate relationships helped me understand why her previous attempts at recovery had failed. I learned that her mother had instilled in June a deep revulsion of the female body; her mother often accused her daughters of being "filthy." This word seemed to apply to anything and everything related to female sexuality. June grew up believing that any sexual response or thought was "sinful." Her most potent rebellion against her mother was to begin to be aggressively sexually active in her teen years. Nonetheless, she had internalized her mother's disgust concerning the female body and displayed it in the way she talked about herself.

Karen's crippling family legacy was more concentrated in her beliefs about what love and parenting should be. She was so neglected by her mother that she had no internal image of maternal protection. Her beliefs about the role of parents were extremely negative and hopeless, and they affected how she approached the possibility of a trust-based relationship with me. She could not allow herself to view me as either trustworthy or nurturing as long as she viewed me as a maternal figure. Learning this important piece of her story helped me to find ways to construct a more acceptable role in relation to her.

Establishing the Therapeutic Relationship

In developing a new therapeutic relationship, it is vital for the TRS client to feel safe and empowered, with maximum control over what is happening to her as she begins therapy. As with any client, a basic "contract" is important to how we begin our relationship.

I start by working with my client to establish boundaries. I clearly explain my own limits for the well-being of both myself and the client. We talk about when I am available for phone contact between sessions, what the limits are on confidentiality, and what my policies are regarding payment for therapy and missed or canceled appointments.

It is of special importance for my TRS clients to know my usual procedure for responding in periods of crisis. Some therapists assure their clients that during times of intense distress, flashbacks, or escalating self-harm, they will be more available than actually turns out to be realistic. This kind of promise can lead to bitter disappointment for the client. If a TRS woman is beginning to believe that finally someone will take on the role of the Protecting Presence and will really be there for her, she will feel set up and confused if the therapist is unavailable to her in a moment of intense crisis or panic. I know that realistically, like any other therapist, I cannot be available twenty-four hours a day. I learned through bitter experience that if I make exaggerated promises of availability, the client will end up feeling as betrayed and abandoned as she did in childhood. The TRS woman feels safer trusting a therapist who states her limitations around anticipated crises long before they occur.

Mail-Order Brides

For both the therapist and client, psychotherapy can provide a significant and intimate relationship. After I had been a therapist for some years, I realized that the process of engaging in this relationship is a bit like a courtship or interviewing for an important job. Courtship involves a series of experiences in which two people are "interviewing" each other, often with the idea of beginning a lifelong partnership, but each knows that it is possible to back out if something is unacceptable about the potential union. The job interview dynamic may be a bit less intense, but again the expectation is that if the fit seems right, a relationship will be formed that will have deep and lasting implications for the person's sense of security and self-esteem.

As I have continued to ponder the complexity of the therapy relationship, I have wondered if perhaps the beginning of the relationship is more similar to the beginning of an arranged marriage. Two strangers meet for the first time, knowing that they may be committing to an enduring and primary relationship. Enormous risks are taken by both the client and therapist. Whether the relationship works or not, the process is central to the client's experience of self-in-relationship and to her recovery, and the success or failure of the therapeutic connection is important to the therapist's professional and personal self-esteem. For the TRS client, the risks are even greater than for many other clients: the TRS woman has been betrayed by would-be caretakers in the past, so she risks betrayal once again. Each time a potentially trustworthy, protective person fails her, she is more deeply wounded and less likely ever to heal.

When I am beginning therapy with a new TRS client, I wonder what it is like for her to walk into an unfamiliar room, knowing that she may eventually talk with me, a stranger, about her most private and distressing moments. If she is one of the many TRS women who have already tried to get professional help, she will be reminded of these other professional relationships and will access the experiences of being helped (or not) and being understood (or not). I am also acutely aware of what each new client represents for me: this newly forming relationship will inevitably remind me of other clients and their stories, and I may also find that parts of my own personal experience are evoked.

Vulnerability

In varying degrees, both the therapist and client are vulnerable. For example, the therapist may be vulnerable in assessing the client's potential for self-harm and in determining the appropriate therapy intervention. If the therapist misses the degree of danger for the client and her intervention is a failure, the therapist will feel the greatest vulnerability in taking responsibility for the failure, even if the client tries to assume the blame. The risks are greater for the client, however. The differences in power, vulnerability, and responsibility are often intimidating to the TRS woman, who is especially reactive to situations in which she feels "one down." The TRS client is likely to feel vulnerable throughout the course of the therapy relationship, at least in part because of the unidirectional flow of information. The client is very sensitive about the information I ask her to divulge, especially at the beginning of therapy. As a therapist, I have the "right" to know or ask about many significant and potentially shameful areas of the client's life. No matter how careful I am, there is no way to avoid the vulnerability my questions impose on the client.

Among the questions I am most likely to ask a TRS client are many relationship-focused questions. Unlike a friend or colleague beginning a relationship with the TRS woman, I may ask some rather direct and personal questions about important relationships, both past and present. These questions touch not only on presumably neutral or positive relationships, but perhaps also on relationships involving abuse, incest, or physical and psychological violence. Even though I try to avoid probing questions about painful or shameful events and relationships in the early therapy sessions, I will inadvertently stir up some degree of painful material by asking what seem to be fairly routine questions.

The work history and current work situation, including difficulties, job loss, conflicts, failures, and disappointments, are important areas to explore with every client. For the TRS client, work may be a more successful arena than some other areas of her life, but she may still feel vulnerable to my questions because of some particular secret. Karen, for example, had a tremendous degree of shame about her work life because of the secret bingeing and purging she often engaged in at work. Even though I did not initially ask anything about her work, except what she did and how she felt about it, she told me later in the therapy that she was sure that somehow I magically knew about her symptomatic behavior at work.

Family problems, both current and historical, including parenting issues, problems, and failures, are also routine for me to explore in early therapy sessions. These questions can feel invasive for the TRS client if they are asked by someone she does not know and therefore cannot readily trust. While she may have chosen to reveal her status as a trauma victim in the first therapy session, it does not mean she is ready to describe family life in detail to me.

Sex is almost always a problematic topic. The TRS woman is especially vulnerable to questions in this area, yet many clinicians in the early stages of therapy ask their clients about sexual orientation, sexual activities, and sexual problems. The client is sometimes asked about her fantasy life, including any sexual feelings the client may have about the therapist, and her dreams, preoccupations, and thoughts, no matter how embarrassing or uncomfortable these topics may be for the client. Asking the TRS woman these kinds of questions is a potential reviolation. In the Outer Circle, I carefully avoid any questions in this domain, allowing the client to decide what she is ready to tell me. If I believe that she is rushing into areas of disclosure where she seems too vulnerable to allow me comfortable access, I will gently try to block her from revealing too much too soon.

I talk to my clients in the first session about another area of vulnerability—my right to divulge information about the client to others under certain circumstances. For example, if I am worried that she may harm herself or someone else, I am legally obliged to tell someone in her family or those providing emergency services: psychiatrists, crisis teams, emergency room personnel, or the police. Conversely, I can receive information about the client from others: medical personnel, other mental health workers, family members, colleagues, and sometimes even friends. I also explain that I not only have the right to divulge information about the client but, if necessary, to invoke social control measures as well, including hospitalization, social service investigations, and criminal justice proceedings.

Laura exemplified one possible reaction among TRS clients to this area of vulnerability. When I explained about the flow of information, she asked bitterly, "And who do I run to to talk about *you* and how safe or dangerous *you* are?" I explained that the client can also invoke larger system controls, such as reporting a therapist to the state licensing board, but I admitted that such actions tend to happen rarely. The fact was, Laura was much more vulnerable to me in this way than I was to her.

An especially delicate and loaded area of vulnerability for the TRS client is hearing irrelevant or disturbing personal information about the therapist. I believe that it is not in the client's best interests to know details about my personal life, including my own struggles with self-harmful behavior or my childhood physical and sexual abuse. Therapists who talk freely with clients about their personal lives are often setting up the client to feel either unsafe or burdened with the feeling that the client should be in a caretaking role for the therapist, which is clearly inappropriate.

Many therapists do not choose to disclose their identity as an incest survivor or as recovering from addiction to food or alcohol. Others feel that such a disclosure is an important part of role-modeling for clients, a demonstration that it is possible to achieve relative health and recovery from these devastating experiences. It is important to note that there is a difference between divulging general information about these experiences and going into the details. Sometimes clients learn details of the therapist's life because they happen to be at the same twelve-step meeting. My opinion differs from many of my colleagues', but I feel certain that even in the context of a twelve-step meeting, therapist disclosure is inappropriate and should be avoided. TRS women have spent their lives in inappropriate relationships with people who were supposed to protect and take care of them. They have had enough of caring for the caretaker and should not be put in that role once more by a therapist disclosing her own needs and pain.

The therapist is charged with abstaining from any kind of dual relationship with the client. This means that no other relationship should exist between a client and myself during the therapy relationship or even after it ends. There are many good reasons for this prohibition, especially in regard to TRS women, for whom there is such longing and fear involved in close relationships. Therapy involves extreme vulnerability and, in the best sense, it replicates the nurturance and protection of the parent–child relationship. If I were to engage in a relationship with my client that extended beyond the parameters of therapy, to the client it could feel very similar to the complications of the abusive relationships in childhood, when she was forced to be a parent's sex partner, confidante, or caretaker. Once again, she is betrayed in her wish for healing, protection, and nonexploitative love.

Power and Responsibility

Although the TRS client is in a very vulnerable position in therapy, she is in control in some significant ways and needs to be aware of them. In early meetings with a TRS client, I point out that she has relative power in determining what kind of information she will share and how open, honest, and direct she will be. To some extent, she has more control than I do over whether the therapy relationship will continue. She is also in control of certain logistical aspects of the session. She is responsible for payment and other contractual agreements about appointments: showing up, canceling when necessary, and being on time.

The TRS client who acts out has control in determining how assaultive or explosive she will become in sessions and between sessions. Similarly, the less flamboyant TRS woman determines how withdrawn or "oppositional" she will be.

In the case of a client who acts out by engaging in dangerous behaviors between sessions, there are numerous challenges to my illusion of control as a therapist. I am put in the position of having to decide whether I should continue to work with the client in individual therapy or if some other form of treatment would prevent, or at least contain, the self-abusive behavior. At these moments, I can easily feel that it is my fault that the client continues to hurt herself. From this perspective, it can feel very much as if the client is the one who is in total control of the therapy and of my emotional responses. Laura certainly created uneasiness in me when she engaged in self-harmful behaviors I could not at first understand. Despite the reality that she was the one in great pain and out of control, her behavior made me feel at times as if I were at the mercy of her father's rage.

The TRS client's major area of control is in attaining or maintaining self-care. As her therapist, I cannot be responsible for her basic needs, work commitments, sexual safety, driving safety, or financial obligations. These areas of responsibility are not easy, however, for the TRS woman. Therapists often spend a considerable amount of time negotiating with their TRS clients about openness in sessions and self-care between sessions.

Finally, I work very hard with my TRS clients to help them be as clear as possible about whether the therapy is "working." Is therapy addressing the issues she most wants to address? Am I responding in the ways she needs or expects me to? If not, should we discuss the problems? Is this style of therapy productive? Does she feel that I am accepting the material we are working on? How successfully are we working together? If not, can we talk about it? Through experiencing control of the relationship and the conversation in therapy, the TRS woman begins the process of becoming more powerful in other aspects of her life.

Other People in Outer Circle Sessions

In the beginning stages of treatment, sessions may or may not include other people close to the client. Sometimes it is helpful for the TRS woman to involve her partner, children, siblings, parents, friends, or anyone else who can help illuminate the context that initiated or maintains the self-abusive symptoms.

The partner's presence can serve several purposes. It can help to diffuse the apparently frightening intensity of the individual therapy setting, in which some TRS women feel trapped, afraid that they will be forced to share more than they want to. It also allows the therapist to explore with both the client and her partner any beliefs that may be keeping them mutually stuck in a shared experience of shame and fear. These beliefs may be about dysfunctional patterns of protecting the internalized abuse relationship and may be pertinent to why the client is keeping her self-abusive behavior secret.

By meeting with Lee, her husband, David, and Lee's therapist, Martha, I could begin to explore with all three of them how and why Lee and David combined forces to keep Lee's cutting secret. The following excerpt from a session in my consultation with them illustrates this kind of exploration.

DM: Lee, do you mind if I ask David about his involvement with the problem?

LEE: No. It's okay. (Notice that Lee is immediately compliant. This is typical of the woman who has grown up in a situation where authority figures—parental figures or men—were entitled to demand information and services simply because of their privileged status. Because of her ready compliance, I am already beginning to make some assumptions about how unsafe Lee would probably feel about resisting any of my probes. I want to find out more about her beliefs concerning female entitlement and about her and David's expectations about sharing information with each other and about each other.)

DM: David, would you expect Lee to give me permission to ask you questions, or are you surprised?

DAVID: Oh, no, I'm not surprised at all. Lee and I try to talk about things, especially about the problems she's been having. I think she kind of depends on me to help her with situations like this, you know, in general.

DM: What do you mean, "situations like this"?

DAVID: Well, uh, like therapy. Or anything where she doesn't know the situation or the person involved and she's hesitant. (He glances at Lee. He seems genuinely concerned about representing her accurately, or so it would seem from his questioning look in her direction. She smiles slightly at him and then looks at me timidly.)

DM: Lee, it sounds like David thinks this is a difficult kind of situation for you? (I look at her. She nods, giving me a small, apologetic smile.)

MARTHA: Dr. Miller, I hesitate to interrupt, but maybe I can add something? (Martha looks more nervous than Lee. She is in the position of deferring to my authority as the consultant and as someone who is considered expert in working with TRS clients. She wants my help, but she also wants my approval, to be reassured that it is not her fault that Lee's self-harmful activities have gotten worse. Although I would prefer that she not jump into the conversation, I also want her to relax and feel less defensive.)

DM: That's fine, go ahead.

MARTHA: If I may say so, Lee, you really don't need David to speak for you. We've worked hard on this. We've talked about how assertive you are in your professional role. You're a very successful businesswoman. You don't need anyone to speak for you.

LEE: (Looking anxiously at me, then at David, seeming to be unable to meet Martha's eyes) Yes, I know. This is sort of confusing. I can't quite understand what the question was.

DM: Perhaps I've created the confusion. I'm really just trying to understand how David sees the problem and how the two of you communicate about it. (I am aware that not only is Lee anxious, but so is Martha. Martha wants me to see Lee as strong and competent and to see her that way too. Lee immediately takes the blame for whatever is going wrong and gets confused, possibly as a way to back out of the discomfort and to protect Martha. I now understand that by asking David to comment on Lee's problem, I am perceived by Martha as undermining Lee's competence and perhaps her own as well. Lee, too, seems to be uneasy with the direction this is going. Now I need to reassure both women, explain my strategy, and then get back to David if I can.)

DM: So let me explain a little bit about what I'm trying to understand here. I want to know if David sees things pretty much the same way you do, Lee, or if he has a different idea about what's going on. I'm trying to find a way that's as comfortable as possible for all three of you to help me understand how much you talk to each other about Lee's predicament. Who talks to whom and when? What are the rules about talking about difficult things? Help me out here, Lee. Tell me a little bit about how you and Martha first decided to include David in some of your therapy sessions.

LEE: I was the one who had the idea. I thought it would be easier for me to tell David about the, uh, the problems. . . . I told Martha I didn't think I could tell him if she wasn't there. It was too scary.

DM: Were you afraid of David? What he would do when he found out? Or . . .

LEE: No. Scared of telling it, not of David.

I went on from there to continue my exploration of the communication between Lee and David and between the couple and Martha. It was significant to me that there was confusion and tension about who could or could not speak for whom and about who could speak about whom. In mapping out this territory, I could develop several ideas about the rules that bound each of the three in their efforts to work together around Lee's self-harming and her dissociative episodes.

Despite Martha's skills as a therapist and her obvious compassion for and commitment to Lee, she too had remained largely unaware of hidden rules that blocked Lee from disclosing the full meaning and extent of her symptoms. Many therapists are not trained to explore these areas or to use indirect questioning methods in approaching the complexity of the TRS woman's story.

Meeting with the couple in early therapy sessions also allows the therapist to probe areas of current functioning, such as asking the partner to assess the TRS woman's current potential for depression or self-harm. In some cases, talking with the partner in the presence of the client allows the secrets in her past to emerge more as reflections on or responses to some aspect of her partner's history. The TRS client then feels more in control of the material, because she is participating in the construction of her partner's story as well as her own. This new dialogue, which includes the partner, helps to avoid the dynamics of blame and shame so common in working with problems of abuse.

In some cases, however, the client may not feel comfortable having anyone in the therapy sessions with her, because she is understandably fearful or feels too ashamed or reluctant to reveal so much about herself. The decision should be made by the client. The process of therapy does not require that anyone else be present. Questions can focus on the couple or the family whether or not they are present.

Working with many TRS women has taught me the importance of developing a strong therapeutic relationship based on mutual trust and shared understanding of central ideas about loyalty, protection, secrets,

and relationship. It is essential that the therapy bond be carefully constructed before the traumatic and complex memories of childhood
abuse and the secrets of the adult self-abuse are confronted. I have also
learned the necessity of involving significant and supportive people in
the therapy process, whether or not they ever actually join in a session.

The journey toward healing is often difficult. The client chooses the
direction. The therapist takes the role of the trusted and knowledgeable
guide. It is the therapist's job to help clear the underbrush and to be
aware of lurking dangers. She accompanies the client and does her best
to make the way safe.

The next chapter describes how to create a network of support in
the middle stages of the recovery process, when the symptoms are confronted and treated directly and when the stage is set for the reworking
of the trauma memories.

8

The Middle Circle

Moving from the Outer Circle to the Middle Circle is a delicate phase of the treatment. It is the stage at which many women drop out of therapy or establish a superficial and excessively cautious level of connection. If the foundation of the Outer Circle is carefully prepared, however, moving into the Middle Circle opens the doors to the possibility of recovery.

There are several tasks to be accomplished in this second circle. The central goals are to begin giving up the symptomatic behavior, to develop a support network, and to prepare for the retelling and reexperiencing of childhood traumas that will happen in the Inner Circle. The network is created so that there will be support for both the client and therapist as they enter the "belly of the beast," the reliving of the trauma. The support network collaborates with the client and therapist in the creation of new, healthier relationships.

Exploring the various functions of the symptoms is a major part of the transition from the Outer Circle to the Middle Circle. Until the functions are understood, it is unlikely that attempts to decrease or stop the symptomatic behavior will be effective. No one should ask women who hurt themselves to give up these forms of communication and these coping mechanisms until their function in the woman's current life is understood.

However, in this second phase of treatment, it is possible to achieve only a partial understanding of the functions of the symptoms. In the Middle Circle, the client is not ready for a full disclosure of her experience of trauma. Because the trauma experience has been silenced for so long, its reenactment through self-abusive behavior can be explored only very slowly and carefully.

Entering the Middle Circle

It is best to enter the Middle Circle by examining the functions of the symptom in currently helping the client to relieve pain, achieve numbness, contain rage, or mediate fear. When more about the client's childhood story is known, it will become possible to understand how the self-abuse recreates familiar feelings of connectedness in order to alleviate unbearable feelings of loneliness.

When Karen first came to therapy, she wanted to work on relationship issues. She did not tell me at first about her bulimia or drinking, nor did she immediately disclose that she had been sexually abused by her father. She did not intend to conceal these important parts of her story from me, but rather she was uncomfortable thinking and talking about them.

When Karen did volunteer the information that she was an incest survivor, her tone of voice suggested that this fact of her identity was no more significant than that she was the eldest child in the family. She was still too ashamed and mistrustful to disclose her bulimia, binge-drinking, or hair-pulling. I speculated that there was a strong probability of self-abuse, but I didn't want to push her. I had to wait until she was ready to reveal the details of her suffering.

After four or five sessions, during which she gave very little information, Karen began to relax. Her story began to emerge in such a way that I could approach conversations about childhood trauma and current self-abuse with a sort of map, a guide to the inner world of Karen's shame. The map that I drew during the Outer Circle phase was filled with details about Karen's family, her beliefs about professionals, and the shame, fear, and complicated connectedness she felt toward her father, mother, and grandmother. Without it, I would surely have fallen into holes, traps, and shadowy confusion. My map gave me important information about family patterns of keeping secrets, as well as the consequences of revealing one's pain and secrets to outsiders, especially professional helpers. I also learned about Karen's areas of most concentrated family loyalty and self/parent identification.

By the time she was ready to leave the Outer Circle, Karen could begin to predict how her disclosures to me might be received. She had observed me over the weeks as together we created an atmosphere of safety based on knowledge of each other's ways of describing and responding to a life story of betrayal.

Following is an excerpt from my therapy notes about Karen as we approached the beginning of the second phase of therapy, the Middle Circle:

> Karen and I have been meeting for four weeks now. She talks about her relationship patterns most of each session, answering my questions (about her family) with such brief responses that I have only a skeleton of a map to work with. I have asked her why it is so hard for her to talk about her family and she answers me with flip remarks: "Oh well, once you've heard one incest story you've heard them all" or "What is there to talk about? My father was a bastard, my mother was an alcoholic. What else do you need to know?"

What I had pieced together by the end of our fourth session was that Karen had a very rigid picture of herself as she wanted to be seen by the world. This picture was an old one; from early childhood on, Karen's family had created a story for her to tell the world outside the family:

> We, the family, look good. We are a pretty picture. We have everything we need. We are better than others. We are the Paul Smith family, envied by others for our big house, our status in the community, our social smoothness, our "pretty picture" family of father, mother, daughter, sons, dog, and station wagon. If Attorney Smith's wife drinks a little too much, who cares! If little Karen Smith looks pale and depressed, who dares to comment? If little John Jr. looks bruised and fearful, who wants to fuel his father's anger by investigating the home life? Don't look too closely and you won't get sued or snubbed or called on the carpet by the school superintendent.

I learned more from what wasn't said about how little protection Karen got as a child and how little attention she and her brothers got from their parents. I began to understand that the Smith family's motto was "What you don't know can't hurt you." It was a family in which the surface had to look good, a family in which neglect was as strong a component as abuse.

The following is a glimpse of Karen's childhood nightmare, showing what it was like to try to get help or protection in her family.

> After my father first started to abuse me, I began getting infections. I went to my mother to ask her to fix the itching between my legs. She scolded me, and I think she might have threatened to tell Daddy. She said that if she told him what I was doing to myself, he would spank me. Then she slapped me when I said Daddy was the one who had been doing something to me.
>
> She took me to the family doctor finally, but she told me if I lied and said Daddy did it to me, I would get spanked, and anyhow, Dr. White would never believe me because he was a good friend of Daddy's. So Dr. White looked at me and then scolded me and told me never to put anything up myself again. That was that.
>
> When my therapist asked me more about this story, I understood why she was asking, but I couldn't really get into the details. I still felt so ashamed, not because I was abused, but because I was called a liar. It's complicated. I can't really explain it.

Karen's story about Dr. White was an important piece of information. It helped me to understand various internalized family rules she had been consciously and unconsciously obeying. It also helped me to understand her capacity to live with contradictions and not necessarily recognize them. I learned that she was not allowed to tell the truth, neither within the family nor outside it. Her story of Dr. White illustrated how she had been trained to take the blame for what was done to her. Lying was an acceptable form of communication. Little Karen learned that women protected men, and men protected each other. Professionals were no more trustworthy than anyone else.

I wanted to understand how Karen, coming from this family, had found a way to believe in herself—or in the abstract reality that professional competence could actually exist—enough to become the dedicated nurse that she was; I did not understand what gave her the courage to trust the psychotherapy process with me, when she had been so betrayed by professionals in her childhood. I only knew about the deficits in her family experience, not the resources. The more positive parts of Karen's story began to emerge when she told me an anecdote about her grandmother.

> My grandmother, Lillian, was a wonderful lady. She lived across town from us, so we only got to see her on Sundays. But she always made me feel special.
>
> One time I remember her holding my hands and looking at them. "You've got good strong hands, Karen," she told me. "Use them. Use these hands and your good strong mind. You can count on these hands and this mind. You're going to be all right, you wait and see."
>
> Gram knew something was wrong at home. I heard her tell my father to get help for my mother, that Mother was drinking too much. But I guess she felt like she couldn't interfere in the family. That is how people are. You don't interfere in how families do things. It hasn't changed. I see the same thing going on with families I see at the hospital.

Her memory of her grandmother was an important part of who Karen was, her one source of hope and potential self-esteem. Grandmother Lillian's love and belief in Karen's strength helped her as a child to develop some capacity for trust and hope in relationship. Understanding these resources in Karen's history was as important for me as understanding the impediments that could keep her from connecting with the necessary supports for successful treatment. But while acknowledging this important connection with her grandmother, Karen continued to tell me that she had felt deeply unprotected.

Karen's story is like many others. Her desire to change her patterns of self-harm and to achieve better relationships was what moved her into the initial phase of therapy. But her courage and desire to change could easily be overwhelmed by discomfort or panic. I needed to remain mindful of Karen's loyalties. Although Karen might state directly that she had no existing loyalty to either her abusive father or her nonprotecting mother, I knew from my clinical experience that there were undoubtedly hidden loyalties, deeply internalized parts of Karen.

The betrayal by her father's friend, Dr. White, had contributed to

Karen's overt contempt for professional helpers. Yet she also had a covert belief that professionals could help victims if only the victim knew how to ask for help. Karen was trapped in a victim-blaming cycle. As a nurse, Karen was endlessly reenacting the wish to help and be helped, but there was another part of her that was overwhelmed by her rage at the doctors with whom she worked. This victim self would not easily open up to me, because on a less conscious level, I was identified in her mind with the doctors.

While it was a step forward to learn this much about Karen, it was not enough to help me decide how to begin the bridge work into the Middle Circle. I needed some kind of anchor from Karen's past that would help us both from being blown off course in the storms of fear and mistrust stirred by confronting the symptoms. Her bulimia and drinking had functioned to keep her from feeling too much pain or rage, to protect her from being too vulnerable, and to keep her in primary, loyalty-bound relationships with both her father and mother. To begin to take away these symptoms would trigger waves of panic and rage. In addition, as Karen began to reveal her shameful symptoms, the threat to the "look good, keep smiling" family portrait would also create intense distress.

I knew Karen could not yet allow herself to trust me; I was, after all, an outsider, a professional. I had to find a way to invoke the presence of someone she could trust. I decided to use Karen's memory of her grandmother as the anchor. The following excerpt from a session in the sixth week of therapy gives a glimpse of how this kind of exploration can happen.

DM: Karen, who would be the most disapproving if you and I began to talk about your drinking patterns?

KAREN: Me, I suppose. I don't get it. What do you mean? Who else would even care?

DM: Besides you . . . would it be your mother or your father or your friend Ellen or your boyfriend or . . . ?

KAREN: Well, let's see. It would have to be my father, I guess. My mother wouldn't like it either, but my father would be so ripped! He doesn't even know I'm getting therapy. And he never will, either.

DM: And who would be the most pleased if we did some work with the drinking and the eating problems?

KAREN: You? I don't know. Is this a riddle?

DM: I don't know, is it?

KAREN: You're the one who's supposed to have the answers. Hey, just kidding. Uh, what was the question again?

DM: Who would be most pleased if we did some talking about the drinking, or the eating?

KAREN: I guess it would be you, because I sure don't want to talk about it. Or maybe I do—I don't know.

DM: Anyone else?

KAREN: What?

DM: Would anyone else think it was a good thing to talk about?

KAREN: Well, my grandmother, I guess. (Her eyes tear up a little. She looks as if she'll cry if she lets herself.)

DM: (After a long pause) What's going on right now, Karen?

KAREN: (Begins crying) I'm so ashamed of how disappointed Gram would be . . . (Cries harder) . . . what I've been doing to myself. She'd never believe it . . . or if she did, she'd be so upset, so disappointed in me.

DM: Would she still love you?

KAREN: (Nods, still crying)

DM: Do you think if she were here with us she'd want to help? Could she understand your pain?

KAREN: (In a little girl voice, still crying) Yes, I think so.

DM: Okay, let's imagine she's here. Where would she think we should start? Would she want you to talk to a friend? Or talk to me? Or try going to a twelve-step recovery meeting? Or pray?

KAREN: (No longer crying) Wow, that's tough. I don't know. She didn't really know anything about therapy or twelve-step meetings. But she probably wouldn't think praying would do much good either. She wasn't that kind of religious person.

DM: How would she say that people heal from pain? What did she do to help others?

KAREN: Find something you're good at and do it. Don't let anyone stop you from your heart's desire, that's what she said. I think she helped me by believing in me.

Here I had an essential piece of the puzzle, an answer to where Karen and I might begin. Karen had identified a belief about healing that she attributed to her grandmother. Thus, she was able to evoke her grandmother's presence. Now I could try out what I thought might be the best initial "fit" for Karen in terms of a support group.

Support groups, which I will discuss in more detail later in this chapter, cover a wide range, from professionally led groups directed at specific symptoms to informal groups united in a common political or social cause. For Karen, a group that focused its efforts on action, developing the competencies of its members, would probably work best. She might, for example, join a self-defense group or a group at her job that targeted women's issues such as daycare or extended health benefits covering mammograms or prenatal and postnatal care. I knew that Karen would have a hard time initially connecting to a symptom-focused group, because she had internalized much of her family's denial system. She felt so much shame anticipating a disclosure of symptoms that she had been unable to connect with any twelve-step group she had tried up to this point. Her internalized message from her grandmother—do something you are good at—suggested that a competency-focused group would be more effective.

Karen's path is only one example of the journey leading to the Middle Circle. Other problems in entering the circle may result from the secrecy surrounding the symptoms or a tendency to attack helpers who get too close. Nancy's experience was very different from Karen's. The process of helping her enter the Middle Circle took a different route.

I am currently in psychotherapy treatment with Dr. Dusty Miller. Dr. Miller is a well-known psychologist, an expert on substance abuse and trauma, I have been told. Frankly, I'm not entirely sure why I am seeing her. I myself am not a victim of child abuse, nor am I a substance abuser. But the internist I've been seeing most recently for my panic attacks recommended Dr. Miller. He thought she could help me with some of my diet-related problems as well as my panic attacks.

Dr. Miller—she asks me to call her Dusty—has been asking me so many questions about my family and my childhood that I'm beginning to think she believes I was abused. Now, that is not the case, the way I see it, but you never really know what to think these days. Certainly I wasn't abused by my father! He was never alone with me. He and my mother left a lot of my care to my grandmother. Dr. Miller asked if maybe some of the ways my grandmother took care of me seemed intrusive. She even asked me if I thought of myself as neglected. Now how could someone from a successful family like mine possibly be neglected?

I told this to my walking partner, Ellie, and she really got a big laugh out of it. Later Ellie and I told the girls we play doubles with that I had come from a neglected childhood, according to Dr. Dusty Miller. One of them took it seriously and told me I ought to think about it. She's the one who's always giving me a hard time about my diets and how thin she thinks I am. I wish!

So this Dusty Miller wants me to tell her how many surgeries I've had. I told Chip she asked me about it, and he advised me to tell her the truth and maybe it would save him some money. He's so insensitive sometimes. Dr. Miller also told me she wants me to go to an Al-Anon meeting because she thinks I would find it interesting. I suppose she thinks Chip drinks too much. I simply can't see myself sitting around with a bunch of wives complaining about their factory-worker husbands. I really wouldn't fit in. Anyhow, I don't really see how I could stop Chip from drinking.

It was a challenge to help Nancy see herself as having serious problems with self-destructive behavior. It was equally challenging to get her to rethink her childhood. She complained readily about how much her grandmother nagged her and violated her privacy, but she had trouble seeing this treatment as causing lasting harm, and she was initially shocked at the idea that she had been a neglected child. Moving into the Middle Circle with Nancy meant finding ways to help her accept the idea that her obsessive dieting, her escalating choice of cosmetic surgeries, her excessive exercise habits, and her careless overuse of prescription drugs all indicated a diagnosis of Trauma Reenactment Syndrome. Nancy had a long way to go before she could see herself as a woman who hurts herself.

Part of helping Nancy understand these self-destructive patterns depended on finding her the right sources of support. She was not a good candidate for traditional eating-disorder groups such as OA, because she did not see her diet and exercise excesses as addictions, and she was also not ready to face the desperation of her situation. I chose

Al-Anon as a good starting place for her. Al-Anon is for people who are or have been affected by someone else's drinking. Emphasizing taking care of yourself, Al-Anon deals with general family problems. In this twelve-step program, I thought Nancy might begin to identify with others' stories of not-so-perfect childhoods.

The other issue for Nancy was her tendency to devalue professional helpers. Because I had learned about this pattern through the questions I explored in the Outer Circle, I knew I needed to find a way to construct a support network that would help both Nancy and me through the inevitable bouts of rage she would soon level at me. It was important to build bridges to other people in Nancy's natural support system who could become our allies in the healing process.

I invited Nancy to bring various friends to our early sessions and also to bring her husband. Several of Nancy's friends, but not her husband, were initially quite willing to become involved in her early recovery efforts. Later on in the work, Chip and one of their children also joined in the process of helping Nancy to stop hurting herself.

The focus of the transitional work into the symptom-based phase of the Middle Circle is determined by the information gathered in the Outer Circle. When the client seems unable to engage in any form of network support, it generally means that important information about the family history, treatment experiences, secrecy patterns, gender and power assumptions, or some other critical area has not been explored fully enough in the Outer Circle. Rather than blaming the client for rejecting support systems, the client and therapist need to explore further what in the family history and belief system might be blocking her at this stage.

Investigating the Symptoms

Working directly with symptoms is an important but treacherous part of the therapist–client enterprise. If the therapy begins to focus on the symptoms too early, the client may be flooded with shame, or feel fear and reluctance at the thought of giving up the symptoms. On the other hand, if the therapy continues too long without addressing the symptoms, the client may feel unprotected or unseen in a way that replicates her childhood experiences.

Hypnotherapist and lecturer David Grove (1989) uses the phrase "interrogating the metaphor" to describe his approach to understanding the symptomatic communications of trauma survivors. He gives the example of a woman who experiences the stored pain of the trauma as knots in her stomach. He questions her about the knots as if they were animate, reasoning creatures, "interrogating" these physically enacted metaphors in order to learn their strengths. He believes that each metaphor not only carries the stories of the client's pain but can also yield strength to rework the trauma. The knot, for example, can become a rope that can be used to help the woman climb up out of the scary cellar of her pain.

In the same way, I investigate the many different ways in which the symptoms have meaning for the client. The four major areas I explore are the history of the symptoms, the severity of the symptoms, what has already been tried in the client's attempts to get rid of them, and what functions they serve in the life of the client. It is only when I have explored all four of these dimensions that I feel comfortable suggesting ways to begin letting go of the symptoms.

History of the Symptoms

Questions about the history of the symptoms can be relatively direct: When did this problem begin? How did you know it was a problem? How disabling was it or has it become?

The language the client uses to describe her symptoms is important because it gives me a sense not only of her history but also what language or terms to use to talk about her symptoms. For example, because June has been active in a twelve-step program for a long time, she describes her early drinking in AA language; she will attach the drinking to her basic description of herself: "I've been an alcoholic since I was fourteen years old. I didn't know what I was back then, of course, but now I know what I was even then, an alcoholic."

Karen would describe her drinking in different language: "I began to drink wine after I came home from work, to unwind. Gradually I kept on drinking more and more. It's not serious, really. It's like the way I stuff myself with food and then throw up. I could probably stop either problem anytime. I'm not really addicted, I'm just in pain a lot."

Someone like Nancy does not see her problems as symptoms and does not relate them to the concept of addiction. Nancy will tell anyone who is interested about the diets, and she will tell her closest friends about her surgeries, but she keeps her addiction to prescription drugs a secret even from herself. Nonetheless, it is worthwhile to ask her about the history of these behavioral patterns, even if she may not identify them as problems.

How Serious is the Problem?

TRS women are likely to minimize the extent of their symptoms. It is important, however, for the therapist or helper to know how big the problem is. Discussions must include questions about the frequency of the behavior and the extent of the injuries or danger to health. When the symptom is an eating disorder, questions should explore how often the cycle of self-abuse occurs and specifically what takes place. With women who cut, burn, or otherwise mutilate their bodies, it is necessary for medical reasons to know the details of what they have done and are currently doing to themselves so that the degree of danger can be assessed. Whatever the form of self-harm, it is important to know the extent to which the TRS woman is hurting her body so that the support system developed in the Middle Circle can include appropriate medical intervention.

When direct questions fail, the TRS woman may be more willing to continue this difficult conversation if the focus is on other people besides herself who might be worried about the problem. In one of my earliest cases as a family therapy trainee, I could not get any direct information about the mother's alcoholism until I asked the whole family who among them was most worried about her and why. All four children said they worried about their mother because she was "sick" and might die. They would not be more specific, but when I continued talking with them, the mother suddenly disclosed her alcoholism, saying that the doctor had told her she would die within a few years if she continued to drink.

There are several reasons why a more indirect approach sometimes works. Perhaps the most obvious explanation is that direct questioning may be threatening to the TRS woman, even when the questions are apparently benign. As a child, she was often intimidated or invaded by adults' questions. She may have learned a self-protective style of response that evades questions, or she may submit helplessly to such questions, believing that she must answer and that she will be punished no matter what her response.

Another advantage to using the more indirect "Who else might be worried or concerned about you?" questions is that it introduces the theme of caring rather than judging or blaming. It also allows the woman to be as direct or indirect as she chooses: she can answer the "who" part of the question without specifying the "why." She can be relatively noncommittal: so-and-so might be worried about her drinking, but she doesn't know why, because she doesn't really drink that much, but perhaps "some people" think she has a problem. This kind of reply sets the tone for the conversation, allowing the therapist to continue the topic carefully, using language that matches the client's: "If so-and-so might see it as a problem, why? What part of her (his) concern do you share?"

What Has Already Been Tried?

In most cases, the client who hurts herself has made efforts in the past to try to stop her patterns of self-harm. Her efforts may have been relatively solitary self-help solutions such as diets, self-imposed abstinence from the behavior, switching to another form of self-harm, or exercise programs, or she may have tried more interactional approaches such as individual psychotherapy, support groups, twelve-step programs, or medical interventions.

One reason self-harmful behavior becomes so entrenched is that the woman gets angry at herself when she keeps failing in her efforts to stop the behavior, and her anger stimulates more self-harm. It seems to be the rule rather than the exception for professionals and nonprofessionals alike to offer repetitions of the "wrong" solution; they often neglect to determine whether the context for the treatment fits the needs and self-image of the individual client.

For example, BJ, my young "punk" client, had been using the mental health system in the same way from the age of sixteen. By the time she began working with me at age twenty-five, she had developed a predictable pattern of demanding professional caretaking in order to feel protected and less alone. She would do something self-destructive or bizarre that made all the helpers perceive her as out of control and unable to be responsible for herself. They would impose safety-based interventions such as hospitalization, powerful antipsychotic medications, and extra "emergency" contact with her primary therapist. She would then reward the mental health system by getting healthier: her caretakers would feel competent, knowing that their interventions had been right. BJ would briefly remain self-sufficient and capable, but as soon as her professional caretakers relaxed their hypervigilance, she would feel panic and anger because she felt abandoned. Then the cycle would begin again.

My first goal with BJ was to create a new set of responses to her out-of-control mode. I insisted that if she needed hospitalization, she should be in a detox unit rather than a psychiatric unit. This was a new solution, because it gave her a substance-abuse label rather than a personality disorder diagnosis and because it forced both BJ and her helpers to hold her responsible for her behavior. I also was able to persuade the psychiatrist who provided her medication to substitute low doses of antidepressants for the high doses of mind-deadening antipsychotic medications that for years had been used to control her.

The most important factor in this change of protocol was the system's collective willingness to try a new approach to BJ's crises. While it took a leap of faith for BJ and all the helping professionals who knew her history, they recognized that the old responses were not working and that she needed a new approach. In fact, she responded positively to the changes.

Letting Go of the Symptoms

There are both dangers and rewards to letting go of the symptoms. The rewards may seem obvious, but the dangers are often hidden, and anyone working with a woman who hurts herself needs to be aware of them. The woman herself knows what these may be, or at least senses them. She is an expert in the area of such dangers and should be treated as such by those who want to help her give up the behaviors.

When Letting Go Feels Bad

Letting go of self-harmful behavior can feel self-abusive. Letting go means giving up a familiar mode of distance regulation, a dependable way of numbing, diminishing, and containing fear, grief, rage, and shame. Letting go means relinquishing a way of feeling not alone, of feeling connection.

Letting go also means getting acquainted with other people in a new way. It means getting to know oneself. It can be both exciting and disconcerting to get in touch with all the parts of the self, including the abused self, the self that has refused to be self-protecting, and the internalized abuser. All this needs to happen in order to begin the work of the Inner Circle, but it can feel almost unbearable. It is a frightening, maddening, and disorienting phase of the work for most women who hurt themselves, and potentially also for those who are involved with them. The client and the therapist may each experience extreme reactions to initial memory fragments of horrific abuse. Both often feel overwhelming rage at the parent who so cruelly betrayed the vulnerable child. The struggle to contain the rage so that the therapy work can continue is a challenge. Pieces of the client's childhood story may feel bewildering, unfamiliar, and disorienting to the client because of her amnesia and fragmented cognitive process. The therapist may feel the same feelings because of her own trauma experience or because each client's trauma story is different; there are always surprising, disconcerting new details to absorb. The therapist and client must unite in this effort so that they can move more comfortably into the individual therapy phase of the Inner Circle, where traumas are confronted without the protection of the symptomatic behaviors.

When Letting Go Feels Good

Letting go of symptoms can feel wonderful. Many women say they feel tremendous relief at ending the secrecy, deceptive communications, and shame involved in self-abusive patterns of behavior. They also feel pride and mastery at no longer being enslaved by their symptoms. A feeling of community and celebration may develop with various helpers, friends, and group members who share the woman's process of letting go. Most powerful of all may be the experience of beginning to feel whole rather than fragmented. This feeling, coupled with the deepening connections with others, may allow the woman who stops hurting herself to feel genuinely lovable and loved for the first time in her life.

Creating Support Systems

Establishing a support network is an essential part of decreasing and then extinguishing the symptoms. When the TRS woman's symptoms are taken from her, she needs a variety of support resources. Expecting all her emerging needs to be met by her therapist is dangerous, both for the client and the therapist. The TRS woman experiences a roller-coaster ride of positive feelings, discomforts, and sometimes unusual health problems as she begins to let her symptoms go, and the therapist alone cannot hold her through this part of the journey. Support systems including medical professionals, therapy groups, twelve-step groups, political and community action groups, and spiritual resources, along with friends and family, all can help the woman get through this challenging and often excruciating phase of recovery.

The Power of Storytelling

The successful sharing of secrets can create a narrative experience that connects us and draws us closer. Through storytelling in therapy, in support groups, in friendships, and in intimate relationships, we heal each other.

Storytelling has long been a source of connection and healing for women and other oppressed groups. In the movie *Fried Green Tomatoes*, storytelling is both the form and the subject of the movie. Octogenarian nursing home resident Mrs. Threadgood (Jessica Tandy) tells a story to her visitor, menopausal Evelyn (Kathy Bates). The story serves to connect and empower the two women, eventually releasing the unforgettable spirit of "Towanda." "Towanda!" becomes the exultant cry of liberation for Evelyn and for millions of female moviegoers.

The story within the story told in this movie is also a testament to female connection and healing in the face of trauma. Mrs. Threadgood tells Evelyn the tale of two young women who join forces to fight male violence. Idgie and Ruth, two young white women in the rural South (circa 1930), and an elderly African-American woman and her son collaborate to protect Ruth from her brutal husband. The story of Idgie and Ruth inspires a deepening affection between Mrs. Threadgood and Evelyn, culminating in an abiding and primary relational commitment.

Fried Green Tomatoes offers an important lesson, because it is not only through understanding, accepting, and loving each other that these women grow in connection and healing, but also through action, breaking the silence, and revealing secrets. *Fried Green Tomatoes* illustrates the power of storytelling in bringing the speaker and the listener closer and enabling the one who shares her secrets to feel truly seen. It also illustrates the importance of context. The story is told in the context of an institutional setting: Mrs. Threadgood is constrained by her role as a resident of a nursing home and Evelyn is constrained by her role as a submissive wife in the institution of marriage. These two women together construct a story of another time that serves their own liberation. Idgie, Ruth, and others at the Whistlestop Cafe join together to fight the institutional violence of both wife-battering and racism: Mrs. Threadgood is able to help Evelyn value herself and fight the oppression of her lifeless, self-abdicating role as a traditional wife and Evelyn, in turn, is able to help Mrs. Threadgood reclaim some of her independence.

Some support groups, such as twelve-step groups, women's support groups, and incest recovery groups, are organized around storytelling as the central healing activity. Storytelling is also part of group therapy sessions at inpatient hospital units or detox facilities. Political and community action groups are organized around the need to turn a story of injustice or need into action. Spiritual and religious groups are also story-centered, although the content of the stories ranges from suffering to enlightenment and revelation.

In any setting where storytelling triumphs over silent shame and secrecy, TRS women can be transformed by telling and hearing the stories of others. When the symptoms no longer dominate, the silence and isolation begin to diminish. Finding the right place to tell the story is a vital step in the Middle Circle phase of recovery.

There are several major types of support which can be helpful in the middle stage of treatment. For some women, only one of these support systems may be necessary. For others, a combination may be right. The TRS woman and her therapist, partner, friends, and others who are helping her through the process of recovery will want to consider several potential areas of support.

Clinical and Medical Options

A woman who hurts herself as seriously as Lee, the victim of maternal abuse, or Laura, the ex–heroin addict, may need to begin letting go of symptoms in a hospital setting. Giving up self-mutilating behavior or extreme drug abuse patterns may trigger uncontainable panic and disorientation. A hospital staff is best equipped to protect the woman from such forms of self-abuse during the initial phase of withdrawal.

The woman who is relinquishing alcoholic drinking or drug abuse may do best initially in a detox program or inpatient substance abuse facility. It is difficult for the chemically dependent woman to let go of the emotionally anesthetizing aspects of alcohol or drugs. When she is faced with the intense emotions, arising from therapy, she is likely to relapse unless she is in a specialized hospital unit.

Anorexia also may necessitate hospitalization. Anorexia is one of the most life-threatening of the self-harmful behaviors. There are many hospitals where the most cautiously and intensively treated psychiatric problem is anorexia. One of the disadvantages to most of these anorexia treatment programs is that they unknowingly replicate the invasive physical acts of childhood abuse through the use of tube-feeding, intravenous feeding, and physical restraints. Nonetheless, this may be the only way to keep some anorexic patients alive.

A major drawback to hospitalization for women who hurt themselves is that for the average hospital staff of the 1990s, the primary goal of treatment is to get the patient out of the hospital as quickly as possible. The management of treatment is controlled by the health insurance industry and managed care. Unfortunately, these systems are guided by a for-profit philosophy. Insurance companies restrict the amount and types of treatment they will cover, and hospitals plan treatment around the companies' formula for the number of days in the hospital allowed for a given illness or condition.

When the patient must be able to leave the hospital before her insurance coverage runs out, she is not encouraged to stay open to the flood of emotions released when she relinquishes her symptomatic behavior. She is also not encouraged to dwell on the memories released by her abstinence from drinking, drugs, or self-mutilation. These emotions and memories must be sealed over so that the patient can resume "normal" functioning as soon as possible.

There are some hospitals where longer treatment is available, anywhere from several months up to a year, but this luxury is available only to a small number of self-harmful women. For TRS women who need hospitalization, it may therefore be better to give a PTSD diagnosis rather than an eating disorder, chemical dependency, or Borderline Personality Disorder diagnosis. PTSD is a new enough label that the length of time needed for successful treatment is less clear, and insurance companies have not yet established a standard number of treatment days. This uncertainty can buy the patient and the staff a little more time to allow some of the uncovering of traumatic material to be done in the safety of the inpatient setting, and can give the patient more time to adjust to the absence of her self-harming behavior.

As increasing numbers of women work through trauma material and achieve successful recovery, we may see alternative crisis-defined treatment programs being developed and staffed by women in advanced recovery for women in the early stage of recovery. Until that time, hospitals can provide safety and more intensive attention during the initial flood of emotion and memory that is activated by stopping the self-harmful behaviors.

Therapy Groups

A therapist-led group may be helpful at this early stage in recovery. Group therapy specifically concentrating on PTSD usually is not a good idea in the symptom-focused work of the Middle Circle, however. Such groups can be valuable in the process of reliving and reworking the trauma memories later on, in the Inner Circle, but they are too intense and overwhelming for most women who are just beginning to give up their symptoms. The therapy groups that seem to work best at the Middle Circle stage are those that focus on more general difficulties in living and that discuss relationship issues in general terms. Women's self-esteem issues may be another relatively safe focus for therapy groups.

There are also therapist-led groups that work on issues of addiction such as eating disorders and chemical dependency. These groups may not use a twelve-step format, but they are symptom-focused and usually incorporate much of what works best in twelve-step programs. Symptom abstinence requires concentrating on "one day at a time" and accepting that one is powerless over the addictive behavior and that one's life will be unmanageable unless the symptom is relinquished. While the feelings of powerlessness may be all too familiar to the TRS woman, at least in the domain of symptoms she can do something concrete—remain abstinent—to combat the powerlessness in her life.

Twelve-Step Recovery Programs

Many books and articles have been written about why the AA and AlAnon twelve-step recovery model works. Rather than repeating the rationale for these programs, I will note why some of their main principles seem to help so many TRS women.

Perhaps the most important vehicle for healing offered by the various twelve-step programs is the possibility of community. When the woman who hurts herself shares her story with others who are struggling with similar issues, she breaks out of her isolation and secrecy. She feels the power of being connected with others who are able to speak of their shame and pain and who have been able to let go of their self-abusive patterns. Each new member of a twelve-step program works with a sponsor, an experienced member who can help her through the program.

Another important aspect of the recovery program is that it offers a simple, manageable frame for making enormous changes in one's life. The admonitions to live one day at a time and to refuse responsibility for the sobriety or health of anyone other than oneself are keys to beginning to organize what has felt like a totally unmanageable life. At this stage of treatment in the Middle Circle, stopping the symptomatic behavior is essential to a sense of gaining control. Relinquishing the symptom is all that the woman should concentrate on initially. At first it may be necessary to put aside the complex meanings and roots of the symptom in order to strengthen oneself for the challenging and complex work that lies ahead in the Inner Circle, when the story of trauma will be retold to give meaning to the symptoms.

There are many variations of the original AA and AlAnon programs. Women who are drug-addicted may find Narcotics Anonymous more appropriate than AA. Women who have eating disorders may find Overeaters Anonymous helpful. OA uses the same twelve-step program as AA but allows its participants to talk about their unmanageable relationship to food.

Although there are women-only AA meetings in larger communities, most AA meetings are attended by both women and men. OA, on the other hand, is frequently a women-only meeting, because so few men acknowledge eating disorders. For that reason, OA may work well for the many eating-disordered women who are also sexual abuse survivors and thus have difficulty feeling safe with men. Although it may seem somewhat more complicated than total abstinence from alcohol, the *relationship* to food is what is given up rather than the actual food itself.

Women who hurt themselves by engaging in compulsive and unsafe sexual activities sometimes attend SLAA (Sex and Love Addicts Anonymous), a twelve-step program that addresses relationship addictions. I do not recommend this program for TRS women who are still at the Middle Circle stage of recovery. They may well be in addictive, self-harmful relationships, but they need to work on their physical self-harming symptoms first. Otherwise, the feelings triggered in SLAA meetings can overwhelm the woman with a sense of her own "badness" and rage, and she will be extremely vulnerable to symptom relapse.

Al-Anon, originally founded for partners of alcoholics, now encompasses partners of people with a full range of the addictions. It is sometimes a useful program for women who hurt themselves. The focus in Al-Anon is on achieving detachment from the addicted partner or family member and taking responsibility for one's own addictive behavior. This kind of relationship work is often necessary for TRS women who have partners or family members who are addicted to some form of self-harmful behavior. However, it should happen later; again, in the Middle Circle, the primary focus needs to be on the woman's own process of relinquishing her symptoms.

There are TRS women for whom the AA/Al-Anon model does not work at this stage of treatment. The most obvious and frequent problem I have encountered is self-disclosure. Although for many the peer group experience is the best aid to letting go of the symptomatic behaviors, for others, exposing their symptoms talking about themselves so directly is too threatening. The woman's reluctance may have to do with historical (family or cultural) rules and attitudes, or it may have some connection in current identity.

For some women, working on their symptoms in a twelve-step group is unthinkable because they are not yet ready to tell their trauma history. They feel that they can't really make the program work for them without being open about this central part of their identity. Many women who hurt themselves are constricted or completely mute when it comes to revealing shameful information, whether it is the shame of what was done to them or what they do to themselves. This shame may be compounded by a history of treatment failure or by feeling additionally unsafe as a member of a stigmatized minority group (including women who are lesbian, bisexual, disabled, nonwhite, elderly, or obese).

Another source of self-imposed silence is one's role in the community. Psychotherapists, religious leaders, teachers, doctors, lawyers, and public administrators are among those who find it especially difficult to disclose personal information in a public forum. Despite the twelve-step program's strict adherence to confidentiality, many people in these professional roles feel uncomfortable disclosing self-abuse and trauma histories in the presence of their clients, members of the congregation, or parents of the children they teach. In larger communities, they may be able to avoid the problem by having a number of different groups from which to choose, but in smaller communities, absolute anonymity is impossible.

Another stumbling block can be the negative response many women have to the concept of turning their lives over to a Higher Power. Loosely translated, this means giving up the illusion of having power over an addiction and trusting in an abstract power (often synonymous with God) for help with the process of letting go. Women who hurt themselves may have trouble with this concept for several reasons: they may be philosophically uncomfortable with the idea of a Higher Power, an omnipotent deity watching over everyone. They may also be resistant to the idea of admitting powerlessness when disempowerment has been the pervasive experience of being female in a patriarchal culture as well as in their own family. Thus, the twelve-step maxim "Let go and let God" may be irritating and unacceptable because it seems further disempowering. There are many ways to help women translate these ideas into more acceptable concepts, but for some it is simply too much like the religion or sexism of daily life that they have rejected. For these women, it may be more useful to find another way of beginning to let go of the symptoms.

One alternative closely related to the twelve-step recovery model is Women for Sobriety (WFS). This program was started in the 1970s by Jean Kirkpatrick, who found herself struggling unsuccessfully with the traditional AA model. The program encourages women to take a more holistic and woman-centered approach to recovery. Women in the WFS program are encouraged to meditate, eat healthy food, smoke less, and treat themselves with love and care. Instead of twelve steps, there are thirteen statements, using non-sexist language and referring to spirituality rather than to God or a Higher Power. Unfortunately, WFS meetings are not widespread, but where they are available, they can be a viable alternative for women troubled by what they consider to be sexist aspects of AA. (Some AA meetings use more inclusive language, but this is still the exception.) The twelve-step model does not help the self-harmful woman to understand her abusive behavior in the larger political context of misogyny. Thus, a woman like June can be actively involved in a twelve-step program and still blame and hate herself when she relapses. Women for Sobriety is able to focus on the woman's addiction problems while also acknowledging that she is a victim of a patriarchal system that engenders and feeds female self-hatred and abuse of the body. If WFS or similar meetings are not available, it is helpful for women who hurt themselves to get involved in community or political action groups as a supplement to the specific symptom focus of the twelve-step group.

Political and Community Action Groups

Not everyone can imagine becoming a political or community organizer, but most of us have participated in some form of community action. Women with children may have participated in some activity connected to their children's school or neighborhood needs. Other women may have been part of some process that attempted to change problems in the workplace. Many women are concerned about low pay and overwork in most aspects of daily life, from jobs to housework. Even if these discussions do not culminate in some form of organized committee or activity, the act of talking is a form of political action.

Many women who hurt themselves are aware of sexism in their daily lives, yet feel powerless to make even the smallest changes in how they are treated. Others may have tried to protest but have been trapped under the weight of their own symptomatic behaviors or have felt discouraged about achieving any real change. But it is never too late to begin believing that change is possible and that in community there is strength.

For many TRS women, the beginning of liberating the self comes from joining with others to make a change in the workplace or community. As the early women's liberation movement stated, "The personal is political." Members of oppressed groups have always found strength in numbers. While a therapist should not impose her own ideas for political or community change, she can help the client explore what might be the most appropriate vehicle for her own particular community involvement. If the work of the Outer Circle has been done carefully, the therapist will have an idea of what might work for the client. Many women, for example, do not consider themselves feminists, so joining a radical women's action group would probably feel inappropriate. Yet these same women might be comfortable joining with others in their workplace to ask, for example, for better health insurance coverage for women's health needs such as annual mammograms or maternity leave.

Many people believe that if it had not been for the consciousness-raising of the women's liberation movement of the 1970s, the current movement to stop child abuse and violence against women would never have been possible. (Herman, 1992).

Helping the client find her social action niche and her political voice is an important part of the Middle Circle work. If she has no sense of community with, and potential support from, others who are also beginning to face their oppressors and fight back, she may be overwhelmed by the terrors of the Inner Circle and her symptoms are likely to recur.

Unfortunately, many therapists are still unaware of the importance of community affiliation for their self-abusive clients. There are also many therapists who insist that the reliving and reworking of the trauma in individual therapy must precede the phase of recovery in which social support and political affiliation take place. Sometimes the TRS woman feels that her therapist is ignoring or avoiding this part of her recovery process; her first political action may be to raise the issue in her therapy sessions and discuss possibilities for political affiliation. Most therapists tend to overprotect their self-abusive clients, believing that they are not ready or that they are too fragile to join in any sort of nontreatment group or activities.

Religious and Spiritual Resources

A striking difference between the current medical model of psychotherapy and the various models of healing in other times and cultures is that we separate psychotherapy (and other healing efforts) from spiritually based healing. In other cultures, the shaman, wise woman, or medicine man has both physical and spiritual healing powers. Gradually, Western medical theories are coming to understand the deep connections between the mind and the body. Doctors can readily make the connection between stress and illness. Alternative healers are also making connections between spiritual disease and mental and physical illness. In working with women who hurt themselves, the importance of connecting mind and body with spiritual healing is central. Women who have been betrayed as children have sustained an enormous psychic injury that eats away at them like a cancerous growth. They may have little reason to trust in any kind of human or spiritual goodness, love, or protection.

Although traditional psychotherapy has avoided spiritual language and practice, there is a way to connect the two realms. Using the information that has been gathered in the Outer Circle, the therapist can help the client determine where to begin the important work of connecting mind and body to spiritual resources. The therapist does not have to share the TRS woman's particular mode or language of spiritual connectedness. For a client who has been raised in a Western faith that has betrayed her trust by either its incapacity to offer protection or its active collusion in child abuse, the path to spiritual healing may need to be Eastern or New Age in its philosophy. The therapist need not believe in the healing power of crystals or flower essences to join the client who does in exploring her new spiritual path. Nor does the Jewish therapist need to accept the Catholic Church's politics to accompany the client who chooses the path of comfort within the church's rituals and spiritual teachings.

On a more practical plane, churches, synagogues, and other spiritual groups generally offer a generous and steady source of community. Many therapists are grateful to the priest, minister, rabbi, or spiritual guide who, with the religious community, offers support during the TRS woman's terrors of reliving the trauma and the desperate loneliness that follows giving up the symptom.

It is unfortunate that in all the religious communities, from Catholicism to fundamentalist Christianity to Judaism to New Age spirituality, women and children have been violated, abused, and silenced under the guise of religious beliefs and practices. It is important to understand how religious ideas, institutions, and people may have participated in the client's history of trauma. Once that has been understood, it is time to find a way to create new forms of spiritual connectedness and comfort for the client.

It is my conviction that recovery is deeper if there is a component of spirituality. There does not need to be an affiliation with a specific group or institution, but there does need to be a sense of spiritual awareness that builds connection to others rather than perpetuating solitude. Spiritual healing can be manifest in the client's appreciation of natural beauty or in her belief in some basic capacity for human goodness and loving kindness. An activity such as whale watching or hiking with others can be a vital source of spiritual connection and healing.

Some sense of a mission to share healing through spiritual awareness seems to be part of many groups with a spiritual component, whether it be the Higher Power aspect of the twelve-step movement, the sharing of responsibility for protecting the earth in environmental groups such as the Sierra Club or Greenpeace, or a specific deity in more traditional institutions such as churches and synagogues. This shared mission to "do good" is an essential part of healing through connection for the TRS woman and is as important as the feelings of empowerment through shared community action.

Physical Activities

The last area in which the woman who hurts herself can develop a base of support is physically focused activity. Because she has been so involved with her body through abusing it, she may need a body-focused activity that continues this emphasis but changes it to self-care. The range of activities appropriate or appealing to these women is broad. A physical activity that can help the woman both take better care of her body and engage with others is preferable to more solitary activities, but even walking or jogging can be done with a friend or a group instead of alone.

For women who are struggling with eating disorders, the choice of physical activity is complicated. The obese woman, for instance, may not be able to engage in vigorous activities, but may begin to swim or walk regularly with others. The anorexic woman for whom compulsive exercise is part of her symptoms should not be encouraged to engage in any form of vigorous exercise; she could join a yoga or stretching class that allows her to focus on her body but does not cause her to burn off vital calories.

Physical activities that should be postponed for most clients until after the Inner Circle work are those that stimulate interpersonal fears and rage, such as self-defense courses. Although they can be wonderful forums for healing and empowerment after some of the trauma has been relived and reworked, the enactment of violence necessary to learn self-defense skills can set off extreme terror in women who have not yet done the Inner Circle work.

When Is It Safe to Move to the Inner Circle?

The decision to move into the Inner Circle should be made very carefully. The client and her therapist should rehearse what can happen when the original traumas are revisited without the familiar securities provided by the symptoms and her old patterns of relationship. They should anticipate using various support systems developed in the Middle Circle. Both should expect the threat of relapse: the original symptoms may reappear or new symptoms may be substituted. The client should not feel judged if she relapses; on the other hand, she should not be given permission to do so. If she or anyone else involved feels significant fear about a possible relapse, revisiting the trauma should be postponed, or at least approached tentatively.

The most important determinant in whether the time is right for the Inner Circle work to begin is the strength of the therapist–client relationship. The client must be able to feel that the therapist knows her well enough, cares for her enough, and is strong enough for the reentry to the childhood trauma experience to be survived. The therapist, too, must have confidence in herself in these three areas. When both client and therapist agree that they can work as a reliable, respectful, and mutually caring team, the Inner Circle work can begin.

9

The Inner Circle

The term "Inner Circle" suggests privacy, sanctuary, a special place of inclusion. It means being close to the source of power. It implies intimacy among those within its bounds. The relationships created in the Inner Circle are transforming for the woman who hurts herself and for those who enter this inner sanctum with her. The healing relationships in this last phase of treatment are private, powerful, and intimate. Being in the Inner Circle provides the experience of deepening and expanding the TRS woman's capacity for connection: she learns to connect fragmented parts of herself as she learns to connect with others.

The Transforming Relationship

Much like the attainment of religious belief, successful partnering, parenting, and enduring sexual compatibility, the successful Inner Circle relationship is based on acceptance and love. For the recovering TRS woman, this transformation through loving relationship can happen in individual psychotherapy, with partners and friends, in spiritual connections, and sometimes in therapy groups.

An important moment of "seeing through the heart" comes to mind from my own experience as a client. As I was flatly recounting some fragment of my abuse history, the tears in my therapist's eyes mirrored the hurting child within me. Her grief, probably stimulated by some part of her own history as well as mine, startled me. Before this time, I had not been able to feel the grief, to see, hold, or love this poor little girl I had been carrying around inside for so long. In the shared moment, an important shift in the healing process began. The Nonprotecting Bystander part of me began being replaced by a tentatively unfolding Protective Presence. This presence first emerged in the person of my therapist and then gradually was incorporated within me.

Although it is not like the love between partners or between parents and children, the love shared by the therapist and client is deep and precious. It is not a love that is enacted physically or in shared life tasks or activities, but it is a form of love that requires a similar commitment. Like a parent, the good therapist loves the client generously enough to remain steady and accepting in the face of rage, fear, and unbearable grief. In turn, the client can feel love for her therapist that is like the best of a child's love for a parent: it is given with trust and without obligation to be the parent's or therapist's caretaker. The bond between therapist and client is also like the love between adult friends in that it allows for mutual responsibility for whatever tasks and challenges must be faced, and at the same time allows for different needs and different capacities between these two people.

Any two people engaged in a healing relationship must begin with mutual trust adequate for allowing truth to prevail. Getting to the heart of the Inner Circle means facing the truth of what happened to the child. When this truth is thoroughly explored in a nurturing, trust-based relationship, the woman in recovery is finally able to begin a new life of healthier relationships and self-nurturance.

Whether the primary healing relationship happens with a therapist or with a partner or friend, the vulnerability and intensity of the transforming relationship is what moves the TRS woman to a new level of change. In psychotherapy jargon, we talk about the difference between "first-order change" and "second-order change." First-order change simply substitutes one set of symptoms for another. For example, an alcoholic may stop drinking but become addicted to gambling, overworking, or caffeine. In second-order change, the alcoholic comes to an understanding of her addictive patterns and develops a new set of beliefs, skills, and relationships that allow for a genuine change in all her dimensions. The depth of the transformation is at the level of the core structure—who the person is, not just what she does. The transformation in the Inner Circle work represents second-order change in that the TRS woman creates new patterns of relationship, self-definition, and lifestyle together with her therapist and loved ones.

The core of the Inner Circle work is remembering and then arriving at a new understanding of the childhood memories. Even if the TRS woman has already shared these painful memories with others, whether therapist, partner, or peer support group, she needs a new experience of reliving and reworking the material. When the earlier work in the Outer Circle explorations and the Middle Circle support-building has been done carefully, the client can better endure the fear, rage, shame, and grief that she will feel in this last phase of recovery. She and her therapist or partner will not be alone in doing this work. There will be a system in place where the symptoms can be checked and daily life connections maintained. The therapist will know which parts of the client's Inner Circle memories will be the hardest to access and the hardest to bear, which ghosts are most likely to rise up in the client's mind to try to block these efforts, and which sources of childhood support may be evoked to help her feel less alone and endangered.

Rage is perhaps the most overwhelming of all the experiences the TRS woman and her therapist (and others who love her) will have to get through together. The rage strikes with alarming intensity as the symptoms abate and the full impact of the client's childhood suffering is remembered and relived. Rage can cause the client to hurt herself in new ways and to lash out at those around her. Most therapists can stay calmer in the face of a client's fear or grief than they can in the face of her rage. Shame, too, is difficult for the therapist to bear, especially if it is a close fit with shame issues of her own. But rage directed at the therapist or at the client herself can be frightening for both of them. Unfortunately, it can trigger the therapist's anger if she is not careful. All of the same statements can be made about the effects of rage on the client's other relationships. Without a structure to contain the rage and support those around her as they endure her rage, the TRS woman can once again be left dreadfully alone.

Although there are a number of ways the TRS woman can work through her painful history, individual therapy is often best suited for dealing with this kind of rage and the shame issues that inevitably emerge. I emphasize individual therapy because it is how I work as a therapist and because it has helped me the most in my own recovery process. It is important to state, however, that therapy is only one part of what is needed to achieve lasting recovery. Healing also occurs in intimate relationships and close friendships and in group therapy where recovery from trauma is the focus. Most effective of all is when the woman who hurts herself is fortunate enough to have several relationships in which the healing work occurs. For example, when the therapy relationship is supported by an intimate relationship or a deep friendship, the client is able to work out her powerful and overwhelming feelings in several different arenas. By doing the work in several different relationships, she can test the endurance and affection of those who support her, and strengthen her recognition that she is no longer alone with her nightmares.

In the following excerpt, Lee describes her experience of the Inner Circle as she and her therapist, Martha, began to work with the memories of her early traumatic abuse.

I never thought I could stand the pain I felt when I quit cutting myself. Funny, isn't it, that I would stop hurting myself and feel more pain than I ever imagined. People talk about how they cut themselves to feel something besides numbness or else they cut themselves to stop feeling pain. I never knew exactly which way I would have described it, but I knew after I quit cutting that I was feeling agonizing pain.

You want to know how I stayed with the pain and didn't go back to cutting? It was because of the relationship I had with Martha. Martha told me over and over again that she would stand by me and that she wasn't afraid of the parts of me that began coming out when I started talking about what my mother had done to me.

Sometimes I would just sit there and barely say a word the entire session. She would sit there with me and wouldn't demand anything. She would just be there with this calm look on her face, almost as if she was meditating or praying. I'd keep on glancing over at her to see if she had fallen asleep or was reading or something, but she'd always be there looking at me, looking kind. I'd really give her a hard time, too. I'd yell at her that she wasn't doing me any good and that therapy wasn't helping and that we were just wasting our time. I'd tell her she couldn't help me, that no one could. She would answer back, as calm and steady as you could imagine, that she knew we were making progress. She would say that she had faith that we would find our way into health together. She'd even sympathize with me, telling me she knew how frightening and painful this was.

"You can't possibly know how I feel," I'd respond angrily.

"Lee, I can't know what you feel like inside," she'd say patiently. "But I can feel the fear and pain with you. You are not alone with it."

"But I am alone," I'd say. "Even David can't get close to me when I feel this way. I hate myself! If I could get away from myself, believe me I would. I just don't understand why you stick around and tolerate all this crap from me. When are you going to kick me out of therapy? Or do you just keep seeing me for the money?"

She would actually smile at me when I said awful things like that to her. She'd sound so rational and so nice sometimes, I just wanted to slap her.

"I want to be in this with you," she'd say. "I think you're feeling very old fear and rage and mistrust when you tell me that I'm seeing you in order to take your money. I understand your rage and your fear. I'm not going to abandon you or stop loving you just because you're in excruciating pain right now. You're very angry and I can hold your rage. We can hold your rage and your shame and your fear. And when you are ready, we can hold your grief."

Martha never seemed to lose her grip on me while I was flailing around in my pain and anger. David had a harder time with me, but then again, he was with me a lot more of the time and I probably treated him even worse than I did Martha. Once in a while, David would come with me to meet with Martha, and she would help him understand what I was going through. She also tried to help him protect himself. She advised him to join a group like Al-Anon, and she also convinced him to go see a therapist himself. I was really grateful she took the responsibility for helping him get some support, because I didn't have any energy left over to help him myself.

Some of the time while we were doing the remembering work,

I felt as if I loved Martha more than I loved David or anyone else in the world. I even began to imagine what it would be like to make love with her. It absolutely flipped me out to have those kinds of thoughts. I was finally able to tell her and she was great! She told me that what I was feeling and imagining probably had all kinds of meanings and that it was wonderful that I could let her know about these feelings and that we could explore them. She told me that I didn't have to worry, because nothing sexual would ever happen between us. She would repeat over and over again how the love I felt for her was safe and good and it would never be abused.

Using the Transference

The feelings of powerful and sometimes erotic longing that Lee was having for her therapist are called "transference" in the language of psychotherapy. Transference is a common phenomenon in therapy: the client works through her feelings and thoughts by projecting them onto the therapist. Lee might have been feeling the childhood desire for physical intimacy with her mother, which she was projecting unconsciously onto Martha as if she were still a child and Martha were her mother.

A good therapist works with the client's maternal transference by accepting the feelings, helping the client feel safe having them, and exploring what they may represent in the client's past or present relationships. The therapist must be sensitive about how much to help the client interpret such feelings; telling the client too bluntly that her powerful feelings are transference feelings rather than actual feelings can be unintentionally hurtful. If the therapist is too heavy-handed in interpreting what the feelings "really" are, those feelings that are also about the therapist–client relationship can be devalued or dismissed. The client then feels once again that her real experience and real feelings are being distorted or denied. Overinterpretation of the transference also robs her of the opportunity to figure out for herself what all the levels of the feelings may be. Moreover, the therapist may offer an interpretation that misses the mark. If the therapist imposes her own interpretations as correct because she is the trained professional, the client can lose the sense of being the expert on her own story and defer to the therapist's story, thus losing precious awareness. Two good clues to the skill of the therapist are the degree to which she allows the client to decide for herself the various meanings of her feelings and the therapist's willingness to welcome and hold all those feelings, even when they are hard to take.

Facing Fear

Entering the Inner Circle can be terrifying. For some clients, fear is masked by cold hostility, yet the therapist may experience it as sharply as if it were her own. For example, because Laura and I had worked hard together for months before we got to the Inner Circle stage, I was prepared to enter her terrifying memories with her despite the distance she tried to create through her hostility. I also knew we had the support of her twelve-step group and her sponsor, so that we were not alone. I had gotten a preview of her story when she had started to disclose it prematurely: I knew it would be chilling, both for her and for me.

June's fear, on the other hand, was more disguised. I did not know how I would respond to it until she slowly created a picture that was terrifying in its emptiness and loneliness. When June was finally strong enough to let go of drinking as her primary relationship, her fear was of being utterly alone. The memories she began to explore were of a little girl who was unloved. She remembered that as a child she would most likely get attention through trying very hard to be a good caretaker of her parents and siblings or through receiving random acts of punishment. No one told her that they loved her, and no one helped her learn how to work out the various puzzles and challenges of childhood.

My response to June's fear was to feel her aloneness and to want to help her run from it. It was very hard to sit with it, to bear it with her, and to allow it to surface long enough for both of us to feel it and know it. Before she could escape this terrible fear of complete, unloved solitude, she had to let herself feel the solitude and explore it. So did I. In my own life, the experience of being alone with fear and shame was familiar. Although I was not a neglected child in the way that June was, I certainly knew the experience of having no one pay attention to what was happening to me. I remembered how trapped I had been by shame and family loyalty. I could still shudder at the memory of what it was like to stay in that prison of silent loneliness well into my adult life. This familiarity meant that I could understand June's fears, but it also meant that I was tempted to avoid them because they triggered my own painful memories.

The other temptation was to rescue June, to snatch her away from that loneliness so that neither of us would have to face it. The memories stimulated such fear that June would do almost anything not to go through it. When she could no longer use alcohol as a companion, she responded to her fear in the same powerless, overwhelmed state she had experienced as a child. She became so depressed that she was temporarily unable to function. She stayed in bed all day, stopped bathing, and avoided contact with her friends and her twelve-step sponsor. The work for her—and for me—was to face the fear, this time knowing she was strong enough to vanquish it.

June's fear needed to become accessible. She had to be able to look at it from every angle and describe it, and then learn how to tame it or control it. Her AA group was a strong support for both of us during this siege. The other sources of support were her deepening spiritual connection with what she called her Higher Power and the support of her oldest friends, two women with whom she had shared the challenges of poverty, child-rearing, and disappointments with men. June's belief in her Higher Power gave her the reassurance that she could face the fear with more resources than just me, her sometimes nervous therapist. Her two friends were able to remind her that they were there—as always—dependable, kind, and full of wry humor.

My healing continued too, as it often has when I have accompanied a client on her journey through pain. By being with June in the presence of her fear, I could continue to remind myself that fear can only overpower us if we try to outrun it. Dealing with fear is like swimming in high surf: the swimmer can survive the wave only by diving into it or riding on its crest. If we try to outrun big waves and big fears, we are knocked off our feet and left awash in the treacherous undertow. The sixties phrase "go with the flow" was June's expression for confronting her fears in the Inner Circle. "Go with the flow, right?" she would say to me when a wave of fear would assault us as we excavated a new memory. We would smile at each other, taking courage that we were not alone on the beach.

The client should pay attention to what her body is telling her about fear. Sometimes the only way she knows she is circling fear is when her body is telling her something her brain has not registered yet. For example, the fear may be manifest in her body as a specific pain or as nausea, a racing heartbeat, or shortness of breath. She may also need to check her responses to how others are reacting to her fear. She should ask if her therapist is aware of her fear and how the therapist is processing it. If she feels that her therapist, partner, or friend is trying to rescue her from her fear instead of allowing her to experience it, she should point this out.

Anger can mask fear. If the client feels angry when anger does not seem to fit the memory or reaction she is investigating, perhaps she is hiding from her fear. She does not have to hide anymore. The client and those supporting her in her work are much more powerful than her fear. They can name it, learn it, dive into it, even laugh at it.

Surviving Rage

Rage is as powerful as fear, and even harder for most therapists and loved ones to endure. As the TRS woman unleashes the memories of what was done to her as a child, she also unleashes her rage. She may be completely unfamiliar with how to feel or express rage. Or she may be in the habit of losing control through rage attacks that serve to push others away and to keep them always at a distance. One or the other extreme is likely, since women who hurt themselves have not been allowed to express healthy, appropriate anger in situations of pain or injustice.

Rage takes many forms in the Inner Circle therapy relationship. Some women are so uncomfortable with their rage that they find a way to sabotage the therapy process by skipping appointments, talking about irrelevancies, or dropping out of therapy completely. Others express their long-stored rage by attacking the therapist.

In my work with BJ, the hardest of her transference feelings for me were not her wild bouts of rage expressed through devaluing my skills or my commitment to her. A much more upsetting expression of her rage— far harder to tolerate—was her grossly explicit sexualizing of our interactions. I understood that she used sexual provocation to attack me when we were getting too close to her pain or shame, but it was nonetheless shocking for me to hear, because I wished to be her Protective Presence, a transferential good mother. Despite my discomfort, it was important for me to understand that her ways of feeling powerful and her familiar method of self-soothing came from being sexually aggressive.

Understanding this did not mean that I sat through her lewd verbal attacks without comment. Instead, I learned to say to her that the barrage of abusive, rage-motivated communication was letting us both know that we were getting too close to something that made her feel scared or ashamed. We needed to recognize it and help her feel safe again. I would then ask her how we could work together to achieve safety. Generally, this approach helped her come back into a more collaborative relationship with me. On several occasions, when she could not stop her angry, sexualized assault, I ended the session. I reassured her that I was not abandoning her and that I cared very much about her. I told her that I was disappointed that we had to end our session early. But she needed to know that I had limits that helped me stay strong and self-respecting, and that I had to protect myself by not allowing her to continue this form of verbal assault.

When the therapist is able to hold the client's rage and at the same time protect both herself and the client, the client can begin to be reassured that the therapist will not enact the roles of Abuser, Nonprotecting Bystander, or Victim. This reassurance is important because of how these three voices become amplified in the Inner Circle work. If the client believes that her therapist is retaliating because she is unable to manage the client's rage, they must talk about it. The therapist may need the client's expert opinion on how the therapist's response feels to her.

Therapists, like other human beings—especially women—are prone to avoid rage. It scares them or makes them want to fight back. The therapist should not let herself be intimidated by the client's rage. Often the client is not only showing the therapist her own rage but enacting the rage of the Abuser as well. The client must not let the internalized Abuser get away with scaring the therapist, too. She needs the therapist in her corner. The client and therapist must find a way for the therapist to respond to the rage that is supportive to the client and does not turn the therapist into a Victim. The client is justified in asking if the therapist needs to seek a consultation if they cannot talk this out.

Releasing Shame

There is probably nothing harder to comprehend and describe fully than the experience of shame for most women in this culture. It seems so pervasive that it could be considered synonymous with being a woman. We are taught to devalue our bodies and to feel shame at the body's continuous imperfection, from childhood right through old age.

Shame is even more powerful when the woman is a survivor of childhood abuse, invasion, or neglect. Shame is what makes the woman unable to find language to explain what she feels, thinks, or does to herself when she is living a life of self-harm. Just as shame rendered her both speechless and powerless as a child, shame traps her as an adult when she tries to give voice to her experience of being violated and of violating her own flesh.

When Lee talked about her shame, it was almost visible, an entity that served to keep Martha, David, and everyone else at a great distance.

Now that I have stopped cutting myself, I feel like my shame is going to strangle me. How can Martha sit there across from me and hear me say the things my mother did to me and not get up and walk out the door?

David would like to walk out whenever I try to tell him what my mother did. He only stays because he is so good and because Martha keeps on explaining to him how okay it is for him to have the feelings he does. I think David is ashamed for me and ashamed for himself. He even seems to be ashamed on my mother's behalf when I tell him about the abuse.

We can't make love anymore. We are both too ashamed.

Why does Martha stay with me? Can't she feel the black slime coming up around us when I start remembering? Can't she see that my shame will poison us both? When she looks at my scars, the places where I used to cut myself, doesn't she see horrible crawling things coming out of my body? I see them and I call them the spawn of my shame.

The shame the client may feel as she begins to relive her childhood can feel contagious to her. For the therapist, it may trigger her own unresolved shame. It may be so distressing that she colludes in the client's avoidance, allowing her to change the conversation abruptly in order to retreat from the shame experience, instead of letting her get to know the shame and then do battle with it.

It is rare for the therapist to get inducted into the client's experience of shame, but it can happen. For example, a therapist responding to BJ's experience of shame might be unable to see it for what it is and therefore express revulsion when BJ acts out her shame and rage by being sexually aggressive. The therapist would then be experiencing BJ's shame as contagious, feeling shame and a desire to flee. In such a case, the therapist would be trying to distance herself not only from the client's shame but from her own as well.

In Lee's case, Martha was able to stand fast in the journey with her client. For many female therapists, hearing the story of maternal abuse is perhaps harder than hearing about any other kind of abuse. We want to be in a positive, caring, maternal role with our clients, and we are horrified by motherhood gone amok. Listening to these stories may be hardest of all for a therapist who is not only female but also a mother. We find it impossible to comprehend that a woman could do such things to her child. We want to distance ourselves from these stories of atrocity. Martha showed great courage and steadiness in bearing witness to Lee's story and in making herself stay connected to what was good as well as to what was dreadful in Lee's mother's caretaking efforts.

Martha also did well in her work with David. She helped him to legitimate his horrified reactions by listening to him with empathy and thoughtfulness. Then she helped him find his own sources of support, so that he could remain connected to Lee throughout her process of remembering and reliving the memories.

Shame is the hardest of all feelings to bear. Once the TRS woman can identify it, she is already more than halfway through the nightmare. She must trust herself to be able to remember and relive it. She is no longer alone with it and she can now understand that It is not Her. She can eventually even allow herself to feel love for the abuser, because he or she is also a victim of shame, even though she remains mindful that the abuser did harm to her and should not be exonerated.

Telling her story to someone who stands by her and continues to love her will free her from shame. Allowing herself to take in love from a partner, friends, support group members, and spiritual sources will also free her from shame. Learning to love herself allows her to give up her shame.

Bringing Other People into the Inner Circle

There are many ways in which a good therapist works closely with other people in the client's support system throughout the Inner Circle phase of recovery. In working with Lee, Martha was able to make use of David's willingness to be involved in the recovery process and his genuine devotion to his partner. Although David could not be expected to do the intensive work of helping Lee relive and rework her trauma memories, he was capable of supporting the process.

Many women who hurt themselves believe that no one can tolerate the horror and pain of hearing their abuse memories. They cannot trust that anyone can stand fast with them as they become rageful, reclusive, or rejecting in the process of relinquishing the symptomatic behavior. Just at the time when the recovering person needs the most love and acceptance, she is most likely to pull back from the sources of that love. Therapists, too, can underestimate the strength and importance of partners and close friends. All too often the therapist colludes in this silence or withdrawal from others, believing that the client cannot endure the exposure of her pain.

Martha's inclusion of David in some sessions with Lee demonstrated her trust in David as capable of hearing Lee and supporting her through the process of reconstructing her trauma memories. It is often especially important to reassure partners that they need to trust themselves to allow their responses to be aired, even though these can be painful for the TRS woman to hear. David, for example, had trouble believing Lee when she began telling him about the sadistic abuse she had suffered at her mother's hands. David had known Lee's mother for many years and had a cordial relationship with her. It was very upsetting to him to know that she had been abusive in the ways Lee described.

The work Martha did with David and Lee together in sessions allowed for David's shock and disillusionment to be processed. Martha took responsibility for helping David work through his initial disbelief, and at the same time supported Lee in her need for David to accept her memories. Had Martha not encouraged David to share all his reactions, no matter how distressing they were for Lee to hear, a subterranean uneasiness would certainly have begun to undermine the relationship. Instead, by airing David's discomfort in therapy sessions, Martha made space for David to understand Lee's pain as he himself worked to assimilate two very different versions of the mother–daughter relationship: the mother and daughter David had observed for years and the relationship Lee was now reliving from her childhood.

Another reason to involve the partner or close friends is to allow the woman to share the memories as she should have been able to do as a child. Instead of being alone with her shameful memories and sense of self, as she was in childhood, Lee could experience the comfort and protection of both her therapist and her partner. Karen, a woman without a partner, could share her experience with the friends who filled the space of family. By sharing her memories, Karen reworked the terrible solitude and hopelessness she endured throughout childhood, when family members were rarely there to protect or reassure her.

It is important for the woman and the therapist to decide who the sharing will involve and when and how it will take place. Generally, the client feels safer if she is able to disclose pieces of her history to her therapist before sharing them with others. But the process of revelation is never easily controlled or predicted. Once the client relinquishes her symptoms, she will begin to be flooded with memories, especially if she is participating in a group where others are also remembering traumatic histories. Often she will remember a terrifying fragment in flashback form when she is making love with her partner, seeing an intense movie with a friend, or visiting a sibling. However the reconstruction of traumatic memory takes place, the partnership with her therapist can help the client to use the experience of remembering to build new connections with her intimate circle of friends, with her partner, and sometimes with her siblings.

It is not always safe to include siblings in the beginning stages of recalling and reliving family trauma memories. There are also situations in which it is the best thing that can possibly happen. Here are two examples that illustrate when including siblings works and when it doesn't.

June decided that she would talk to her sister about the way she remembered many childhood episodes of severe parental neglect. She reminded her sister of the time that no adult had been home for three nights in a row, and how she, at age nine, had tried to feed, clothe, and comfort her younger siblings. She told her that she believed this kind of home life had played a major role in her becoming an alcoholic. She confided in her sister the shame she now felt about her alcoholism, and told her how much she had wanted to turn to the sister for help. But she had been afraid of her sister's judgment and condemnation, especially because June had been married three times, while her sister had remained married to the same man for twenty-five years.

June's sister responded to this disclosure with denial and anger. She told June that if she had only opened her heart to Jesus, she would not have lived the depraved lifestyle she did. She also insisted that June was fabricating the memories of neglect. June knew that her sister had been beaten severely by her husband more than once but was committed to continuing the marriage because of her religious beliefs. June was heartbroken that her sister could not share in remembering and recovering from their shared history of childhood neglect. She was also shaken by her sister's denial of family history. Stunned by her sister's response, she became further depressed about her own capacity to survive and create better relationships in her current family. Her unsuccessful reaching out to this sister caused her to start drinking again.

Nancy, on the other hand, had always had a close relationship with her brother, Allen. When Nancy and her therapist invited Allen for a therapy session, he and Nancy were able to share similar memories of invasive family patterns that had contributed to Nancy's later self-harm. Allen too had been tormented for years, desperately lonely in his young adult years, when he had a succession of unsuccessful relationships.

Allen and Nancy both cried as they pieced together their childhood memories and the shame that had kept them separated from each other. Both grieved that they had not been able to talk to or support each other in their silent suffering. Allen was later able to tell Nancy that he was gay and that he had been living happily with his partner for ten years. He was delighted that Nancy was able to accept his lifestyle. Allen and his male partner became one of the principal sources of support for Nancy in the Inner Circle work that followed.

Transforming the Triadic Self

The central work of recovery for a TRS woman is finding the particular configuration of the Triadic Self that fits her history and her particular ways of enacting self-harm. Each woman has her own unique way of retelling and reliving a painful childhood through how she hurts herself. The secret of achieving second-order change in the Inner Circle is for the TRS woman and therapist to find ways not only to relive this story together, but also to comprehend its meaning fully and to connect it with current problems in the client's life.

Identifying the Three Voices

By the time the Inner Circle work begins, it is often relatively easy to identify what parts of the abusive adult and what parts of the nonprotecting bystander the woman is enacting when she hurts herself. The wounded child within, the Victim, is usually unmistakable. As the TRS woman begins to retell her story in such a way that she relives it, each of the three parts becomes as real and painful to her as if she were actually back in childhood. The first phase of Inner Circle work should be concerned with keeping the three voices from getting too big and too threatening.

The three voices—the Victim, the Abuser, and the Nonprotecting Bystander—are represented by the symptomatic cycle. The harming behavior is the Abuser. The protesting part of the self that wants to resist self-harm is the Victim. The voice who says "But I can't help it, I can't stop myself from doing this" is the Nonprotecting Bystander. Together the therapist and client develop a detailed picture of how these three forces operate within the woman who hurts herself. How does the cycle begin? What are the warning signals that the dangerous dance is about to start?

An important turning point in the work is uncovering whom each of these voices represents in the client's actual childhood memories. Who was the Abuser? If there was more than one, who is most prominent at the moment of the adult's self-harming cycle? Who was the Nonprotecting Bystander? Sometimes the Abuser and the Nonprotecting Bystander can merge into one figure; then the internal battle becomes dyadic rather than triadic. Whoever the characters are, it is important to identify them, try to separate them out from the adult self, and begin to confront them.

There are several writers who, like me, have suggested ways to explore internalized voices and then to externalize them, making them less frightening and thus more manageable. David Grove (1989) works with symptoms that have been toxic and powerful, to develop a metaphor in which the malignant image is transformed into a helpful

ally in healing ("interrogating the symptoms to learn their strengths").
Michael White (1988, 1989), an innovative Australian family therapist,
has developed a different kind of model in which fears, bad habits, and
nightmares become externalized and turned into cartoonlike characters.
White reduces the power of the distressing behavior by teasing it outside the child or adult, turning the problem into something silly to
make it manageable. My approach to working with the Triadic Self
also externalizes the symptoms, giving them identities as familiar figures from childhood. Once they are identified in this way, the client can
begin the work of confronting them and changing her adult relationship to them.

This identification obviously requires a leap of imagination, for both
the therapist and client. It may be relatively easy to make the connection between the act of self-harm and the *physical* or *sexual* abuse the
child experienced; but it is somewhat harder to make the connection in
a case like June's, where the abuse was a peculiar combination of
neglect and devaluing. June's mother seems to be represented by June's
drinking (the Abuser), as well as by the failure to take care of herself
(the Nonprotecting Bystander). Nancy's situation is the most confusing
of all, because her grandmother, the very person who loved and protected her, also unknowingly violated her through invasive caretaking.
Sometimes the best way to externalize the Triadic Self is to identify the
pattern of how the child felt with abusive and nonprotective adults,
rather than trying to be too precise about which adult figure is represented by each part of the self-abusing cycle.

The process of identifying the three parts of the self and then banishing them by stopping the symptoms creates a deep loneliness for most
TRS women. This is why it is so important for them to do this work in
therapy rather than alone. The TRS woman can learn to identify the
Triadic Self, and she can find ways to give up these familiar figures
from childhood as she gives up her self-harmful behaviors or symptoms, but the next step is enduring the emptiness. The good therapist
can go through this process with the client and help her feel less alone.

Replacing the Symptom with the
Therapeutic Relationship

The therapist replaces the symptoms in the client's relational system
during the Inner Circle work. The therapist steps into the space left

empty when the symptoms are abandoned and becomes the woman's primary relationship, much as the symptoms were. This relationship is only temporary and eventually shifts to partners, children, and friends.

In Karen's case, I took the place of Karen's drinking and bulimia. Karen had used these symptoms to comfort herself, to contain her anger (or sometimes to release it), to feel a familiar sense of connection, and to reproduce the old abusive relationship with her father. In her cycle of self-harm, she also reproduced her relationship with her non-protective mother by refusing to save herself from self-abuse.

When she was able to give up the self-abusive behaviors, she was left with anger, fear, shame, and loneliness. Although her various group activities were a source of support and comfort, she felt overwhelmed by the intensity of her feelings. At that point, she was tempted to return to her symptoms. Karen had close friends and a solid sense of her competence at work, but her needs could not be met by friends or work. If she had had a partner, I would have involved that person in some of our sessions. However, even women with sympathetic partners need to do much of the intensive work with a therapist, simply because the partner has neither the training nor the neutrality of the therapist.

When I became the substitute for the symptoms, Karen developed a variety of feelings toward me that she had previously attached to her symptoms. Sometimes she projected onto me her father's violence and the anger at him that she had previously enacted through her symptoms. For example, she might be furious with me for seemingly small mistakes such as being two minutes late for our appointment or forgetting a small detail of her daily life. I had to stay steady in the face of these sudden rage attacks and understand what she was communicating and reliving.

At other times she was overcome by feelings of idealized love for me and viewed me as all good. These feelings were equally distressing for her, because she would feel shame at her own imperfection. She feared that I would reject, neglect, or abandon her. At still other times, she combined the feelings of rage with the overidealized longing for my accepting love. She would be devastated that I was not powerful enough to protect her from herself or from the disappointments of daily life. In this situation, she seemed to be projecting the Nonprotecting Bystander onto me and experiencing me as being much like her ineffectual mother.

Another common transference is to project the Victim role onto the therapist. Karen did this if I was ill or injured. For example, I broke my toe, and Karen experienced me as far more disabled and helpless than I actually was. My vulnerability terrified her, and she responded by missing several therapy appointments, although she had no conscious awareness that my injury could have any bearing on why she was suddenly missing appointments after more than a year of regular attendance.

Gradually, Karen and I were able to identify the various parts of the Triadic Self that she had transferred from her cycle of self-harm to the relationship with me. When she was able to see what she was enacting with me, she began to settle into a solider feeling of trust for me and tolerance of her own pattern of intense feelings. The next step was for us to begin to develop within her a Protective Presence on which she could count. As with all TRS women, this was the most difficult step of all.

Cultivating the Protective Presence

The development of the Protective Presence is a three-part process. First, the TRS woman and the therapist must look back into the client's childhood to see who there was who provided moments of protection and affirmation for the traumatized child. Then the therapist works with the client to act as a temporary stand-in for what will eventually be an internalized Protective Presence. (In this process, a temporary Protective Presence can also be provided by a twelve-step group, a therapy group, or a Higher Power.) Finally, the client is able to develop an internalized Protective Presence of her own.

The client and her therapist or group must decide on the best way to begin to create a relationship with the appropriate Protective Presence. A number of techniques are helpful. One way is to imagine that the therapist is present for the client whenever she feels the compulsion to hurt herself. Instead of the disappointing Nonprotecting Bystander, the therapist is now there to help the child fight off the Abuser within, so that the client begins to believe that she is not alone. She can now visualize the therapist when she needs a Protective Presence (or she can visualize her support group, therapy group, or Higher Power). The client may need some sort of object to help her feel connected to the new protector, like a blanket she brings with her to therapy sessions, or a sweater or stuffed animal.

Some women like to have a tape of their therapist reading a comforting children's story to them. I found it especially comforting to have a tape of my therapist reading *The Runaway Bunny*. This story is about a little bunny who imagines running away by transforming himself into many different forms, and a mother rabbit who transforms herself to mirror him and keep him safely with her. I found the story reassuring because the little bunny is so obviously sure that his mother will validate his various fantasies of adventure and yet never let him run off into danger or lose what is loving and protective in their relationship.

The client will find that she can begin to summon up a variety of Protective Presences when she needs them. In addition to her therapist, group, or Higher Power, she may recall those people from childhood who were at least occasionally there for her: an aunt, a teacher, a family friend, another child, a pet. When she has the images dependably in her mind, always available to her mentally when she feels alone, frightened, or enraged, she will be able to resist turning to her old patterns of self-destruction. She will have succeeded in developing a composite group that makes up an internal Protective Presence. One day she notices that she simply acts spontaneously in a self-protective way, resisting self-harm, without having to summon up those other images. She is beginning to know that she has her own Protective Presence who has taken up permanent residence.

There is great variety among the people and images each TRS woman chooses as the representation of her Protective Presence. As with many other TRS women, my Protective Presence has changed over the years. The first was the image of a therapist I went to for many years who provided the experience of abiding affection and stability for me over a long period of my tempestuous young adult life. The next Protective Presence appeared to me quite unexpectedly when I was having coffee with a friend, and was suddenly and inexplicably filled with the sense of some other presence entering my consciousness. As skeptical as I was about anything even remotely spiritual, after a number of similar experiences, I accepted this spirit guide who appeared in the form of a dolphin. For more than twenty years I have summoned the spirit of the dolphin when I need strength and the feeling of lightness. The dolphin is especially helpful to me when I am bearing the pain of someone else's story in my role as therapist and supervisor.

My most enduring representations of the Protective Presence have been two women who have each played deeply important roles in my life. One of them, although not actually a blood relative, functioned as my aunt and was an important source of nurturance and affection throughout my childhood. The other image is my therapist. At this point in my life, it is not usually a conscious act to invoke any specific representation of a Protective Presence, but rather something that happens without my even noticing that I have been able to act in a self-protective way.

For some women who are first discovering a Protective Presence, the very act of experiencing hope can trigger the expectation of disappointment and therefore rage. Any TRS woman who has begun the process of developing trust in an image, person, or fantasy knows what it is like to expect betrayal. Sadly enough, many women experience the slightest setback as if it were a major disappointment, overreacting because they were primed to doubt the possibility of hope and trust. Part of successful recovery is to learn that the Protective Presence is fallible.

When Karen began to experience my image as her transitional Protective Presence, she was extremely distressed when the flesh-and-blood Dusty Miller was momentarily inattentive or had to cancel an appointment. She went through months of therapy when she would politely cancel appointments, come in late, or avoid working on important issues as a sort of payback for my transgressions. She was eventually able to talk with me about her feelings of rage when I would fail to live up to the image of Protective Presence she had created in her mind. A turning point was reached when together we were able to validate her internalized capacity for self-protection while at the same time accepting that, in the real world, I was far from perfect. When she could separate me from her internalized Protective Presence and claim the voice as her own, she was truly achieving recovery from TRS.

Not all TRS women can or should use the therapist as the primary transitional Protective Presence image. For a woman like June who was severely neglected and devalued by her mother, it was safer to use her Higher Power and her friends as the images she could internalize to protect herself. When she tried to use me in this way, she could not stop herself from hearing a critical "Big Brother" voice criticizing her efforts. Although she clearly felt comfortable with me in our sessions, and was able to trust me and allow herself to know that I genuinely cared about her, she could not transform her mistrust of anyone in a powerful authority role to create a safe space for me in her fantasies of protection. It was important for me to understand this and not try to push my way into a role that was not safe for her to accept. What I could do was support her as she began to use the internalized images of her friends and her twelve-step resources to create a Protective Presence of gentle, loving voices, no longer drowned out by the harsh, critical voices she had heard for so many years.

The shift from hearing only judgments from her twelve-step sponsor and supporters to hearing these same voices as accepting and compassionate was the most significant work we did in the Inner Circle. June began to understand how she had been hearing her mother's critical, nonprotecting voice in how she had responded for years in AA meetings. She finally could make sense of why she had continued to relapse. I played the role of guide in my work with June, showing her that she was lovable and helping her to develop compassion for herself that allowed her to connect more closely to the resources in her life that had been there all along.

Nancy created an interesting composite Protective Presence. She was able to hold firm to the positive aspects of her grandmother's love and to internalize those parts of the relationship. Her sessions with her brother, Allen, were especially helpful in this process, because we were able to recreate wonderful memories of times when Nancy and Allen had each felt cherished by their grandmother. Her friends were also part of her development of Protective Presence, because of their loyalty to her and acceptance of her struggle to begin letting go of the quest to remain forever young. In one session, Nancy and her two closest friends wept together as each shared the anguish of coming to terms with the inevitable process of aging.

I was both touched and amused by Nancy when she told me that I too had become part of her Protective Presence. "You've really taught me something," she said, "because you really seem to feel good about yourself even though you don't have—you know—the perfect body or the perfect hairstyle or great clothes. I guess I'm trying to say that you seem really okay with just being kind of ordinary."

Lee had a difficult time holding onto any of the images of the Protective Presence that she created. I consulted regularly to her and Martha, encouraging both of them to stay with the hard work they were doing. Martha had become a symbol of protection for Lee over the many years they had worked together, and David, too, represented a strong external source of protection. The problem seemed to be that Lee became quickly terrified of any fantasy image she was able to create. It finally occurred to me that Lee needed to begin creating an image of something less dangerous to the terrified Victim self than an adult person. I suggested to Lee and Martha that they collaborate in helping Lee visualize a fantasy image of another child or an animal that might be less threatening to her child self.

Two weeks later I got a call from Martha. "Guess what!" she said delightedly. "It worked! Lee has a new image and it's really great for her." Martha went on to describe the fantasy child created by Lee to help her escape the dark places she kept mentally revisiting. The child was a sort of alter who could help Lee feel safe without having the potential of an adult to turn on Lee and overwhelm her. Soon Lee was able to add another representation to her slowly forming Protective Presence, a large lion who reminded her of a favorite stuffed animal from childhood. Over time, Lee was able to expand her repertoire of protective images, until she finally could visualize Martha, then David, and eventually herself as representing powerful internal forces of protection. Although Lee had relapses when she could not remember ever having experienced the existence of a Protective Presence, the relapses became increasingly infrequent and also much easier for her to predict and thus prevent. The core work for Lee was to integrate the fragmented parts of herself, including the fragmented parts of the Protective Presence, until she could feel a more dependable sense of self-cohesion. Because she had suffered such severe trauma in childhood, there was more serious damage to her capacities for attachment and integration of self than many TRS women have to face. Her achievement of any form of Protective Presence was especially impressive in this light.

Neither Laura nor BJ was able to finish her therapy with me because I moved to another area and had to terminate therapy before our work was finished. Had I understood what I do now about Trauma Reenactment Syndrome during the years I worked with them, I believe we would have accomplished major changes together. My guess is that each would have created a lively Protective Presence, although not without some equally lively struggles with her therapist.

Resolving Old Pain

A part of the recovery process to be done at the end of therapy is to resolve and repair those relationships that can be salvaged. When responsibility for past abuse and neglect is fully accepted by the TRS woman's family members, she is then able to move toward acceptance of those parts of the relationships that she values.

This stage of the work may involve members of her current support system, including her current family, supportive members of her family of origin, and friends. It may also include face-to-face meetings with the abusive or nonprotecting parent. The goal at this stage is to work through past unresolved relationships, to confront the past abuse, and to build connections to people in the client's current life.

Not every woman who has worked through her history of childhood abuse and neglect will be able to confront her abuser or resolve relationships with other family members in person. Some TRS women cannot do the work of confrontation and resolution directly because the parent or other family member is dead or no longer in the picture. But whether or not the abuser or nonprotecting bystander is available, the work of the TRS woman is to confront these family members with their betrayals, either directly or in her memory.

The confrontation can take place in the therapist's office or in a carefully planned family meeting that includes an advocate for the TRS woman. Even when the family member is not literally present, the confrontation is healing, because it is the time when the Victim self relinquishes all responsibility for the abuse and places the responsibility squarely in the laps of the abuser and nonprotecting bystander. However they respond, the next step is to move toward resolution of the relationship.

In the Inner Circle, the TRS woman has already done the work of banishing the internalized Abuser and Nonprotecting Bystander. She is therefore able to separate the abusive and neglectful relationships from her sense of self. The Inner Circle work of accepting herself as "not bad" and no longer alone allows her to achieve the strength she needs in approaching the resolution of the external family relationships. Either face-to-face or in her mind, she must be able to confront those who abused her and failed to protect her, and to withstand their possible refusal to acknowledge their betrayal. If she attempts the confrontation before she has completed her healing of the Triadic Self, she will not be able to summon her Protective Presence to help her transcend the disappointments that are likely to be part of this work.

Perhaps the best way to end this book is through the voices of my clients, those heroic women who have taught me so many ways to think about the problem of Trauma Reenactment Syndrome and how to transform pain into strength, how to experience fully what the psychologist Judith V. Jordan (1990) calls "courage in connection."

Nancy is a good example of the complementarity of Middle and Inner Circle work. She says today that she truly is "a work in progress." In therapy, Nancy talks about the difficulty she has had letting anyone get close: Chip, Allen, her friends, and her children. She says that the willingness of her friends, brother, and husband to come to therapy with her gave her the courage to trust in these relationships and in the therapeutic relationship itself. Here she shares her insight about how her therapy and her network of support both contribute to her newfound mental health.

NANCY

I have found a therapist who is willing to continue to work with me. She has not abandoned me, even though I gave her every opportunity to do just that. In fact, I inadvertently worked at pushing her away. I tested her and she passed the test. Today I use therapy to foster and encourage the Protective Presence within myself.

Chip and my friends still tease me sometimes about how much time I spend fixing my hair, buying clothes, generally trying to look as good as possible. But it's very different now from how it was when I was having all the surgery and going on the crash diets. When I start getting frantic about wrinkles or age spots or gaining a pound or two, I can almost always stop myself and recognize that voice in my head from childhood.

I know that some of the messages I got from my grandmother were not healthy for me. I am really glad, though, that I can feel so much love for her in my heart. I can forgive her for the mistakes she made, just like my friend Babs has been able to forgive me for the ways I treated her in our business when I didn't know the difference between her needs and my own. Babs and I are much closer friends now, just like Chip and I have gotten much closer too. I still go to therapy sometimes to talk with Dusty when I start getting freaked out about old worries, but I know that I have the answers inside my own head.

June's use of the therapeutic relationship led to a new appreciation for her twelve-step program.

JUNE

My therapist got so that she was kind of like a teacher to me—or maybe a cheerleader. I'm not sure which. But somehow she got me to change my attitude about going to my twelve-step program. Those slogans that I hated—"Let go and let God," "Easy does it," and the Serenity Prayer, "God grant me the serenity to accept the things I cannot change, the courage to change the things I can, and the wisdom to know the difference"—I have now taken them to heart.

I am changing my life. I don't know if I would call it a Protective Presence, but I am recovering. I have a sponsor and I am learning through her to become honest with myself.

My therapist also pointed out that I am being a better parent to my children than I ever experienced that parents could be. I am learning to forgive my parents and myself. When a new problem arises, I sometimes "turn it over" or talk it over with my sponsor. Now when she sends me back to therapy, I can go, knowing that I am not being punished. She's sending me to get the help that I can ask for and accept.

I know that recovery is a lifelong process, but with my sponsor, my group, and a therapist I can go to when I need her, I'm happy to be in the process. I've even come close to appreciating the saying "progress, not perfection." Sometimes.

Lee has found a new stage of therapeutic healing in her work with David in couples therapy.

LEE

On the surface I looked so good. I "brought home the bacon and cooked it up in a pan," and I had a man who loved me.

Therapy was the most painful experience. Not because it was

bad. It's just that in therapy I got in touch with so much pain, oh, so much pain. Pain I had pushed down until it came out as such violence against myself. I remember feeling so ashamed. That shame was as painful as any of my childhood memories.

I am not hurting myself anymore. So much of what I turned inward, what you might call "acting out," is really "acting in." I don't do that anymore. You might think that I would be happy about that. Well, I am and I'm not. I'm glad that all the conflict I feel isn't going on inside me anymore. I'm not so glad about how so much of the conflict now is between David and me. Martha says that it is understandable, even to be expected.

I want to be grateful to David for the ways he stood by me, and I am. But that's not all there is. I get angry with him and he gets hurt and feels rejected.

We have begun couples therapy, and I think it's going to be hard work, but I have every hope that we are going to make it.

Karen's story expresses the best of what the TRS woman can achieve through her courage in making connections with others. Her growth in self-esteem and in creating more genuine closeness in relationship shines as a beacon of hope for all TRS women.

KAREN

You are not going to believe this, but I'm happy. Oh, I'm not happy every moment of every day, but for the first time in my life, I can honestly say, "I'm happy." Maybe after all these years my luck has changed, but I feel lucky and I deserve it.

I am involved in therapy and a women's group. I have found ways to assert myself through the nursing association. I don't just boil inside and then go home and take out my rage on myself. With my friends I am even becoming honest. It's scary, but I'm doing it step by step.

Therapy, which I first approached with such mistrust, is really working. I have begun to understand that someone can get close and not abuse or neglect me. Learning ever so slowly to trust my therapist so that I could share my deepest, darkest secrets—that was the most wonderful gift I have ever received. She really is trustworthy. Now there's a word that I could not have said a few years ago. She showed me unconditional love and respect. That's probably what allowed me to finally get into a women's support group. With her I had experienced acceptance, so that when people in the group talked about unconditional love, I had an idea what they were talking about.

Today I am even in a relationship. I want to share my joy about it. I was never able to stay in a relationship before—couldn't let anyone get close—couldn't trust anyone, remember?

Well, that's not altogether true for me anymore. You see, I have someone to love and someone who loves me. Her name is Anne. We met in my women's group. She has four years of sobriety in a twelve-step program, and she is committed to her recovery—and to me.

My therapist listened as I shared all my scared feelings about loving a woman. She is right there, working with me as I continue to struggle with intimacy. Her nonjudgment of me has led me to be more fully self-accepting. I'm happy today. I don't hurt myself anymore and I don't even feel really tempted to do so. I have confronted my mother with her not protecting me in childhood, and I even confronted my father about the sexual abuse. It was a pretty big deal—a lot of yelling and crying and denying and accusing. But I came through it okay. My father's second wife has made him go to therapy, and she will not allow him ever to be alone with their kids, even though my dad and the kids swear he never did anything inappropriate to them. My dad denies the full extent of what he did to me, but he has at least admitted that he was "sexually inappropriate" and has asked me to forgive him. I'm not ready to do that, nor do I want to have contact with him. Maybe after he does some really hard work in his own therapy that will change.

My mother and I have had a lot of meetings, both with Dusty and by ourselves. We have cried a lot and gone through a lot of remembering together. I know she suffered, too. I have been able to hold her accountable for not protecting me, but also to know that she is finally able to acknowledge what went on and her part in it. She is going to twelve-step meetings with my partner, Anne, and she's been sober for over a year.

Dusty and I are going to finish our work together by the end of the year, around the same time I will have been abstinent from both the bulimia and the drinking for two years. I'm really thrilled, because I've been accepted for an advanced degree in psychiatric nursing, so I'll be able to use what I've learned in my own life with my own patients one of these days.

BIBLIOGRAPHY

American Psychiatric Association. 1987. *Diagnostic and Statistical Manual of Mental Disorders*. 3d ed., rev. Washington, D.C.: American Psychiatric Association.

Bass, E., and L. Davis. 1988. *The Courage to Heal: A Guide for Women Survivors of Child Sexual Abuse*. New York: Harper & Row.

Benjamin, L. 1993. *Interpersonal Diagnosis and Treatment of DSM Personality Disorders*. New York: Guilford Press.

Bepko, C., and J. Krestan. 1985. *The Responsibility Trap*. New York: The Free Press.

Bepko, C., and J. Krestan. 1990. *Too Good for Her Own Good: Breaking Free from the Burden of Female Responsibility*. New York: Harper & Row.

Bepko, C., and J. Krestan. 1993. *Singing at the Top of Our Lungs*. New York: HarperCollins.

Bollerud, K. 1992. "Long Night's Journey into Day: The Treatment of Sexual Abuse Among Substance-Abusing Women." In S. Shapiro, ed., *Sexual Trauma and Psychopathology*. New York: Lexington Books.

Carter, B. 1990. Personal communication.

Courtois, C. 1988. *Healing the Incest Wound: Adult Survivors in Therapy*. New York: Norton.

DiCello, D. 1993. Personal communication.

DiCello, D. (in press). "On the Borderline" (unpublished manuscript).

Fairbairn, W. R. D. 1952. *Psychoanalytic Studies of Personality*. London: Routledge & Kegan Paul.

Ferenczi, S. 1932. "Confusion of Tongues Between Adults and the Child: The Language of Tenderness and of Passion." In *Final Contributions to the Problems and Methods of Psychoanalysis*. New York: Basic Books, 1955.

Fisher, S. 1985. "Identity of Two: The Phenomenology of Shame in Borderline Development and Treatment." *Psychotherapy* 22 (1): 101.

Ganaway, G. K. 1989. "Historical Versus Narrative Truth: Clarifying the Role of Exogenous Trauma in the Etiology of MPD and Its Variants." *Dissociation* 2: 205–20.

Gelinas, D. 1983. "The Persistent Negative Effects of Incest." *Psychiatry* 46: 312–32.

Goldner, V. 1987. "Feminism and Family Therapy." *Family Process* 24: 31–47.

Goldner, V., et al. 1990. "Love and Violence: Gender Paradoxes in Volatile Attachments." *Family Process* 29: 343–64.

Grove, D. 1989. "Use of Metaphor." Public lecture in Hartford, Conn.

Hare-Mustin, R. T., and J. Marecek. 1990. *Making a Difference: Psychology and the Construction of Gender*. New Haven: Yale University Press.

Herman, J. 1992. *Trauma and Recovery*. New York: Basic Books.

Herman J. L., J. C. Perry, and B. van der Kolk. 1985. "Childhood Trauma in Borderline Personality Disorder." *American Journal of Psychiatry* 146: 146–49.

Herman, J. L., and B. van der Kolk. 1987. "Traumatic Antecedents of Borderline Personality Disorders." In B. van der Kolk, ed., *Psychological Trauma*. Washington, D.C.: American Psychiatric Press.

Imber-Black, E. 1988. *Families and Larger Systems*. New York: Guilford Press.

Imber-Black, E., ed. 1993. *Secrets in Families and Family Therapy*. New York: Norton.

Janoff-Bulman, R. 1992. *Shattered Assumptions: Towards a New Psychology of Trauma*. New York: Macmillan.

Jordan, J. 1990. "Courage in Connection." Working paper. Wellesley, Mass.: The Stone Center.

Jordan, J. 1991. "The Meaning of Mutuality." In *Women's Growth in Connection*. New York: Guilford Press.

Kernberg, O. 1975. *Borderline Conditions and Pathological Narcissism*. Northvale, N.J.: Jason Aronson.

Kluft, R. 1984. "An Introduction to Multiple Personality Disorder." *Psychiatric Annals* 14 (1984): 21–24.

Kluft, R., (1993). "Multiple Personality Disorders." In D. Spiegal, ed., *Dissociative Disorders*. Lutherville, Md.: The Siddran Press.

Kreisman, J., and H. Straus. 1989. *I Hate You, Don't Leave Me*. New York: Avon Books.

Krestan, J., and C. Bepko. 1993. "On Lies, Secrets, and Silence: The Multiple Levels of Denial in Addictive Families." In E. Imber-Black, ed., *Secrets in Families and Family Therapy*. New York: Norton.

Landecker, H. 1992. "The Role of Childhood Sexual Trauma in the Etiology of Borderline Personality Disorder: Considerations for Diagnosis and Treatment." *Psychotherapy* 29: 234–42.

Lerner, H. 1993. *The Dance of Deception: Pretending and Truth-Telling in Women's Lives*. New York: HarperCollins.

Linehan, M. 1993. *Cognitive-Behavioral Treatment in Borderline Personality Disorder*. New York: Guilford Press.

Loftus, E. 1993. "The Reality of Repressed Memories." *American Psychologist* (May): 518–37.

Lorde, A. 1984. *Sister Outsider*. Trumansburg, N.Y.: Crossing Press.

Luepnitz, D. 1988. *The Family Interpreted: Feminist Theory in Clinical Practice*. New York: Basic Books.

Mackinnon, L., and D. Miller. 1987. "The New Epistemology and the Milan

Approach: Feminist and Sociopolitical Considerations." *Journal of Marriage and Family Therapy* 13: 139–56.

McCann, L., and L. Pearlman. 1990. *Psychological Trauma and the Adult Survivor: Theory, Therapy, and Transformation.* New York: Brunner/Mazel.

McCann, I., and D. Stang. 1978. *The Pollyanna Principle: Selectivity in Language, Memory, and Thought.* Cambridge, Mass.: Schenkman.

Miller, D. 1983. "Outlaws and Invaders: The Adaptive Function of Alcohol Abuse in the Family-Helper Supra System." *Journal of Strategic and Systemic Therapies* 2: 15–27.

Miller, D. 1988. "Interrupting Deadly Struggles." *Journal of Strategic and Systemic Therapies* 7: 16–22.

Miller, D. "Family Violence and the Helping System." In L. Combrinck-Graham, ed., *Children in Family Contexts.* New York: Guilford Press.

Miller, D. 1990a. "The Trauma of Interpersonal Violence." *Smith College Studies in Social Work* 61: 6–26.

Miller, D. 1990b. "Women in Pain: Substance Abuse/Self-Medication." In M. Mirkin, ed., *Social and Political Contexts of Family Therapy.* New York: Allyn & Bacon.

Miller, D. 1991. "Are We Keeping Up with Oprah? A Treatment and Training Model for Addictions and Interpersonal Violence." In C. Bepko, ed., *Feminism and Addiction.* New York: Haworth Press.

Miller, D. 1993. "Incest: The Heart of Darkness." In E. Imber-Black, ed., *Secrets in Families and Family Therapy.* New York: Norton.

Mirkin, M., ed. 1990. *Social and Political Contexts of Family Therapy.* New York: Allyn & Bacon.

Ofshe, R. J. 1992. "Inadvertent Hypnosis During Interrogation: False Confession Due to Dissociative State, Misidentified Multiple Personality and the Satanic Cult Hypothesis." *International Journal of Clinical and Experimental Hypnosis* 40: 125–56.

Olio, K. 1993. "Truth in Memory: Comments on Elizabeth Loftus's 'Reality of Repressed Memories.'" Unpublished article.

Putnam, F. 1989. *Diagnosis and Treatment of Multiple Personality Disorder.* New York: Guilford Press.

Rich, A. 1979. *On Lies, Secrets and Silence.* New York: Norton.

Ross, C., et al. 1990. "Multicenter Structured Interview Data on 102 Cases of Multiple Personality Disorder." *American Journal of Psychiatry* 147: 602.

Rush, F. 1980. *The Best Kept Secret: Sexual Abuse of Children.* Englewood Cliffs, N.J.: Prentice Hall.

Russell, D. 1986. *The Secret Trauma.* New York: Basic Books.

Shapiro, S., and G. Kominiak. 1992. *Sexual Trauma and Psychopathology.* New York: Macmillan.

Spiegel, D., and A. Rosenfeld. 1984. "Spontaneous Hypnotic Age Regression: Case Report." 45: 522–24.

van der Kolk, B. 1987. *Psychological Trauma.* Washington, D.C.: American Psychiatric Press.

van der Kolk, B., J. Perry, and J. Herman. 1991. "Childhood Origins of Self-Destructive Behavior." *American Journal of Psychiatry* 148:12.

Watters, E. 1991. "The Devil in Mr. Ingram." *Mother Jones* (July–August): 30–33, 65–68.

White, M. Summer 1988/89. "The Externalizing of the Problem and the Re-authoring of Lives and Relationships." Dulwich Centre Newsletter.

Winnicott, D. 1965. *The Maturational Processes and the Facilitating Environment: Studies in the Theory of Emotional Development.* New York: International Universities Press.

INDEX

AA. *See* Alcoholics Anonymous (AA)

Abandonment fears: Borderline Personality Disorder (BPD) and, 156, 160, 161; relationships and, 117, 126–27

Abuse. *See* Childhood trauma; Sexual abuse

Abuser: attachment and loyalty to, 29, 47; cognitive confusion and, 103; gender identification and assumption of characteristics of, 110; identification of child with, 106, 107, 144, 189; secrecy about abuse and, 81; sibling as, 145; similarities between adult relationship partner and, 136; timing of questions from therapist about, 189–90

Abuser (Triadic Self), 31, 113; Inner Circle work with, 249–50, 257; lesbians and, 140; reenactment of childhood trauma and, 31, 32; relationships and, 117, 121, 136, 140

Acting out: Borderline Personality Disorder (BPD) and, 164; expression of pain from childhood trauma by, 6; sexual activities and, 136, 138

Addiction. *See also* Alcoholism; Drug abuse and addiction; Prescription drug abuse

Addiction treatment programs. *See* Recovery programs; Twelve-step programs

Addictive Personality Disorder, 41

Agoraphobia, 125–26

Al-Anon, 20, 125, 215–16, 226, 227

Alcoholics Anonymous (AA), 8, 83; June's experience with, 19, 20, 21, 36, 94, 241; Karen's experience with, 35–36, 41, 217; as support group, 226–27, 229; treatment approaches with, 35

Alcoholism, 3; abuse by mother and, 108; body as battleground and drinking in, 27; detox programs for, 220, 224; diagnosis of, 154; family therapy and, 176; fragmentation of self in, 42; gender identification issues related to, 108, 110; June's experience with, 8, 19–22, 43, 49–50, 67, 68, 95, 127; Karen's experience with, 11–15, 42, 67, 68, 212–13; link between childhood trauma and, 6, 10; Middle Circle work on, 212–13; parental, 14, 19–20, 21, 36, 48; as protective relationship, 67, 68; questions from therapist on symptoms of, 218; relapse and blame in, 93–94; relationships affected by, 117, 127, 129; relief from feelings through, 49–50, 51, 55–56; secrecy and, 28–29; self-protection and, 95; social and cultural acceptance of some forms of, 40; space and boundary issues in, 98; Trauma Reenactment Syndrome (TRS) with, 9; treatment approaches to, 35–36, 38; Triadic Self and, 112; twelve-step programs for, 35–36

childhood trauma through, 10; Borderline Personality Disorder (BPD)
and, 162; diagnostic issues in,
164–67; link between childhood
trauma and, 6; reenactment of childhood trauma through, 7; suicide risk
with, 168; treatment approaches to,
37–38. *See also* Alcoholism; Drug
abuse and addiction

Suicide and suicidal behavior, 3, 4; Borderline Personality Disorder (BPD)
and, 156, 168; depression and, 168;
Lee's family and, 26, 64; link between
childhood trauma and, 6

Support groups, 42; choosing, 214,
215–16; creating, 222–33; depressed
TRS woman and, 169; Middle Circle
work and, 182, 207, 214, 215–16,
222–33; storytelling in, 82–83,
222–23, 227–28. *See also* Alcoholics
Anonymous (AA); Recovery programs; Twelve-step programs; *and
specific groups*

Surgeries: numerous elective, 16. *See also*
Cosmetic surgeries

Symptoms: as clues to history of abuse,
62; communications about, 217; disclosure process and exacerbation of,
174–75; history of, 217–18; indirect
approach of questions about, 218–19;
Inner Circle work with, 250–52; letting go of, 220–21; meaning of,
through use of metaphor, 217; Middle Circle work and, 207, 208,
216–20; past treatment approaches
to, 219–20; relationships affected by,
117, 120, 142; seriousness of problem and, 218–19; survival skills in
childhood as, 9; timing of work on,
217; in Trauma Reenactment Syndrome (TRS), 9; in TRS treatment
approach, 38

Therapist: attitudes of TRS woman
toward, 211–12, 216; Borderline Personality Disorder (BPD) and, 160;
cognitive confusion and perceptions
of, 103; craving for arousal and treatment approach of, 60–61; crisis periods and response from, 197; decision
to reveal personal information to a
client by, 200–201; depressed TRS
woman and, 168–69; difficulty of
identifying TRS woman by, 41–43;
disclosure of abuse and centrality of

relationship with, 87–88, 91; distortion of client's attempts at disclosure
by, 85–88; divulging information
from the client, 200; dual relationship
between client and, 201; earlier treatment approaches and, 219–20; establishing the therapeutic relationship in
Outer Circle by, 183, 196–202; gender identification issues and ambivalence about, 111; indirect form of
questions from, 191–92, 196,
218–19; Inner Circle work and relationship with, 234–35; Inner Circle
work toward new understanding of
memories and, 236–40; June's experience with, 20, 21–22, 36; Karen's
experience with, 193–95; Laura's
experience with, 60–61, 114; Lee's
experience with, 24–25, 26, 36–37,
62–64, 89–90, 120–21; letting go of
symptoms and, 221; need to keep at a
distance, 61; Outer Circle work and,
182–83; power and responsibility in
therapeutic relationship with, 201–2;
Protective Presence during Inner Circle work and, 252–53, 254–55; questions about abuser asked by, 189–90;
rage during Inner Circle work and,
242–43; recovery of memories of
childhood abuse and, 22–23, 84–85;
relationships of TRS women with, 33,
119–20, 124–25; seriousness of problem determined by, 218–19; shame
released during Inner Circle work
and, 243–45; TRS treatment
approach and, 38–39; timing of
retelling and reexperiencing and,
183–84, 188–89; transference used
by, 239–40; trust between client and,
205, 235; vulnerability to some questions asked by, 198–201

Therapy. *See* Psychotherapy; Treatment

Therapy groups, 39, 154, 225

Time, and boundary issues, 97–98

Tranquilizer addiction, 20. *See also* Drug
abuse and addiction

Transference, and Inner Circle work,
239–40, 251

Trauma in childhood. *See* Childhood
trauma; Incest; Sexual abuse

Trauma Reenactment Syndrome (TRS):
body as battleground in, 27–28; central characteristics of, 8–9, 26–34;
craving for excitement in, 49; cycle of
thoughts, feelings, and behavior in,